Site Unscene

Site Unscene

The Offstage in English Renaissance Drama

✦

Jonathan Walker

NORTHWESTERN UNIVERSITY PRESS
EVANSTON, ILLINOIS

Northwestern University Press
www.nupress.northwestern.edu

Printed in the United States of America

10 9 8 7 6 5 4 3 2 1

Library of Congress Cataloging-in-Publication Data

Title: Site unscene : the offstage in English Renaissance drama / Jonathan Walker.
Description: Evanston, Illinois : Northwestern University Press, 2017. | Includes bibliographical references and index.
Identifiers: LCCN 2017000593 | ISBN 9780810135024 (cloth : alk. paper) | ISBN 9780810135017 (pbk. : alk. paper) | ISBN 9780810135031 (e-book)
Subjects: LCSH: English drama—Early modern and Elizabethan, 1500–1600—History and criticism. | Offstage action (Drama)
Classification: LCC PR651.W26 2017 | DDC 822.309—dc23
LC record available at https://lccn.loc.gov/2017000593

∞ The paper used in this publication meets the minimum requirements of the American National Standard for Information Sciences—Permanence of Paper for Printed Library Materials, ANSI Z39.48–1992.

To my parents,

Patricia Hansen and Richard Walker

For my daughter,

Harriet

No sweeping exits or offstage lines
Could make me feel bitter or treat you unkind

—Mick Jagger and Keith Richards, "Wild Horses"

CONTENTS

ILLUSTRATIONS

ACKNOWLEDGMENTS

Many others have stood behind the scenes to give encouragement, advice, perspective, and insight to the ideas and arguments that follow. I am grateful to Clark Hulse for zeroing in on the single chapter in my dissertation that I had slated to study the offstage and for persuading me to refocus the entire fledgling project on palpable but unseen phenomena in Renaissance drama. Mary Beth Rose encouraged the project from early on, and she has been a source of support throughout the extensive process of writing the book. In addition to their support, their judicious criticisms have significantly influenced my thinking through the project, and I am happy to remain deep in their debt.

I wish to thank the exceptional teachers who have both given so freely and demanded so much of me: Lisa Freeman, Diana Fuss, Judith Kegan Gardiner, Thomas N. Hall, John Huntington, R. Barry Levis, Michael Lieb, Maurice O'Sullivan, Charlie Ross, Natalie Crohn Schmitt, and Paul Whitfield White.

During this book's long writing and revision process, I have benefited immeasurably from many friends and colleagues who have offered their ideas, asked questions, shared conversations and expertise, and given me intellectual companionship: Shannon Ambrose, Sarah Bartlett, John Beer, Heidi Brayman Hackel, Thomas Cartelli, the late Duncan Carter, Christy Desmet, Terry Downs, Julie Eckerle, Oscar Fernández, Tom Fisher, Tim Francisco, Amy Greenstadt, Stephen Guy-Bray, Alastair Hunt, Susan Kirtley, Matt Kozusko, Carole Levin, Bishupal Limbu, Erika T. Lin, Kris Luce, Karin Magaldi, Michael McGregor, Randy McLeod, Lauressa Nelson, Liz Obert, Helen Ostovich, Michelle Parkinson, Isabel Jaén Portillo, Rachel Reynolds, Anya Riehl Bertolet, Christine Rose, Marjorie Rubright, John Smyth, Tiffany Stern, Alan Stewart, Paul D. Streufert, Sean Twomey, Steven Urkowitz, Heather Wolfe, and Leni Zumas. I am especially thankful to Gina Buccola, Josh Calhoun, Liz Ceppi, Alice Dailey, Brad Greenburg, Maude Hines, and Marie Lo for their steadfast support in ways that are too fundamental and varied to list. I owe thanks to Jeffrey Masten not only for introducing me to "The Booke of Sir Thomas Moore" over brunch somewhere on the north side of Chicago, but also for his encouragement and keen advice at the publishing stage. Peter Carafiol deserves special recognition for his searching questions, spirited conversations, good sense, better wit, and editorial magic, without which this would be a very different book.

Much of the material in this book first appeared at various conferences and seminars, including the Renaissance Society of America, the Group for

Early Modern Cultural Studies, and the Shakespeare Association of America. I would like to thank James A. Knapp, Jeffrey Knapp, and Travis D. Williams for organizing the SAA seminars as well as the participants and auditors for their helpful questions and ideas on my work. During the collaborative Andrew W. Mellon and Newberry Library Workshop at the University of Warwick in 2006, "Culture, Space and Power: Peopling the Built Environment in Renaissance England, c. 1450–1700," I received invaluable feedback on chapter 3, and in particular I thank the workshop leaders Steve Hindle and Beat Kümin, as well as James R. Brown, Will Cavert, Matthew Hansen, Sean McWilliams, and Matt Milner.

At Northwestern University Press, I would like to express my gratitude to acquisition editors Gianna Francesca Mosser and Henry Lowell Carrigan as well as to press staff Maggie Grossman, Marianne Jankowski, Nathan MacBrien, and J. D. Wilson. The two anonymous readers each provided incisive criticisms that have shaped my final revisions on the book, and I gladly thank them here.

My appreciation goes to the generous staff of the following institutions: the British Library, London; the Folger Shakespeare Library, Washington, D.C.; the University of Glasgow Library; the Huntington Library, San Marino, California; MOLA (Museum of London Archaeology); the Newberry Library, Chicago; the Portland State University Library; and the Utrecht University Library. Melissa Scholl in my own Department of English has been a great help. I am thankful to Portland State University for awarding me two Faculty Enhancement Grants, one to conduct research on chapter 4 at the British Library and another to subsidize the cost of the book's illustrations.

An earlier version of chapter 1 was published as "Rhetorics of the *Obscæne*" in *Theatre Survey* 48, no. 1 (2007), and I am grateful to the journal's editor, Harvey Young, for permission to reproduce some of that material here.

I dedicate this book to my parents, Patricia Hansen and Richard Walker, who have always been unwavering in their love and support, and above all to my daughter, Harriet, who in her four short years has carried me on longer journeys, and more steadily, than I have her.

A NOTE ON TEXTS

Premodern typographical features such as nonstandardized spellings, page layouts, and press-exigent irregularities retain traces of their material production, yet they also foreground how the production of literary meaning is always embedded within particular material conditions. A central preoccupation of this book, material conditions slow the observer down and estrange sometimes familiar dramatic moments when they appear in their earliest textual environments. My quotations of early texts therefore preserve many of their typographical features, while also acknowledging that they are representations and not the thing itself. I have silently modernized most ligatures and the long *s* throughout, but I have reproduced original spellings, abbreviations, italics, i/j and u/v graphs, brevigraphs, and the general layout of the texts. Unless otherwise noted, square brackets within quotations contain my additions or my deletions with ellipses. All references to plays in the First Folio are to through-line numbers (TLN) in *The Norton Facsimile: The First Folio of Shakespeare*, ed. Charlton Hinman (New York: W. W. Norton, 1968).

PREFACE

In *Shakespeare and the Popular Tradition in the Theater*, Robert Weimann argues that the English Renaissance stage inherited from native performance practices a complex and informally coded dialectic of theatrical space. In medieval playing the *locus*, which produced "a heightened level of mimetic representation," exemplified the space of the dramatic fiction, whereas the *platea* "provided an entirely nonrepresentational and unlocalized setting," which was more adjacent to and sometimes even coincided with the space of those gathered to observe and hear that dramatic fiction.[1] As he cautions, however, the relationship between the two spaces "is not the *confrontation* of the world and time of the play with that of the audience, or any serious *opposition* between representational and nonrepresentational standards of acting, but the most intense *interplay* of both."[2] On the Renaissance stage, these interactive spaces evolve and are carried around by the actors and their language, synthesizing the medieval dialectic of *platea* and *locus* into what Weimann calls *Figurenposition*, an analytic that incorporates an actor's physical location onstage with the character's mode of speech, degree of action, and level of stylization.[3] "This *Figurenposition*," he writes, "should not be understood only in the sense of the actor's physical position on the stage, but also in the more general sense that an actor may generate a unique stage presence that establishes a special relationship between himself and his fellow actors, the play, or the audience."[4]

Like Weimann, I would like to propose another spatial category that early modern dramatic characters convey through their persons and their language, one which often stands in contrast to the mimetic space of the stage itself but which also engages in a "most intense *interplay*" with it, shaping and also warping our understanding of and knowledge about the performed dramatic fiction. This book investigates the "offstage" space of the English Renaissance theater, a vast, manipulable, and ultimately unmappable region that spectators never actually see. Because it is governed by narrative principles rather than produced by the more conventional techniques of theatrical performance, offstage dramatic space would at first seem best approached through a literary critical methodology. Although the offstage raises elemental questions about the division between dramatic and narrative modes of representation—questions that traditionally reside squarely within the domain of literary criticism—the epistemological disturbances that the offstage activates as a live theatrical event require a critical approach that is likewise attuned to Renaissance performance conditions and to questions of rhetoric, too. Yet just as these particular modes of representation determine how audiences come to understand both onstage and offstage spaces, the media through which those audiences perceive dramatic events necessarily modify those spaces and their representations, which demand careful attention to be paid to the material structures of Renaissance amphitheaters on the one hand and of Renaissance dramatic texts on the other.

Site Unscene will therefore have to behave in a critically promiscuous fashion, traversing the bounds not only of literary criticism and performance studies but also premodern and modern dramatic theory, rhetoric, theater history, and textual studies, with occasional jaunts into the fields of archeology, architecture, and visual culture. Marshaling the resources of these fields will allow us to apprehend a conceptual and dramatic space that has for the most part eluded critical commentary—not least because when one is looking for the offstage, there doesn't seem to be a *there* there (to adopt a contemporary idiom). Nevertheless, the power of such absence to transform the dramatic material that's most apparently *there* will give an investigative principle to the pages that follow, where the offstage stakes its own *Figurenposition* in the drama to "generate a unique stage presence."[5] If whatever happens onstage has typically, not to mention logically, occupied our critical and aesthetic attentions, then it has also obscured an immense dramatic environment that actually determines the physical and epistemological boundaries of the Renaissance stage. By elucidating this offstage dramatic space, *Site Unscene* not only throws new light on the more familiar topographies of Renaissance drama but also traces how our coming to knowledge in the theater is formed by calculated ignorances that mark its limits.

Site Unscene

INTRODUCTION

When the Venetian Duke demands a response to Brabantio's accusation of witchcraft, Othello tells him a story. "Rude am I, in my speech," Othello warns, "And little bless'd with the soft phrase of Peace," but "I will a round vn-varnish'd Tale deliuer."[1] Unvarnished or not, his tale is indeed multilayered, recounting the scene of Brabantio's invitation to tell it in the first place as well as how hearing parcels of it had sparked Desdemona's desire and request to hear this tale, too. At the center of these storytelling occasions—first before Brabantio, then Desdemona, and now the Duke—lies what Othello calls "my Trauellours historie" (TLN 484). Like all narratives, Othello's features a double-time structure: it is both localized in its telling and dispersed by what is told. His story spans great lengths of time: "I ran it through, euen from my boyish daies, | To th'very moment that he bad me tell it" (TLN 477–78). The narrative traverses immeasurable distances and extreme terrains "of Antars vast, and Desarts idle, | Rough Quarries, Rocks, Hills, whose head touch heauen" (TLN 485–86). It proceeds through "most disastrous chances," "mouing Accidents," and "haire-breadth scapes," describing how his fortunes had declined and recovered: "Of being taken by the Insolent Foe," of being "sold to slauery," and "Of my redemption thence" (TLN 479–83). It tells of wonderfully bizarre peoples and their customs, such as "the Canibals that each others eate, | The *Anthropophague*, and men whose heads | Grew beneath their shoulders" (TLN 488–90). "These things to heare," Othello explains, "Would *Desdemona* seriously incline," "and with a greedie eare | Deuoure vp my discourse" (TLN 490–91, 494–95). This onstage embedding of one tale within a series of others theatricalizes storytelling for playgoers while at once absorbing them into an auditory circuit of a self-perpetuating narrative progression, one in which story begets more story. As soon as Othello concludes his speech, the Duke admits: "I thinke this tale would win my Daughter too" (TLN 517), which reveals that Othello's rhetorical ability to craft a captivating and influential narrative is but an alternate beguilement to the witchcraft that Brabantio accuses him of having used on his daughter.

If the scope of Othello's narrative is vast and shifting, then the scene of its narration, the actual telling of the story, is quite fixed. Within the dramatic fiction, the scene transpires in Venice, it is nighttime, and Othello tells his story "at the Dukes," as Cassio says (TLN 253). Theatrically speaking, Othello's narration would of course occur onstage with physical action probably limited to a few bodily gestures, while the particular stage on which the King's

Men performed *Othello* early in the seventeenth century would be the first Globe's and, after 1609, that of the company's indoor venue, the Blackfriars, as the 1622 quarto states on its title page.[2] But the scene also produces a significant representational surplus that is not fully governed by the mimetic economy of theatrical performance. The offstage expanses of Othello's story, in other words, relocate and displace the immediacy of the scene's visible action and audible dialogue. Dislocating the here and now, Othello draws his audience's ears and minds' eyes from Brabantio's initial questions about "the Storie of my life, | From yeare to yeare," moving on to "Battaile, Sieges, Fortune," then to "Flood and Field," and to "th'imminent deadly breach"— "Such was my Processe," he says, compressing the procession of historical events (*fabula*) into the sequence of their telling (*sjuzhet*) (TLN 474–75, 480–81, 487). Yet suddenly Othello transports his audience back to Brabantio's home, where Desdemona had overheard only portions of the story because "the house Affaires would draw her hence" (TLN 492), and reveals how he "Tooke once a pliant houre, and found good meanes | To draw from her a prayer of earnest heart, | That I would all my Pilgrimage dilate" (TLN 496–98). After he tells his tale yet again, this time to Desdemona,

> She thank'd me,
> And bad me, if I had a Friend that lou'd her,
> I should but teach him how to tell my Story,
> And that would wooe her. Vpon this hint I spake,
> She lou'd me for the dangers I had past,
> And I lou'd her, that she did pitty them. (TLN 508–13)

This scene exceeds the theater's representational economy because, even though the narration is fixed upon the stage and at a specific fictional locale, the narrative itself explodes those spatiotemporal limits into an unseen dramatic space that this book will call "the offstage."

Such a space is not unfamiliar to scholars and students of Renaissance drama. Innumerable scenes of great moment and abiding effect occur there. When Iago declares to Brabantio that "Euen now, now, very now, an old blacke Ram | Is tupping your white Ewe" (TLN 96–97), he invokes an unseen offstage sphere that the play will repeatedly conjure up to tantalize and torment the imaginations of its characters. The Turkish armada's threat to Cyprus, Cassio's brawl with Montano as well as his adulterous somniloquy, the strawberried handkerchief's mystical fabrication, Desdemona's alleged infidelities: familiar as their details are, each of these key events in *Othello* happens, or supposedly happens, offstage, and the play represents them solely as narrative reconstructions. The offstage is also where Hamlet grapples with the pirates, and it is where Ophelia sings and sinks "To muddy death."[3] The offstage houses the bedchamber where Macbeth murders Duncan in his sleep. It frames the window where Hero appears to converse with Borachio. And it enfolds Leontes's joyful reunion with Perdita, a reunion "which lames Re- | port to follow it, and vndo's description to doe it."[4] Tamburlaine conducts his bloody battles there. Sejanus saves Tiberius Caesar's life inside a collapsing cave there. Giovanni cuts the heart from Annabella's dying breast there. Offstage dramatic spaces can conceal the seat of real but unembodied power, like that exercised by the unnamed Henry VIII in "The Booke of Sir Thomas Moore." These spaces can give local habitations and names to the fears and violations that characters endure, such as the Duke's offstage rape of Brancha in WOMEN BEWARE WOMEN: "I saw that now," she says, "Fearful for any womans eye to look on."[5] They can mark sites of wonder and desire, as when Enobarbus tells of Cleopatra's gilded barge gliding upon the River Cydnus.

These occasions of unseen action and staged narrative provide a point of entry for this book's discussion of four distinct manifestations of the offstage: in premodern dramatic theory, in Renaissance dramatic literature, in London amphitheaters of the period, and in early printed play-texts. Within these four frameworks that collectively represent the field of "Renaissance drama," I analyze not only how offstage phenomena create drama's enabling conditions but also how they persist as ghostly presences that threaten the drama's coherence and rationality should they come too visibly into view. As the literary form of visibility and immediacy par excellence, drama obscures those features of itself that do not operate according to its theatrical logic. Aristotle, Philip Sidney, and others define drama as the specular literary mode because it puts palpable persons and objects on display, thus favoring (and encouraging its audiences to favor) that which is directly perceptible to the eyes and ears as the basis of their knowledge in the theater. This book demonstrates, however, that the mode achieves its defining qualities of visibility and immediacy by obscuring, erasing, or diminishing offstage phenomena that are in fact foundational to the dramatic mode.

I therefore pursue questions not only about the rhetoric of literary form and the maneuvers that dramatic theorists make to draw formal boundaries but also about the way physical theaters and texts make an exhibition of dramatic action precisely by concealing the mechanisms and assumptions that make such action accessible and intelligible to audiences in the first place. Because each of these contexts shapes, embodies, and provides an experience of the dramatic mode, the project is strategically multidisciplinary and investigates how the drama jettisons, segregates, or brackets fundamental aspects of itself to achieve the illusion of direct and unmediated representation. The offstage, in other words, functions as an animating force within each dramatic context. That which surrounds dramatic action, which cannot or should not be exhibited, which provides a platform or environment for it, and which enables it to attain the highest degree of visibility and immediacy are what will constitute "the offstage" in this study. The most productive methodology for thinking through these phenomena is rhetorical analysis. Because the triangulated relationship that we will see between the stage, the offstage, and the audience consistently foregrounds issues of persuasion, credibility, and belief, rhetorical analysis will provide a responsive instrument to the problems of form, representation, and knowledge that are the subject of *Site Unscene.*

Since the offstage is a necessary condition of the stage itself, it is useful to consider, in the most basic terms, the assumptions by which the stage works, which will bring the various manifestations of the offstage into sharper focus. A stage, first of all, is designed to elevate performing figures above an adjacent spectatorial space, which not only marks a boundary between them but more importantly heightens and concentrates the visibility of that which treads its boards. In addition, the stage delivers its business in real time, which means that spectators perceive its events in a direct and immediate fashion. We should also bear in mind that these formal qualities of visibility and immediacy mutually reinforce one another through the ocularcentric assumption that "seeing is believing." For instance, William N. West shows how the Latin *theatrum* inextricably links "conceptions of vision and knowledge," a conjunction that appealed to early modern humanists for its rich pedagogical value: "*Theater* shares its stem with the word *theory*, meaning literally 'a looking,' and thus also *theory*'s sense of abstraction and knowing."[6] The offstage, in contrast, occupies abjected, nonvisible, disregarded, or transparent spaces to which audiences gain access only through mediated or oblique means. If the stage represents the right-here and now, then the offstage exemplifies anything that may be dramatically relevant but that dwells elsewhere, in the periphery, and/or in the past. Offstage phenomena emerge in different ways within dramatic theory, dramatic literature, Renaissance amphitheaters, and early play-texts, and as a result they activate distinct critical discourses and require different terms of analysis. Although the offstage takes the form of narrative in both dramatic theory and literature, premodern theorists and Renaissance playwrights hold divergent opinions about the uses and abuses of storytelling characters on the stage. On the other hand, amphitheaters and play-texts each present a particular dramatic medium within which audiences exercise a specific literacy, and these media possess certain material conditions that disappear as offstage spaces to enhance the visibility and immediacy of the drama. Taking a comprehensive approach to Renaissance drama, my examination of the offstage will disclose a repeated but site-specific operation within the four major nodes of dramatic theory, literature, amphitheaters, and texts.

Site Unscene makes three broad arguments about offstage phenomena in the period. The first argument is that Renaissance playwrights modernized theatrical representation by dilating the physical limits of the stage with narrative more frequently and more intricately than in classical and medieval drama. To be sure, ancient, medieval, and early Tudor plays also feature onstage reports about unseen events—Oedipus's murder of his father is perhaps the readiest example in Western drama—but in these earlier plays the offstage action remains relatively simple, and, more often than not, the space in which it occurs sits just beyond the stage's fictional locale. In late sixteenth-century London, by contrast, playwrights transform this once peripheral space into a highly adaptable and far-flung location for events, conversations, and realities as dramatically intricate and vital as any produced in full view of theater audiences. What made this transformation possible is storytelling, not only because it is unrestricted by the time and space of live performance but also because it can represent dramatic action according to a narrative and purely verbal logic that defies the logic of theatricality and eyewitnessing. As we shall see, Renaissance plays feature extensive spatial environments and complex but unseen dramatic events that narrative depicts in sophisticated new ways in the period.

These developments in Renaissance drama, I want to suggest, arise from a wider cultural interest in the rhetorical strategies of *amplificatio*, *dilatio*, and *narratio*. Noting that "countless Renaissance rhetorical handbooks" offered advice on how to amplify and dilate a discourse, Patricia Parker writes:

> "To dilate," in Renaissance English, meant not only to expand, disperse, or spread abroad but also to put off, postpone, prolong, or play for time [. . .]. The specifically rhetorical meaning of "dilate"—the amplifying and prolonging of discourse—involves both an expansion and an opening up, the creation of more copious speech through the explication, or unfolding, of a brief or closed, hermetic "sentence," widening the space between its beginning and ending and generating much out of little, many words (or things) where there had been few.[7]

That Renaissance plays are, on average, much longer and contain more spoken lines than classical and medieval plays suggests that one way dramatists dilated their plots entailed simply multiplying staged scenes and lengthening characters' speeches. But critics have not thoroughly examined how playwrights use offstage events to dilate scenic action beyond the stage's spatial bounds, and few have attended to characters' use of narrative to achieve temporal dilation during performance. Lorna Hutson has recently traced the rapid growth of storytelling on the English Renaissance stage to the "judicial pedagogy of narrative," which taught how to produce facts—in courts of law or otherwise—through the forensic strategy of *narratio*.[8] The implications of these dramatic developments are both formal and epistemological: on the one hand, onstage scenes exhibit complex temporal and spatial relationships with the dramatic events that playwrights have dilated into offstage spaces, and, on the other, the veracity of narrated action frequently remains open to question. Any understanding of dramatic form in early modern England, I suggest, calls for the analysis of both the narrative mode and the dilatory space of the offstage because the stories that characters tell about unstaged action are definitive and irreducible features of this period's drama.

My second argument proposes that playwrights' spatial and narrative dilation of dramatic action created rhetorical conditions that encouraged playgoers to become more discerning, skeptical, and analytical in their engagement with the drama. By juxtaposing live drama and verbal narrative onstage, the Renaissance theater confronted audiences with two distinct epistemologies that call for interpretation and reconciliation. We might consider these conflicting epistemologies between the stage and the offstage in terms of anamorphosis. As an artistic technique, anamorphosis draws overt attention to the importance—but also to the limitations—of a viewer's perspective by staging two images that cannot simultaneously be perceived aright from the same vantage point: when one image comes into focus, the other suffers visual distortion. Hence as a play's staged action presents one highly visible and immediate point of view, the offstage delivers another perspective that either cannot be seen or that supervenes or interferes with the stage itself, which distorts the enacted drama that audiences witness firsthand. When Bushy comforts the Queen after King Richard departs for Ireland, he attributes such distortive power to "sorrowes eye, glazed with blinding teares," which

> Diuides one thing intire, to many obiects,
> Like perspectiues, which rightly gaz'd vpon
> Shew nothing but confusion, ey'd awry,
> Distinguish forme[.][9]

Such perspectivism, I argue, confers validity and truth-values on separate and often incompatible viewpoints, producing the epistemologically ambivalent ground from which deliberation and interpretation arise. In dramatic theory the offstage appears as a disruptive incursion of narrative form onstage, in dramatic literature as characters' subjective and unverifiable stories about unseen but decisive events, in theater architecture as the expansive and socially raucous auditoria that playgoers occupied, and in printed plays as the speech headings and stage directions that comprise drama's indispensable but transparent textual apparatus. As a result, when the offstage intrudes into each of these contexts, it compels audiences to view and understand the drama from conflicting points of view, which creates the rhetorical circumstances that provoke active deliberation.

The third argument claims that the offstage both enables and threatens drama's distinctive, genre-defining power to represent unmediated and fully visible fictions. Because offstage phenomena comprise the material contexts from which drama emerges, they directly produce the illusion of dramatic presence by resolving into the background, thereby accentuating the visibility and proximity of the stage and its representations. But the offstage also demystifies drama by encroaching upon and calling into question certain self-evident truths about its theory, live performance, theater environment, and play-texts. A potent subversive absence in drama, the offstage lays bare the limits of the genre. Since visibility and immediacy are the dramatic mode's chief characteristics not only within the context of performance but also in its theory, in the technology of theaters, and in its texts, the offstage must pass unobserved for the drama to appear. The premodern discourse about what makes drama a unique art form regularly defines it as nonnarrative, which turns narrativity itself into a founding element that inhabits offstage regions and that always imperils the confined and rational business of the stage. In theaters, and especially in amphitheaters, we see another of drama's enabling conditions in the offstage space of the auditorium, whose own visible and immediate goings-on all too easily distract playgoers' attentiveness from the stage, as seasoned actors and playgoers well know. Finally, speech headings and stage directions are distinctive traits of virtually all dramatic texts, which make characters' lines intelligible by signaling offpage events, but they also occupy a different textual space from those lines and function according to a separate referential logic, which conjures the illusion of "direct speech" on the page. Whenever it exhibits itself in the theory, in performance, in amphitheaters, and in texts, the offstage destabilizes each of these dramatic environments by revealing the myths, the fictions, the material conditions, and the assumptions by which drama operates.

The offstage ground that this book charts is almost entirely new territory because the secondary criticism is almost nonexistent in the fields of premodern theory, the architectural history of theater, and textual criticism, while in literary studies the scholarship on Renaissance drama usually focuses only on specific Shakespearean plays or scenes. Scholars have used Aristotle's and Horace's comments about messenger speeches to discuss those figures in classical theater who report offstage events.[10] But the delineation of dramatic from nondramatic modes in the *Poetics* and the *Ars Poetica* as well as the theoretical work of Evanthius, Aelius Donatus, Lodovico Castelvetro, and Philip Sidney have yet to be examined as the conceptual origins of inestimable offstage spaces and events, which they create by limiting what the stage itself may portray. Although theater history and textual criticism do not typically ask the kinds of questions that would elucidate the offstage as a founding concept in drama, I highlight a specific network of language in these fields that corresponds with manifestations of the offstage in the theory and in the literature: space, rhetoric, dramatic form, narrative, and the logic of supplementarity. Aside from Bruce R. Smith, who details the acoustical properties of Renaissance amphitheaters, and Pauline Kiernan, who addresses the spectatorial space of the reconstructed Globe in London,[11] no one has analyzed the offstage space of the auditorium as a rhetorical medium that utilizes its material conditions within a particular geometry to produce a complex and variable stage/nonstage dynamic. The offstage as a textual phenomenon is even more elusive, but critics such as Roman Ingarden and Pascale Aebischer have formulated a bilevel structure in dramatic texts that consists of dialogue and paratextual matter, and I elaborate this structure to show how it works as an analogue to onstage and offstage spaces.[12]

The literary criticism on the offstage, as piecemeal as it may be, is worth looking at in some detail here because the chapters that follow synthesize each of the three main approaches that critics have taken to the subject. These approaches focus (1) on the material conditions of early modern performance, (2) on literary form, and (3) on fictional dramatic space. By far the most widespread approach considers offstage scenes in terms of dramaturgy and the amphitheaters' stage conditions. In 1968, M. C. Bradbrook wrote, "No playwright nowadays would stage Ophelia's first interview with Hamlet 'off', or Leontes' recognition of Perdita; the audience would want to see it, and the actor to act it."[13] This distinction between modern and early modern aesthetic temperaments initiates many of the dramaturgical treatments of offstage scenes, prompting the question, "why does he [i.e., Shakespeare] choose the form of the reported scene instead of the more direct and more dramatic form of straight performance?"[14] Francis Berry sums up two possible answers to this question, arguing that for most offstage scenes "the dramatic poet turns narrative poet because either he cannot show them on the stage or he chooses not to show them."[15] B. G. Tandon writes about scenes of execution: "Though Shakespeare shows no inhibition against violence on the stage, he keeps hangings out of it. The Elizabethan spectators would have liked to watch them, but here he exercises restraint."[16] And Peter Holland, discussing the "dramatic form of journeys," says, "Placing a voyage on stage is, of course, a direct route to dramaturgical difficulty. The readiest way to demonstrating the limitations of the stage is to try to move spaces. For all the vaunted flexibility of the Elizabethan stage's response to place it is always liable to appear only too well aware of its own limitations when a journey is at issue."[17]

When such critics ask why playwrights plotted action off the stage, the dramaturgical answer results in two kinds of arguments that they occasionally link together. The first and most prevalent argument is that the Renaissance theater lacked the technological and representational capacities to stage many of its playwrights' scenes, which required moving them to offstage locations and depicting them through storytelling. The second argument exalts Shakespeare's gifted dramaturgy at the expense of either the dramatic work or the playgoing tastes of others. Studying the offstage as a problem arising from live production (as these critics do) would seem to be intuitive because many of the scenes they examine—Ophelia's drowning, for example, or Cleopatra's barge—do seem patently unstageable. Yet counterexamples—such as the drowning of two soldiers onstage by tritons in "The 2. Noble Ladys," or the staging of storm-tossed ships in *THE TEMPEST* and in *Pericles*—reveal the limits of this "unstageable" argument. If we conclude simply that the constraints of Renaissance theaters restricted the period's dramatic production, then we have only speculated about a pragmatic question at the expense of more pressing aesthetic ones. Why do Renaissance playwrights deploy onstage narrative so frequently, so unnecessarily, and with such poetic verve? What kind of aesthetic work does offstage action accomplish in the drama? And how does the nondramatic mode of narration thrust audiences into new rhetorical and interpretive positions? These are questions that *Site Unscene* answers.

In addition to considering the material conditions of performance, critics have also approached the offstage in terms of literary form, though few find it to be an exceptional formal problem. Recent books by both Richard Meek and William Gruber, however, refute the view that narration is compensatory to the supposed deficiencies of the Renaissance stage. Concentrating largely on visual art and ekphrasis in his *Narrating the Visual in Shakespeare*, Meek explores how "Shakespeare seems interested in the interplay between narrative and drama, and the extent to which both modes of representation are capable of eliciting a powerful emotional response from his audiences and readers."[18] And, in *Offstage Space, Narrative, and the Theatre of the Imagination*, Gruber surveys dramatic work from classical Greece to postmodern Europe and North America to "demonstrate the dramaturgically productive tension that has always existed between narration and enactment as modes of image-making in the theatre and to show how dramatists configure unseen people and events in ways that tap spectators' imaginations."[19] Although my discussion shares only a couple of primary texts with Gruber's, I take as axiomatic his assertion that "in some circumstances those things that are beyond the mimesis can be central to it, just as things that are not seen on stage may in some ways be experienced with greater intensity and satisfaction than if they were fully visible."[20] In the same vein, Andrew Sofer's *Dark Matter: Invisibility in Drama, Theater, and Performance* attends to "*whatever is materially unrepresented onstage but un-ignorable*."[21] Though he takes a phenomenological approach to the offstage rather than a literary formal one, Sofer insists that audiences wrestle with the profound weight of unseen action and the radical unknowability that it offers.

Performance-oriented critics inflect a third and final literary approach to the offstage, which critics regard as a space within drama that signifies powerfully across many historical periods. By differentiating various sign-systems in the theater and how these systems impart knowledge about the dramatic action, many of these theorists favor a semiotic method and, especially among French writers, propose new terminology to distinguish between onstage and offstage spaces. Michael Issacharoff separates "mimetic" from "diegetic" spaces, for instance, while Hanna Scolnicov speaks about onstage and offstage as "the difference between perceived space and conceived space."[22] Marvin Carlson argues that the very existence of a dramatic fiction upon a stage must bring a corresponding offstage sphere into being: "One of the most basic conventions in theatre, as basic as the assumption of character and closely related to it, is that the fictive world in which these characters exist is not restricted to what we can see on the stage, but spreads out into contiguous fictive areas which those characters inhabit when we cannot see them."[23] Peter Womack describes this metonymic relationship between onstage and offstage as "*fictional adjacency*," and Tim Fitzpatrick claims that Renaissance playwrights consciously devised such adjacent areas through a system of staging and dialogic conventions, which situated onstage spaces in complex but specific relations to offstage "counter-places."[24]

One important study that takes a nonsemiotic approach to dramatic space is Henry S. Turner's *The English Renaissance Stage: Geometry, Poetics, and the Practical Spatial Arts 1580–1630*, a book that demonstrates how emergent technological discourses, especially that of geometry, shaped early modern dramatic form every bit as much as classical literary theories and traditional theater practices did. He "concentrates on how the boundary between onstage and offstage space delineated what critics have come to regard as the early-modern theatre's most fundamental unit of representation—the 'scene'—and the way in which the 'scene' as a theatrical unit gradually became inseparable from a fictional idea of location, or 'place.' "[25] "On stage in performance," Turner writes,

> the "emplotment" of a dramatic action—the selection of episodes from out of a larger potential continuum of events and their arrangement so as to produce probability, complexity, and interest—required a mastery of *space*, and not simply of time, as the mimetic medium in which that action took place. Above all, it required a playwright to manage the all-important boundary between onstage and offstage space, as this appeared in the entrances and exits of the actors or, more concretely, in the backstage wall of the theatre and the structural features that were associated with it.[26]

Mariko Ichikawa, too, examines "the relation between onstage and offstage spaces and [. . .] the audience's awareness both of the imaginative world created by the play and the wood, lath and plaster reality of the playhouse itself—that is to say, the balance between fiction and theatre."[27] When Turner, Ichikawa, and I step off the stage through the *frons scenae* (stage wall), however, we arrive in very different places. In their studies, "offstage" usually means the theater's "backstage," which Turner describes as "a negatively determining limit, an unrepresentable invisibility behind the wall,"[28] whereas Ichikawa addresses how early modern performance manipulates visibility and audibility to great effect at the threshold of the *frons scenae*. For me, in contrast, the offstage comprises all of those integral spaces, times, and events that reside within the dramatic fiction but outside of its staged action, as well as the various constitutive phenomena that the theory, theaters, and texts try to remove from the audience's view.

Each of these three critical foci—the conditions of performance, literary form, and dramatic space—is a necessary but insufficient factor for analyzing the offstage as a practical, aesthetic, and theoretical problem. In contrast to the literary criticism on the subject, *Site Unscene* significantly expands the investigative scope to include, first, premodern theoretical work, which addresses both literary form and hypothetical dramatic space; second, the rhetorical environment of Renaissance amphitheaters, which draws in performance conditions as well as the practical representation of dramatic space; and, third, the structure of dramatic texts, which transforms dramatic space into textual space by adhering to the precepts of literary form. In analyzing each of these contexts, I demonstrate a remarkable continuity between distinct formations of the drama, which consist of not only those qualities and effects such as high visibility and immediate perception that we most associate with the genre but also a substratum of nondramatic elements that the genre cannot accommodate without contradicting its assumptions. When it comes into view, this substratum of nondramatic elements—what I broadly call "the offstage"—splits the audience's perspective and challenges them to interpret and reconcile the disparity. As a result, these offstage intrusions urge audiences to become more engaged and less passive, which intellectualizes dramatic pleasure. In a word, the drama is necessarily "bifocal," and "onstage" and "offstage" are its governing terms.

The emblem in figure I.1 illustrates these bifocal perspectives. From within a curtained booth, we see a right hand reach out and inscribe on a floating scroll: "MENTE.VIDEBOR," which translates as "by the mind I shall be seen." The figure is almost entirely obscured by the curtain, although it does disclose the clothed forearm, the hand, and the pen, which replaces the voice by mediating it with writing. The image bifurcates our perspective in two ways. It emphasizes, first of all, that two visual points of view are at work: that of the onlooker who witnesses this curious writing event, and that of the active composer whose own visual perspective from behind the curtain faces exactly opposite, causing the script to appear upside down from our vantage point. To read the scroll right side up, we must physically invert the book to see it from the writer's perspective, which brings the text into focus while now distorting the rest of the page. The emblem offers a simple anamorphosis, but it still does the trick. The second perspectival split is epistemological. In the same moment that the hand and scroll reveal a figure to be present, they also announce that there is much more to be seen and known, much more than even the rest of the figure's body, which means that the image overtly dispenses an immeasurable quantity of acknowledged ignorance along with a minimum amount of knowledge about the writer. The emblem implants this ratio of knowledge and ignorance into the viewer's own mind—"MENTE.VIDEBOR"—to provoke reflection on and analysis of the incomplete and ambiguous evidence.

As we shall see, ambiguous evidence and divergent perspectives crop up just as frequently and disruptively in the theory, theaters, and texts as in the literature itself, yet it is in the literature that the most recognizable examples of bifocalism appear, and thus why they have garnered the most critical attention. Gertrude, for instance, tells of Ophelia's demise:

Figure I.1. Henry Peacham, MINERVA BRITANNA OR A GARDEN OF HEROICAL *Deuises* (London: by Wa: Dight, 1612), A1r (detail). Photograph courtesy of The Newberry Library, Chicago, Case W 1025 .657.

There is a Willow growes aslant a Brooke,
That shewes his hore leaues in the glassie streame :
There with fantasticke Garlands did she come,
Of Crow-flowers, Nettles, Daysies, and long Purples,
That liberall Shepheards giue a grosser name;
But our cold Maids doe Dead Mens Fingers call them :
There on the pendant boughes, her Coronet weeds
Clambring to hang; an enuious sliuer broke,
When downe the weedy Trophies, and her selfe,
Fell in the weeping Brooke, her cloathes spred wide,
And Mermaid-like, a while they bore her vp,
Which time she chaunted snatches of old tunes,
As one incapable of her owne distresse,
Or like a creature Native, and indued
Vnto that Element : but long it could not be,
Till that her garments, heauy with her drinke,
Pul'd the poore wretch from her melodious buy,
To muddy death.[29]

If this long and detailed story about Ophelia's drowning is true, that raises serious questions about why Gertrude (or some unnamed observer) failed to intervene; if it is untrue, why does she fabricate the story? Or consider a more elaborate example from *THE TEMPEST*. After Prospero reveals to Miranda how his brother had usurped his dukedom, he tells another story of his initial beneficence to Caliban when they arrived on the island. But Caliban then tells the story of Prospero having usurped the island from him, and his alternate account of this unseen event throws suspicion on both stories because audiences are unable to verify either one. The visible action onstage confirms only that Caliban is now Prospero's slave, but their two accounts confront the audience with "evidential uncertainty" about how exactly this state of affairs came to be.[30] Since neither Prospero's nor Caliban's story can be true simultaneously, the play puts forward anamorphic perspectives that confront audiences with the problem of how to get at dramatic truth when the reality presented onstage is entirely dependent upon conflicting evidence that simply cannot be authenticated. The multiplicity of perspectives and the irresolution between them therefore disputes the dramatic reality that the stage portrays as self-evident through its visual immediacy. Seeing, in this case, is not the same as believing.

Yet, intrusive and perplexing as they may be, such dramatic challenges of bifocalism and conflicting evidence are productive, I argue, because they intellectually engage the audience by encouraging them to think and to deliberate, rather than purely to seek pleasure from the passive consumption of theatrical entertainment. "Nothing needs less justification than pleasure," says Bertolt Brecht, but I want to suggest, along with Brecht, that a certain pleasure also derives from contemplating the conflicting perspectives to which this bifocalism gives rise.[31] The theory of the "alienation effect" (*Verfremdungseffekt*) that Brecht devised for his epic theater illuminates the bifocalism I analyze in subsequent chapters because they both raise questions about the self-evidence of dramatic appearances. In *The Messingkauf Dialogues*, for example, Brecht writes, "The *self-evident*—i.e. the particular shape our consciousness gives our experience—is resolved into its components when counteracted by the A-effect and turned into a new form of the *evident*."[32] At base, the A-effect estranges the "natural," the ordinary, the familiar in order to provoke analysis. His motivation for theorizing and practicing the A-effect in the theater was a fundamentally political one, aimed at prompting audiences to see that history and social systems are created by human effort rather than simply received: "*Historicizing* involves judging a particular social system from another social system's point of view."[33]

English Renaissance drama, among other theatrical traditions, nourished Brecht's extended development of the A-effect and the ways it makes the natural or self-evident seem unfamiliar. Arguing that "Jacobean tragedies, including the majority of Shakespeare's, were more radical than has hitherto been allowed," Jonathan Dollimore observes that "Brecht recognised in Jacobean theatre a prototype of his own epic theatre," which "involves a positive rejection of 'order'—in the universe, society, and the human subject—as ideological misrepresentation. What is at stake here [. . .] is nothing less than opposing conceptions of reality and, even, of rationality."[34] S. L. Bethell, too, has argued that the nonnaturalistic, presentational style of acting and staging in English Renaissance theaters produced in audiences a "double consciousness of play-world and real world," which had the effect from the outset of "'distancing' a play, so that the words and deeds of which it consists may be critically weighed in the course of its performance."[35] Extending the work of these and other critics, this book takes the sharp distinction that Renaissance drama makes between onstage and offstage phenomena as a ubiquitous and meaningful mechanism for representing "opposing conceptions of reality and, even, of rationality," through a kind of alienation effect. By depacifying audiences in these ways, the Renaissance theater created the possibility for more complex, more nuanced, and more contested dramatic meaning than earlier theater had tolerated—much as Dollimore argues—not because this particular theater made some positivistic advancement but because it helped inaugurate a new and protomodern notion that knowledge is situated, perspectival, nonuniversal, and always subject to revision.

Renaissance playwrights devise an unofficial counterdiscourse to a traditional understanding of how dramatic form was supposed to function, to the prescriptive and/or descriptive codifications of dramatic theorists, and to the classical dramatic work of skilled playwrights. Renaissance playwrights do so, I want to suggest, by inventing elaborate offstage environments and events that characters bring to the stage through storytelling. Despite the productive work that the offstage makes possible here, onstage narrative continues to be repudiated long after this period, an attitude which survives even in the modern literary criticism that sees it as merely compensatory to a nonnaturalistic stage. In the PREFACE *To his* EDITION *of Shakespear's Plays*, for example, Samuel Johnson explains why verbal storytelling is inappropriate in the theater, while also dignifying Shakespeare's facility with it:

> In narration he affects a disproportionate pomp of diction and a wearisome train of circumlocution, and tells the incident imperfectly in many words, which might have been more plainly delivered in few. Narration in dramatick poetry is naturally tedious, as it is unanimated and inactive, and obstructs the progress of the action; it should therefore always be rapid, and enlivened by frequent interruption. *Shakespeare* found it an encumbrance, and instead of lightening it by brevity, endeavoured to recommend it by dignity and splendour.[36]

In chapter 2, I will show that "Narration in dramatick poetry" is quite often mesmerizing rather than tedious, as the effects of Othello's story suggest. And while it may be "unanimated and inactive" because the audience perceives it in a mediated way, such narrative actually propels "the progress of the action" forward by taking playgoers on intricate itineraries within the dramatic fiction but beyond the visible stage.

Johnson's critical desire to segregate narrative from performance pervades most other premodern discussions of dramatic form. Chapter 1 therefore surveys the most significant theories of drama down to the end of the sixteenth century, examining how writers distinguish (often with the aim of purifying) the two modes of enactment and narration, a distinction which directly affects whether playwrights plot dramatic episodes either on or off the stage. Among the theorists I consider—Plato, Aristotle, Horace, Evanthius, Donatus, Castelvetro, and Sidney—each isolates dramatic from narrative forms, though the rationales that they offer for this isolation differ as much as do the writers' historical contexts. Aristotle, for instance, routinely specifies those actions that should and should not appear in the drama, using probability and rationality as measures to determine their proper inclusion. When dramatic events, however, happen to be essential but also improbable or irrational, he excludes them from the stage while still allowing messenger figures to report those events, which creates a populous and far-reaching offstage sphere that becomes a necessary condition of Aristotle's ideal onstage space. In THE DEFENCE OF *Poesie*, Sidney appeals to "*Aristotles* precept, and common reason" to critique contemporary theater practices, "where you shall haue *Asia* of the one side, and *Affricke* of the other, and so manie other vnder Kingdomes, that the Player when he comes in, must euer begin with telling where he is, or else the tale will not be conceiued."[37] What Sidney finds preposterous here is the multiplication of dramatic times and places, which requires disruptive announcements by characters that inhibit—precisely because they attempt to facilitate—playgoers' understanding of the presented action.

The so-called unities of place, time, and action are familiar Aristotelian tenets, amplified and codified by later theorists through their commentaries on the *Poetics*. In chapter 1, I argue that a common problem subtends not only these particular concerns for dramatic unity but also the related concerns for credibility and intelligibility that such writers as Horace, Evanthius, and Donatus stress in their treatises. This common problem entails the perceptual and cognitive work that playgoers perform. All of these premodern theorists deliberate on how theatergoers perceive and comprehend dramatic events as they unfold through the space and time of performance, which are more important considerations in drama than in other genres because of the immediate and visible contact between the audience and the art form. Thus the successful playwright must balance what theatergoers know and when they know it by accelerating and decelerating their understanding at crucial moments in the action. Control over the epistemology and, by extension, the intellectual perspective of theater audiences thus becomes paramount in premodern conceptions of the dramatic mode. On the one hand, the strategic introduction of offstage events through narrative supplies an effective means for playwrights to achieve this epistemological control, which likewise offers a structural principle for emplotting successive scenes. But, on the other hand, narration in the midst of enactment frequently defies ideals of dramatic unity, credibility, and intelligibility, which can then destabilize playgoers' knowledge. The possibility of having confused and incredulous playgoers convinces most of these critics to dissociate storytelling from the stage, except under special circumstances. Chapter 1's discussion of premodern dramatic theory argues that the offstage and its representational form of narrativity have always been foundational to the theater. Yet, because of its uncontainable expanses and disruptive itineraries, theorists have converted narratives about the offstage into a theatrical surplus, a ghostly element at once residing inside and outside dramatic form.

The conceptual tensions that premodern theorists register between enactment on the stage and narrative from elsewhere continue to exercise certain quarters of late sixteenth-century English thought, as Sidney's remarks in the DEFENCE make plain. Nonetheless, this historical juncture witnesses popular playwrights diverging from classical dramatic principles (whether deliberately, indifferently, or ignorantly) not by resolving these tensions between enactment and narration but by exploiting them. Instead of viewing this divergence simply as an erosion of classical dramatic values, I propose that, through the development of its representational practices and the routing of action offstage, the Renaissance theater formulates a counterdiscourse to the received critical consensus. That is to say, the offstage becomes one site of contest where dramatic innovations are either promoted or resisted. Although premodern theorists had ordinarily designated fictional offstage space as a kind of waste ground that is typically unfit for dramatic use, London playwrights develop that ground as one might a piece of prime real estate, putting it to work in their plays while appropriating the narrative mode for live performance.

Chapter 2 turns, then, from theory to the practice of dramatic form, examining the rhetorical uses to which writers as well as characters put the offstage by introducing narrative at strategic moments in the action. Instead of designing dramatic plots that are as proportional, rational, and credible as possible to theatergoers, as premodern theorists had so often advised, Renaissance playwrights map a new course by designing plots that make proportionality, rationality, and credibility contested issues within the dramatic fictions themselves. The offstage is a ubiquitous site of contention in this period's drama because it is not visible or immediately accessible. Although characters leverage offstage events to radically different ends, these plays consistently demonstrate the power of verbal narration to influence other characters' beliefs, to make and break social alliances, and to alter the trajectory of dramatic action. I will argue that Renaissance drama showcases narrative as a valuable object of social exchange between characters, as adaptable to different rhetorical circumstances and goals as it is elastic in its spatiotemporality. Examining one comedy, two histories, and three tragedies, the discussion focuses on six plays written between the 1580s and the 1630s: John Ford's *PERKIN VVARBECK*, Thomas Kyd's *THE SPANISH TRAGEdie* [*sic*], part 1 of Christopher Marlowe's *Tamburlaine the Great*, Thomas Middleton's *WOMEN BEWARE WOMEN*, and William Shakespeare's *Henry the Fift* and *Much adoe about Nothing*. Onstage storytellers self-interestedly manipulate how and when playgoers as well as other characters acquire knowledge about unseen dramatic events. Characters thus tactically modulate unauthenticated knowledge to effect social change to their advantage, which is also a structural principle for playwrights to depict dramatic conflict for a playgoing public whose culture frequently uses narrative both to affirm and to contest belief.

While chapters 1 and 2 address the theoretical and the practical questions educed by offstage phenomena, chapters 3 and 4 investigate how the media of Renaissance amphitheaters and texts construct their own peculiar forms of offstage space. Recent archeological discoveries in London have transformed our understanding of the physical composition of Renaissance amphitheaters, those large, purpose-built playhouses usually polygonal in shape, erected outside the medieval city walls, and tiered with galleries to accommodate up to a couple thousand playgoers at a time: the Theater (1576), the Curtain (1577), the Rose (1587; remodeled 1592), the Swan (1595), the two Globes (1599; rebuilt 1614), the two Fortunes (1600; rebuilt 1623), and the ill-fated Hope (1613). Until 1989, the most substantial evidence we possessed about the construction of these amphitheaters had been documentary and pictorial. Two building contracts in particular furnish theater historians with exact measurements and details of design for the Fortune and the Hope (and, anecdotally, for the first Globe), whereas the pictorial evidence includes a variety of period landscapes and "views" that depict playhouse exteriors in both Shoreditch and Southwark. The 1989 discovery of the Rose and the Globe sites in Southwark as well as the discoveries of the Theater site in 2008 and of the Curtain site in 2011, both in Shoreditch, have contributed to these documents and drawings tangible evidence about the amphitheaters' architectural footprints and nominal substructures, of which the most capacious features are the offstage spaces of their auditoria.

In chapter 3, I analyze how the interior geometry of Renaissance amphitheaters distributed playgoers' bodies and senses in space, creating oblique and disunified perspectives on the stages' action. I posit that such perspectives are physically analogous to the epistemological distortions that onstage narratives produce within dramatic form, as discussed in earlier chapters. Just as offstage action introduces unverifiable dramatic knowledge that competes with the visible scene, the offstage space of the auditorium establishes visual and aural challenges to the performance by positioning the audience at least 270 degrees and perhaps as much as 360 degrees around a thrust stage on as many as four vertical levels, yielding a vast array of intersecting sight lines and thereby disunifying the actual physical perspectives that playgoers occupy in relation to the stage. Moreover, because plays were performed in continuous light before audiences that were anything but docile and stationary, spectacle and noise from the auditorium contended with the action onstage and, as the evidence suggests, distracted playgoers from the performance on a regular basis. Prologues and choral figures, for example, habitually appeal to the audience for "*Rare silence*,"[38] which indicates a cultural disposition to theatergoing that did not reflexively direct itself with deference to the stage but rather one that the stage actively worked to persuade and charm to attention.

Chapter 3 brings together theater and architectural history with depictions of the power of rhetoric in action, including both woodcut illustrations and textual accounts, to produce what Henry Turner would call a "topographic" rendering of amphitheatrical space. Turner explains that

> we may define topographesis as the representation of place by texts of all kinds but also by maps, diagrams, paintings, or images, and even by built structures such as buildings and monuments, particularly when these are approached as "texts" with a coherent semiotic structure and a communicative function and especially when they are described verbally or portrayed in visual, graphic form.[39]

The spatial rhetoric of these auditoria consists of a geometrically balanced but perspectivally dispersed configuration of playgoers circulated around a thrust stage. What this physical design gains in maximized sight lines and, according to Bruce Smith, exceptional acoustics[40] it loses in perceptual uniformity among the audience. No two playgoers witness dramatic events from the same perspective, in other words, which is one facet of the performance experience that later proscenium-arch theaters will attempt to modify and that court masques were already reimagining.[41] The chapter links the aim of traditional rhetoric—that is, to persuade listeners to adopt a particular position on a disputed subject—to the rhetoric of space to show how the geometry of the auditorium positions playgoers' bodies and senses in connection to the dramatic disputations taking place onstage. Because the offstage space of the auditorium builds into its material conditions thousands of physical positions for playgoers to take up in relation to the onstage action, it multiplies their perspectives even while individualizing their points of view. I argue that the amphitheater's geometry works as a rhetorical strategy, which proliferates playgoers' interpretive stances by activating or deanesthetizing their physical and perceptual relationships to the stage.

Site Unscene is centrally occupied with the relationship between visible and nonvisible aspects of the drama and especially with how that relationship structures the apprehension and interpretation of Renaissance plays. Failing to attend to this mutually constitutive relationship weakens our understanding of the dramatic mode in both theory and practice, just as overlooking the offstage space of the auditorium neglects a principal rhetorical feature of the amphitheaters' material conditions. In chapter 4, the final chapter, I turn to early modern play-texts to explore how the printed medium of this literary form organizes its textual material according to a binate logic of visibility and transparency. The chief formal differences between narrative and drama—that is to say, a governing narrative voice that delivers characters' utterances indirectly, as opposed to characters speaking in their own persons outside of a prevailing locutionary authority—have always required that drama employ "didascalia," those unique textual conventions such as speech headings and stage directions that convey to the reader information that either a narrator or a live performance would typically supply. As Linda McJannet has shown, the evolution of didascalia has a complex history, but toward the end of the sixteenth century these textual features develop a "self-effacing" quality, which I connect to the offstage.[42] Whether they provide the reader with elaborate stage business or simply with basic knowledge about who speaks and when characters enter and exit the stage, didascalia tend to pass unobserved at the moment characters' lines come alive on the page. I argue that dialogue and didascalia each signify in different literary registers, and that these signifying practices foreground dramatic speech precisely by diminishing stage directions and speech headings to the point of transparency within the text.

The institutional process of transmitting characters' dramatic lines from the manuscript to the mouths of actors and eventually into print is an intricate, irregular, and still insufficiently understood series of practices in the period. Whether on page or stage, however, dramatic lines always remain discursive phenomena, moving back and forth from written to oral language. When Polonius asks, "What do you read my Lord?" Hamlet's reply, "Words, words, words," describes the objects on his page as well as the sounds in his mouth.[43] In contrast, neither the stage direction "*Enter Hamlet reading on a Booke*" nor the speech heading "*Ham.*" that precedes his response to Polonius in the text[44] would be verbalized by an actor playing Hamlet onstage because he is immediately and visibly identifiable to playgoers as he enters and speaks. Didascalia therefore impart essential elements of performance that are absent from characters' speeches—they signify offpage events—by providing printed plays with the textual infrastructure that makes those speeches intelligible to the reader. Yet because speech headings and stage directions substitute for visible but unspoken cues onstage, they acquire a secondary and, ironically, nearly invisible status within the dramatic text. Of course didascalia are not actually invisible on the page, but their secondary status, literarily speaking, causes them to oscillate between visibility and transparency. The material conditions of the dramatic text, then, highlight characters' speeches not only by positioning them in central textual columns but by marginalizing didascalia (at times literally on the page) and by obscuring the work that they do.

While most critics who discuss stage directions and speech headings naturally concentrate on their origins around the vicissitudes of live performance, my interest in didascalia extends to how they function as *textual* phenomena that are independent of performance events. The chapter examines the relation between dialogue and didascalia during the act of reading, and in particular the way that their two literary registers operate in tandem to create bifocal perspectives within the dramatic text. I show that didascalia function in terms of the Derridean *parergon*, the work outside the work of art, "a form which has as its traditional determination not that it stands out but that it disappears, buries itself, effaces itself, melts away at the moment it deploys its greatest energy."[45] Because stage directions and speech headings are at once "essential to this type of literary work" and "almost [able to] be omitted," as Roman Ingarden says,[46] we tend to read them according to what I call the "supplemental hypothesis," a reading practice that grants to didascalia the indispensable responsibility of making dramatic lines intelligible while also divesting them of literary meaning. Didascalia perform the work of the offstage by setting up the conditions that allow printed texts even to produce dramatic meaning in the first place, but they must efface themselves for characters' speeches to appear to be immediate. As removed from the stage as they are, printed dialogue and didascalia function like onstage and offstage space by compelling the reader to navigate two kinds of representation at the same time. Because didascalia both enable characters to speak and are superfluous in and of themselves, they disappear on the page to produce drama's hallmark qualities of being directly perceptible and unmediated.

In *The Production of Space*, Henri Lefebvre comments, "One wonders just how many errors, or worse, how many lies, have their roots in the modernist trio, triad or trinity of readability–visibility–intelligibility."[47] In the case of drama, the roots of this triad reach back to the earliest assertions on the subject, and we have not shaken them yet. The stage, being the theater's chief instrument of representation, is suitably the privileged site of drama because the immediate visibility of live action and the direct audibility of characters' lines comprise the prerequisites of dramatic readability and intelligibility. Yet *Site Unscene* will tell a different story about how the offstage, by virtue of its exclusion, outfits the stage with the enabling and material conditions that make drama possible. The offstage establishes drama's founding mythology by isolating the knowable stage from the unknowable beyond, which institutes the genre's unique and unrivaled contribution to the representational arts: the illusion of a fully visible and immediate aesthetic experience. In short, the offstage makes theater live.

Part I

The Offstage in Theory and Practice

Chapter 1

✦

Scene Individable, or Poem Unlimited

Premodern Theories of the Dramatic Mode

In a short footnote to a discussion of theatrical transvestism in classical Greek drama, Froma I. Zeitlin writes: "We may remember that obscene, *ob-scaenum*, in its usual etymology, means 'off stage,' i.e., off the 'serious' stage."[1] Without pursuing the matter any further, she suggests here that *obscaenum* is etymologically linked with the unseen sights of the offstage, yet in the same breath she associates the word with Greek distinctions in theatrical forms, which judge tragic subjects to be more serious than comic ones: "comedy," as Aristotle says, "is an imitation of baser men."[2] In the quasi-classical Athens of A MIDSOMMER *Nights Dreame* dwells a group of artisans whom the play depicts as just such base or "Hard handed men," who mishandle language and perform their "tedious breefe Scene of yong *Piramus*, | And his loue *Thisby*; very tragicall mirth" to unintended comic effect.[3] The play also features a kind of offstage space in the comic inversions of the Athenian wood, which stand in contrast to the serious business of Theseus's court and its preparations for the royal wedding, where the head of state conducts his own political drama through his misappropriation of Hippolyta. Opposite to Theseus, Nick Bottom serves as the artisans' de facto leader, despite trying to misappropriate the others' theatrical roles, and he just happens to describe the secluded and unobservable space of the Athenian wood as an "obscene" one when he affirms Peter Quince's plan to meet there to rehearse their play:

> *Quin.* [. . .]
> But masters here are your parts, and I am to intreat you, request you, and desire you, to con them by too morrow night: and meet me in the palace wood, a mile without the Towne, by Moone-light, there will wee rehearse: for if wee meete in the Citie, wee shalbe dog'd with company, and our deuises knowne. In the meane time, I wil draw a bil of properties, such as our play wants. I pray you faile me not.

> *Bottom.* We will meete, and there we may rehearse more obscenely, and couragiously. Take paines, bee perfect, adieu. (TLN 358–69)

Quince's rationale is to conceal their rehearsal and dramatic devices from the prying eyes of competing players, so they intend to rendezvous where they will not be seen on the scene in Athens, but remain unseen on the obscene in the wood—which is the same strategy Lysander and Hermia adopt, not to mention Pyramus and Thisby.

Zeitlin's note about the offstage would encourage us to read Bottom's "obscenely" as a rather felicitous use of language, even if he frequently speaks acyrologically—that is, with words opposite to his intention. Might Bottom mean "openly"? "More freely"? "Less offensively"? Be that as it may, the offstage sense of "obscene" toward which Zeitlin gestures does not derive from *obscaenum* at all, nor is its etymology based in either theatrical practice or dramatic vocabulary. Instead the word combines the Latin prepositional prefix *ob-* ("before," "in front of") with the Greek noun *caenum* ("filth")—the word itself putting Latin before Greek to form an impure and preposterous morphology. The logic is that "filth" is not offensive when it is in its proper place and hidden from view, but it becomes obscene when it is placed "before" or "in front of" one's eyes. The common etymological assumption is that the *s* in *obscaenum* derives from the Greek root *scaenum*, which refers to a theatrical scene, but the single letter actually appears to be a phonological accretion that smoothes the transition between the Latin prefix *ob-* and the root *caenum*. "Obscene," in other words, has nothing whatever to do with the stage or the theater, though it makes for a clever pun when naming offstage events, especially when those events are too sexually or violently graphic to perform in plain sight.[4]

Offstage events, in both graphic and less spectacular cases, have the signal effect of limiting playgoers' sight and knowledge while revealing that there is something important to see and know, making such events not unlike Bottom's dream. The offstage confounds the senses: "The eye of | man hath not heard, the eare of man hath not seen, mans | hand is not able to taste, his tongue to conceiue, nor his | heart to report, what my dreame was" (TLN 1737–40). It resists articulation: "I had a dreame, past the wit | of man, to say, what dreame it was" (TLN 1732–33). And it renders the investigator who ventures into its realm a fool: "Man is but an Asse, | if he goe about to expound this dreame" (TLN 1733–34)—an observation reinforced by the fact that Puck translates Bottom into an ass precisely when he steps offstage into their hawthorn brake of a tiring house to investigate and "see a noyse that he heard" (TLN 904). Yet, also like Bottom's dream, the offstage bestows on audiences "a most rare vision" (TLN 1732) by metamorphosing dramatic action into the powers of language while obstructing the faculty of sight, as we will see more fully in the next chapter.

In this chapter I argue that offstage events constitute an unexamined substructure to premodern theories of the dramatic mode. Critics from Aristotle to Philip Sidney stipulate in their treatises that certain kinds of dramatic action must regularly be removed from the stage and beyond the audience's sight, making it less immediate and therefore more palatable. But these critics also concede that such action is often dramatically indispensable, which requires that audiences somehow learn about those events that they never actually witness in order to comprehend those events that they do. When these theorists formulate the parameters of dramatic form—excluding that which belongs to epic and narrative, and including that which only theater can or should represent—they construct two spheres in which a play's action can occur: that of the stage, where the sights and sounds of performance reach playgoers directly, and that of the offstage, which serves as a repository for dramatic incidents that are, for one reason or another, ill suited for theatrical display and for the sensibilities of theater audiences. The language that these writers use to differentiate drama and narrative is invariably the language of rhetoric, emphasizing how the two modes persuade, or fail to persuade, audiences to invest their belief into the stage's representations. My argument is that these premodern theorists bestow the stage with representational power only by producing offstage spaces that can contain and neutralize essential but problematic material in the drama. Although their appraisal of unseen dramatic action varies significantly, the classical and early modern critics who will concern us in this chapter consistently deploy the offstage as a "theatrical necessity," the third term that allows them to make sharp distinctions between dramatic and nondramatic literary modes.

In addition to appraising the offstage in different ways, these critics sometimes address it only in an oblique manner, as a sort of shadow to onstage representations. Despite the indirectness with which Aristotle and others speak of the offstage, it is a compulsory and tacitly understood spatiotemporal reality within drama, one that in a sense goes without saying. Marvin Carlson, for example, cites "the simple trestle stages of the popular theatre from the classical period onward," stressing,

> Behind the acting area is a curtain that serves on a utilitarian level to mask backstage areas, but by usage and decoration it converts those areas symbolically into the fictive offstage world [. . .]. In the earliest printed editions of Terence, slots in this curtain have signs above them indicating that they are to be taken as doorways into bedchambers or into individual houses.[5]

While these curtains and signs certainly point to an unseen world offstage, they continue to function in these contexts as onstage scenic properties, which Keir Elam terms "scenic synecdoches": theatrical elements that "stand [. . .] for only part of the dramatic world in which the action takes place."[6] These properties both direct *and* obscure the spectatorial gaze toward offstage

Figure 1.1. Josse Bade, woodcut illustration for *Andria*, in Terence, *Guidonis Iuuenalis natione Cenomani in Terentium familiarissima interp̃tatio cũ figuris unicuiq3 scœnæ præpositis* (Lyon: Jean Trechsel, 1493), b8v (detail). Photograph courtesy of The Newberry Library, Chicago, folio Incunabula 8602.

spaces. Such onstage directives Carlson elsewhere calls "indexical signs," which guide the playgoer's visual, aural, and imaginative attention.[7] Even if doors and curtains on the stage evoke the existence of offstage worlds, they are but tantalizing apertures through which playgoers are unable to gain direct access in the theater.

In the early imprints of Terence that Carlson mentions, several woodcuts push the stage's visible boundaries inward by drawing the viewer's eye past these curtains, where the reader can peer a short distance into the plays' offstage spaces. In the opening act of *Andria*, for instance, Mysis steps out of Glycerium's house and then turns back at the doorway to speak to her fellow maidservant Archylis, a nonspeaking character who never comes onstage. The woodcut that accompanies this eight-line scene in Jean Trechsel's 1493 edition obscures Mysis's face as she speaks to Archylis, who is shown seated within, head tilted upward, attentive to her companion (figure 1.1). When Pamphilus arrives at his in-laws' house in *Hecyra* to find his wife Philumena in labor with a child he isn't expecting, he stands furtively at the door to hear the bustle inside. The 1493 illustration of this moment in the play shows him crouched and listening to the commotion while trying to silence his servant Parmeno with an upraised palm, but Pamphilus's mother-in-law, Myrrhina,

Figure 1.2. Josse Bade, woodcut illustration for *Hecyra*, in Terence, *Guidonis Iuuenalis natione Cenomani in Terentium familiarissima interp̃tatio cũ figuris unicuiqꝫ scænæ præpositis* (Lyon: Jean Trechsel, 1493), N3r (detail). Photograph courtesy of The Newberry Library, Chicago, folio Incunabula 8602.

is also visible through the curtain as she tries to hush her daughter's painful cries (figure 1.2). And in the third act of *Adelphi*, Demea laments the profligacy of his two sons and his brother Micio when he is met by his brother's servant Syrus, who gives specific orders at Micio's door to two offstage servants, Dromo and Stephanio, to clean fish in preparation for a meal. The woodcut for this particular scene shows Dromo and Stephanio offstage with a fish and a knife, while Syrus approaches Demea onstage (figure 1.3); curiously, the image also anticipates Hegio's (but not Geta's) entrance later in the act, when the three men converse together about Demea's sons.

These and other woodcuts in the Trechsel edition illustrate for the reader interior action that is not typically visible during performance, yet it remains integral to Terence's plays and contributes to presumptive but unseen dramatic realities beyond the stage. As William Gruber says, "Terence's inventiveness makes the offstage seem part of the entire signifying space of the theatre."[8] In premodern dramatic theory, however, offstage realities pose vexing problems to the integrity of dramatic form because audiences cannot see, learn about, or access them in conventional theatrical ways—that is, with their own eyes and ears. These theorists define drama using a kind of litotes that is grounded in the rhetorical circumstances of particular literary events. In other words,

Figure 1.3. Josse Bade, woodcut illustration for *Adelphi*, in Terence, *Guidonis Iuuenalis natione Cenomani in Terentium familiarissima interp̃tatio cũ figuris unicuiqȝ scænæ præpositis* (Lyon: Jean Trechsel, 1493), &2r (detail). Photograph courtesy of The Newberry Library, Chicago, folio Incunabula 8602.

to affirm that the direct and eyewitness apprehension of a dramatic fiction is a more persuasive and credible literary experience, premodern critics tend to deny that drama has anything to do with the indirect and auricular representations of narrative, which require a mediating figure who may be unreliable or deceptive. Aristotle notes that "everyone embellishes the stories he tells as if he were adding something pleasant to his narration" (24.1460a17–18). As we will see in the next chapter, Renaissance playwrights modernize their theater by capitalizing on unreliable or deceptive characters and their stories. But premodern critics attempt to defend the stage from offstage narrative incursions because the process by which an audience invests in, acquires knowledge about, and evaluates the credibility of a narrated story differs considerably from the rhetoric of drama.[9]

Locus Classicus

The premodern criticism on the offstage chiefly traces concerns about either aesthetic decorum or formal integrity. The problem that usually motivates these aesthetic and formal concerns is how a given audience comes to trust in the fictions that it either sees or hears, which serves in classical contexts, at least, as one measure of poetic competence. In his *Ars Poetica*, for instance, Horace first identifies two varieties of dramatic exposition and then distinguishes their effects on an audience's belief:

> Either a scene is acted out on the stage or someone reports the events that have occurred. Actions that have been admitted to our consciousness through our having heard them have less of an impact on our minds than those that have been brought to our attention by our trusty vision and for which the spectator himself is an eyewitness. You will not, however, produce onstage actions that ought to be done offstage; and you will remove many incidents from our eyes so that someone who was present might report those incidents [. . .].[10]

Either acted or reported, representations onstage appeal to either spectators or auditors, eyes or ears—though of course in either case both senses continue to function. Actions perceived through sight, Horace maintains, affect the theatergoer more profoundly than those reported, not because spectacle necessarily takes precedence over speech or language but because "our trusty vision" lends action more credibility than do our ears.[11] Witnessing a scene directly, "the spectator himself is an eyewitness" to every aspect of a dramatic event, both seen and heard. But there are limits. When one places "onstage [those] actions that ought to be done offstage [*ex oculis* (line 184)]"—such as Medea's filicides or Cadmus's metamorphosis—then they repulse spectators' sensibilities while also making them dubious. Yet, since such actions inevitably have their place within dramatic stories, especially tragic ones, Horace advises that they be narrated so as to obviate the shock, and perhaps the poor taste, of their visual immediacy.

The consideration that Horace gives to enactment and to narration on the stage is governed thoroughly by their effects on playgoers' perception. Further, he acknowledges that both modalities have appropriate duties in the theater, with the division falling roughly between scenes of mundane or conventional dramatic action and those of fantastical or theatrically demanding events. "Medea," he insists, "should not slaughter her children in the presence of the people, nor abominable Atreus cook human organs publicly, nor Procne be turned into a bird, Cadmus into a snake. Whatever you show me like this, I detest and refuse to believe [*incredulus odi* (line 188)]" (13). Significantly, Horace expends no effort in condemning or proscribing such events within dramatic performances. His effort lies, rather, in defining the expositional form in which those events should be presented, which correspondingly influences the kinds of response the performance should elicit from playgoers. Gruber observes, "Rather than attribute Horace's injunctions to decorousness, as that term is commonly understood, it may be more accurate to say that for Horace, 'decorum' is essential for verisimilitude as well as for decency."[12] Thus decorum definitely affects the mode through which dramatic action is to be presented, but it is not strictly a moral decorum that Horace advocates, nor does he bar indecorous events from the stage: a sense of theatrical propriety there certainly is, yet he estimates that propriety according to how effectively the stage action inspires the audience's belief.

Although the crimes of Medea and of Atreus, as well as the transformations of Procne and of Cadmus, might very well give moral offense when enacted on the stage, for Horace they are difficult to bring off credibly in the visual dimension of theater. The aural dimension, however, is another story. When the depictions of certain sights reach the limits of plausibility, spoken accounts must then replace them. Horace gauges stage representations by their ability to persuade spectators. He first privileges seeing over hearing because "the spectator himself is an eyewitness" to the events, but once visual credibility cannot be satisfied, its substitution by verbal report becomes a priority. Horace implies, then, that verbal narration will no longer challenge the authenticity of the reported event, which simply becomes a fait accompli. The *Ars Poetica*'s logic is that incidents of this kind cannot be disentangled from plays without damaging them. Whether acted or reported, they continue to be fundamental to the dramatic action.

If Horace addresses the issue of offstage action in an explicit manner, then Aristotle approaches the subject much more indirectly. Actions that take place *ex oculis*, beyond the audience's sight, seem at first inconsequential to his discussion, not least because, as O. B. Hardison explains, "action" in the *Poetics* refers to "the process of change that takes place between the beginning and end of the play" rather than to the physical activity upon the stage, which he identifies with "spectacle," or to the dramatic events that occur in a play's individual scenes, which Aristotle calls episodes.[13] Julie Stone Peters argues that most neo-Aristotelians in the Renaissance will misinterpret his notion of "action" as belonging to the actor on the stage, which for Francesco Robortello, Antonio Minturno, Lodovico Castelvetro, Philip Sidney, and others comes to dominate their discussions of dramatic form.[14] In contrast, Aristotle's notion of action pertains to the overall proportionality of the tragic plot, the construction of which should limit the sort of events or episodes that playgoers witness in the first place. When Aristotle does mention offstage events directly, the references appear almost always as examples from specific plays, such as Sophocles's *Oedipus Tyrannus*, Euripides's *Iphigeneia in Tauris*, and Theodectes's lost *Lynceus*. Notably, few of his references to offstage action are to entr'acte events: most either precede the opening lines of a play or are anticipated to follow well after the actors have removed their masks.

In two important instances, however, Aristotle pauses over certain kinds of events in drama that *should* reside offstage. In chapter 15, he says:

> The *deus ex machina* must be reserved for the events that lie outside the plot, either those that happened before it that are not capable

> of being known by men, or those that occur after that need to be announced and spoken of beforehand. For we grant to the gods the power of seeing all things. There should, then, be nothing improbable in the action; but if this is impossible, it should be outside the plot as, for example, in Sophocles' *Oedipus*. (15.1454b2–8)[15]

Hardison supplies crucial insight to this passage:

> Here the reference is to incidents that influence the action but are far removed from it in time. These incidents may precede or follow the play's action; but they must be described *in the play* if the audience is to appreciate the action and its consequences. Aristotle suggests that the *deus ex machina* is particularly suited to the role of expositor of the past or prognosticator of the future, because the gods have "the power of seeing all things"—past, present, or future (lines 38–39).[16]

Again, one of Aristotle's tasks here is to maintain the proportionality of tragic plots so that the dramatic action presented by a play remains unified and does not exceed the bounds of the stage's direct and visible representation, which can strain mimetic plausibility and thus destroy the audience's ability to believe the action. But if the dramatic poet finds it impossible to compose his plot without incorporating implausible events—implausible because they are "incidents that influence the action but are far removed from it in time"[17]—then the deus ex machina provides the poet with a solution for including the "improbable in the action" while at the same time locating it "outside the plot." Because "we grant to the gods the power of seeing all things," a play's action will be more rational if a god delivers the news about a vital but distant event than if one of the human characters does so.

Toward the end of chapter 24, Aristotle revisits this conjunction of improbability, irrationality, and offstage action, again using examples from plays to illustrate his point:

> The use of impossible probabilities is preferable to that of unpersuasive possibilities. We must not construct plots from irrational elements, and we should especially attempt not to have anything irrational at all in them; but if this is not possible, the irrational should be outside the plot (as in Oedipus' ignorance of how Laius died); it should not be in the drama itself, as occurs in the *Electra* concerning those who bring news of the Pythian games, or in the *Mysians*, concerning the man who has come from Tegea to Mysia without speaking. To say that without the use of such incidents the plot would have been ruined is ridiculous. For it is necessary, right from the beginning, not to construct such plots. (24.1460a26–34)[18]

Aristotle states here that the plot of a tragedy—and, accordingly, the performance and reception of one—should ideally contain no incidents that truck in improbability, irrationality, human reports about distant events or oracles, or other factors that lie outside of the knowledge or experience that an audience acquires during a given theatrical event. Yet, insofar as such incidents cannot be extricated adequately from a unified dramatic action, they must nevertheless take place, he instructs, "outside the plot," and "not be in the drama itself."

These are curious remarks, and not just because Aristotle constructs the offstage sphere as a sort of unknowable territory where dramatic irrationalities can run free, like gods. In these passages, Aristotle sets up an opposition between the ordered, proportional, and rational business of the stage and its antithesis, which would seem to dwell beyond a given play's mimetic action and outside the apprehension of theatergoers. What is so curious in Aristotle's distinctions is how irrational and otherwise troubling events can remain necessary components of dramatic plots—how they can remain *in and part of those plots*—while simultaneously being located outside of those plots and off of the stage.

Through these passages, Aristotle attempts to establish the spatiotemporal boundaries and the ratio-mimetic conditions of the Attic stage by making the offstage its founding repudiation. To mark the limits of tragedy, Aristotle expels from it all that is disproportionate, excessive, unknown, irrational, even as he accepts that, at times, these elements are intrinsic to the operation of the drama. Discussing classical Greek tragedy, Hanna Scolnicov argues that a "wider geographical area accommodates the various events that are excluded from the concentrated plot which unfolds in the visible theatrical space," and thus it is the offstage or "the theatrical space without that guarantees the [Aristotelian] unity of place in the theatrical space within and, along with it, also the two other unities."[19] While it exemplifies the wild and unpredictable landscape outside the theater's bounds, the offstage aspects of tragedy bring into being the controlled conditions on its stage.[20]

The concerns that Aristotle expresses about tragedy's "irrational elements" belong properly in his theoretical schema to the tripartite component of "objects," which comprises plot, character, and thought (6.1450a7–12): these are the things that irrationality afflicts. Related to these concerns are other, less articulated ones regarding narrative and enactment, which are the "modes" of imitation.[21] In elevating tragedy over epic, Aristotle tends to want to make its qualities unique, or at least to portray them as the most refined developments to date in the representational arts. He discerns drama's origins not only in dithyrambic and phallic songs but in the narrative mode as well, particularly as Homer practiced it: "just as Homer was especially the poet of noble actions (for he not only handled these well but he also made his imitations dramatic), so also he first traced out the form of comedy by dramatically presenting not invective [as in Old Comedy] but the ridiculous"

(4.1448b34–38). Moreover, Aristotle readily sanctions the coupling of narrative with dramatic dialogue in the Homeric epic: "using the same means and imitating the same kinds of object, it is possible for the poet on different occasions to narrate the story (either speaking in the person of one of his characters as Homer does or in his own person without changing roles) or to have the imitators performing and acting out the entire story" (3.1448a20–24).[22] But for tragedy Aristotle has reservations about giving narrative anything like a stable footing on the stage.

Reinforcing his modal distinctions, Irene J. F. de Jong argues:

> According to Aristotle *Poet.* 1449b24–7, an important characteristic of drama is that it proceeds through the mode of action [enactment] and not of narration [. . .]. At first sight this would seem to imply that messenger-speeches, which are after all a form of ἀπαγγέλια [*angelia*, narrative], are not at home in drama. This conclusion is, however, unwarranted, since by δι' ἀπαγγελίας Aristotle means the assuming of the role of narrator *by the poet* (as Homer does in the narrator text of the *Iliad* and the *Odyssey*). This indeed never happens in drama.[23]

Yet because characters who report offstage events engage simultaneously in verbal narration and direct enactment, the distinction that Aristotle makes (and that de Jong affirms) holds only at the compositional level, especially considering that, according to Aristotle himself, the "performing and acting out [of] the entire story" is effected by actors, not by the dramatic poet. He reiterates the distinction between the two modes at several points in the *Poetics*, in particular when he emphasizes tragedy's eminence over epic: "Now epic poetry follows the same pattern as tragedy insofar as it is the imitation of noble subjects presented in an elevated meter. But epic differs from tragedy in that it uses a single meter, and its manner of presentation is narrative" (5.1449b9–12). "Tragedy," he soon specifies, "is presented in dramatic, not narrative form" (6.1449b24–27).[24]

So how is one to deliver vital but external—if irrational—information to theatergoers without introducing a narrator to reveal that information? The most effortless way is simply to refrain from associating a humble, usually unnamed *angelos* or messenger with the responsibility of narrating, even if, as de Jong points out, narrative is the technical mode within which all Greek messenger figures speak.[25] In other words, Aristotle is able to dissociate dramatic messengers from the mode of narrative through a kind of hyperrational logic that insists on the impermeability of his categories. After he subordinates character to action—"Poets do not, therefore, create action in order to imitate character; but character [i.e., 'personal qualities'] is included on account of the action" (6.1450a16–18)—he declares that the very point of the dramatic mode is to represent action rather than character: "without action tragedy would be impossible, but without character it would still be possible" (6.1450a23–24). Aristotle would therefore view a messenger's job of narrating offstage events as an attribute of the role and not as a part of the mimetic element of mode, which would properly belong only to the tragic poet who manages the entire design. That dramatic characters actually *do* narrate offstage events, regardless of the poet's initial or compositional control of those characters and their stories, means that the hierarchy of plot and character is not a necessary or even an internally consistent one.

Although the *Poetics* addresses itself to offstage action rather circuitously, such action is in fact imperative to Aristotle's project of designating, through calculated exclusion, a legitimate space for tragic poetry, its theory as well as its practice. I say a legitimate space since the *Poetics* is ordinarily understood to be engaging on some level with books 2–3 and 10 of *The Republic* and countering particularly Plato's attitudes there toward the problem of representation. Indeed, the teacher and student divide their representational modes identically: just as Aristotle describes a specular mode, a narrative mode, and a mixed one (3.1448a19–24), Plato earlier had Socrates describe "'one kind of poetry and tale-telling which works wholly through imitation [. . .] tragedy and comedy; and another which employs the recital of the poet himself [. . .]; and there is again that which employs both, in epic poetry and in many other places.'"[26] But while Socrates and his interlocutors go on to determine "'whether we shall [even] admit tragedy and comedy into our city or not'" (3.394d), Aristotle embraces drama as the most "superior" art (26.1462a14). To be sure, he tries to keep his own analytical categories firm and discrete. Yet unlike Plato, who decides finally to exile drama from his ideal state (10.606e–607b), Aristotle need only banish from the tragic stage that which is "improbable," "irrational," or "common." He says: "if whatever is less common is better, that art would be superior that is directed at the more discriminating audience; and it is very clear that the art that imitates every detail is common" (26.1461b27–29).[27]

One of Aristotle's concerns in the *Poetics* is to maintain the superior position of plot or action at the expense of character, as well as to limit the scope of the action that the playwright represents: an effort to define the qualitative and quantitative parts of action. When weighing the relative excellence of epic and tragedy he says that, aside from the occasional problem of poor acting, "it is apparent that tragedy, since it is better at attaining its end, is superior to epic" (26.1462a14–15). Aristotle harbors a great respect for epic, and especially Homer's facility with it, so to claim tragedy's superiority, he demonstrates that it has everything epic has—and more. Yet his hierarchy of tragic elements ("plot, character, diction, thought, spectacle, and melody" [6.1450a9–10]) comes into conflict with that of poetic form ("invariable narrative voice" and "direct enactment of all roles" [3.1448a21, 24, Halliwell's translation]), which puts him in a double bind with regard to the exact status of narrativity. And this conflict is aggravated by the fact that he authorizes "combining narrative with direct personation" in epic (3.1448a21–23,

Halliwell's translation), but pointedly not in drama. He sees a need on one hand to distance storytelling from drama because the mode belongs to epic. But, on the other hand, Aristotle wants to endow tragedy with all of epic's potency, which leads him to say that tragedy "contains all of the elements that epic has" (26.1462a14–15). In the *Poetics*, then, narrative serves as a fulcrum point by which Aristotle raises tragedy above epic at the formal level and lowers character below plot at the elemental level. Because he is unable to perform both of these maneuvers at the same time, the mode of narrative—the primary form through which offstage events appear—becomes itself a sort of phantom element in the formation of tragedy. In the same way as offstage action occupies multiple locations in its absent–present story form onstage, the narrative mode ultimately resides both within and outside of Aristotle's theoretical system.[28]

If the offstage sphere is always threatening to force its irrationalities into the regulated space of the stage, as Aristotle suggests, then two late classical treatises on comedy actually promote the narration of offstage events to prevent onstage action from itself becoming too irrational. Deriving from a collection of commentaries on Terentian comedy, Evanthius's *De fabula* and Aelius Donatus's *De comoedia* each locate all narratives about offstage events within dramatic prologues, which are the first of comedy's four elements, as Evanthius explains:

> Comedy is divided into four parts: the prologue, *protasis*, *epitasis*, and *catastrophe*. The prologue serves as a kind of preface to the play; it is the only part in which it is permissible to tell the audience something which is external to the plot, either for the sake of the poet or of the play itself or of the actor. The *protasis* is the first act and the beginning of the play. The *epitasis* provides the growth and development of the complications and is, one might say, the knot of the whole problem. The *catastrophe* is the turning of events to a happy outcome through the discovery of the facts being revealed to all.[29]

For Evanthius the protasis "is the first act and the beginning of the play," but the prologue still precedes the protasis. The effect of this partitioning is to transform the prologue into a kind of liminal theatrical element, which nevertheless remains one of comedy's "four parts" but which also "serves as a kind of preface to the play," like front matter in a book.[30]

In *De comoedia*, however, Donatus expands Evanthius's discussion by differentiating and naming the various themes that might occupy the speaker of a prologue: he may recommend the play to the audience, for instance, or pronounce a curse on a rival dramatic poet (273). But occasionally a prologue must relate critical offstage action that has occurred during a play's prehistory, and this he calls "*dramatikos* or narrative [*argumentativus*], explaining the plot of the play" (273–74). Donatus goes on to say that "Some wish to make this distinction between prologue and *prologium*, namely, that it is a prologue when either the poet justifies himself or commends the play, but it is a *prologium* only when something about the play is stated" (274). Hence, according to both Evanthius and Donatus, whenever a prologue speaks about crucial offstage events, it does so to avert confusion about and to make *more rational* the ensuing action on the stage. Evanthius adds, furthermore, that "Terence often uses a device which other authors do not handle with ease: *protatika prosopa*, that is, characters drawn in from outside the plot [*personas extra argumentum accersitas*], so that by bringing them in the plot may easily be made clear" (270).

Evanthius's use of *protatika prosopa* to describe "characters drawn in from outside the plot" helps highlight not only the prologue's liminal status in relation to a play's staged scenes but also the displaced and displacing effects that offstage action brings about when narrated onstage. Originally meaning "face" or "countenance," *prosopon* eventually becomes associated with "character"—think of the rhetorical figure *prosopopoeia*, personification—whereas *protatikon* is an adjective related to spatiality, meaning "placed in front of"—recall the etymology of the word "obscene." In addition, *protatikon* is the adjectival form of the noun *protasis*, which Evanthius defines dramatically as "the first act and the beginning of the play." But, crucially, *protasis* also functions grammatically as the "if" clause in conditional sentences.[31] The phrase *protatika prosopa*, then, designates characters whom the playwright has "placed in front of" or before a play's action in a temporal sense, much as dramatic narrators bring offstage events into the presence of the stage in a spatial sense. Further, any narrative that *protatika prosopa* place in front of playgoers might be viewed as a kind of conditional dramatic or scenographic statement about prior action, which creates for the audience the possibility, epistemologically speaking, for understanding whatever events might follow on the stage.

The narrative prologues that Evanthius and Donatus detail in their treatises resemble Aristotle's uneasy notion about offstage space and events insofar as they are at once internal and external to the plot, indispensable to the performed action but not exactly suitable for the fiction on the stage. Yet whereas Aristotle works to limit the level of irrationality that might appear on the stage by making its spatiotemporal dimensions coincide almost entirely with its dramatic representations, Evanthius and Donatus encourage the introduction of offstage events (though restricted to prologues) to reduce the degree of dramatic ambiguity that performances are liable to produce. The eruption of such offstage situations within the Aristotelian theater threatens the coherence of dramatic action by calling into question the boundaries that define the stage and how playgoers come to knowledge about its representations. But at the same time, as Evanthius and Donatus state outright, offstage events are often theatrically de rigueur, requiring prologues to furnish essential dramatic background so that a play's subsequent onstage action may be sufficiently intelligible. For Horace, onstage narratives become absolutely necessary when the theater is unable to pull off convincing representations, making playgoers' belief in the dramatic fiction the most decisive factor. The language of persuasion, credibility, and belief permeates all of these discussions and, while their rhetorical standards for these dramatic qualities differ, each writer achieves his ideal stage conditions precisely by creating some form of offstage space that playgoers may only access through the mediation of story.

When offstage action appears as narrative within a live setting, the storyteller works in a doubly subjunctive mood, which comprises both the enacted what-if-ness *of* the performance and the narrated what-if-ness *within* the performance. With its effects of spatial and temporal dislocation, narratives about offstage events have the extraordinary effect of arresting the performed activity onstage while simultaneously advancing the action of the play.

The Impractical Spatial Arts

> Now is there not one end, and one only, in philosophical exposition, in oratory, and in the drama? Assuredly such is the case. All have one and the same end—persuasion.
>
> —Julius Caesar Scaliger, *Poetices libri septem*

In *The English Renaissance Stage: Geometry, Poetics, and the Practical Spatial Arts 1580–1630*, Henry S. Turner argues that early modern English dramatists "began to conceptualize problems of theatrical representation in terms that derived not simply from neo-classical literary theory, [. . .] nor simply from the legacy of medieval staging and the Tudor interludes, [. . .] but from contemporary developments in early-modern technology, applied mathematics, and pre-scientific thought."[32] Coincident advancements in "literary and scientific epistemologies"[33] were spurred by common needs in both fields to justify in a coherent and replicable fashion their theoretical underpinnings, tested and testable methodologies, and domain-specific objectives. Turner shows persuasively how early modern playwrights as well as literary critics increasingly adopted the language of geometry and other "practical spatial arts" to understand the range, limits, topography, and conceptual grounds of theatrical representation in the period. When he comes to examine Philip Sidney's THE DEFENCE OF *Poesie*, Turner finds that it engages with an older curricular tradition steeped in rhetoric, dialectic, and other neoscholastic pursuits while at once holding up poesy as a field of knowledge that possesses "an analytic value" beyond a "prescriptive, moral one."[34] Turner explains:

> In the first place, his [Sidney's] essay defends poesy as a specifically *linguistic* epistemology and does so [. . .] as a response to

> the contemporary emphasis on dialectic and rhetoric as intellectual instruments in the production of knowledge that was typical of the university curriculum when Sidney was himself a student at Oxford and when he composed the *Defence* in approximately 1579–80. Secondly, his essay attempts to defend mimesis, or "imitation," as the primary method used by poesy as an epistemology, and so the essay defends poesy as a mode of knowing through *formal representation*—what Gabriel Harvey will call an "iconic" mode of representation, as we shall see—in a way that dialectic or rhetoric were not.[35]

The stress that the DEFENCE puts on "poesy as a mode of knowing through *formal representation*," as Turner suggests, has important implications for how Sidney thinks about theatrical space and especially about offstage space, both of which resound with certain Aristotelian echoes.

These echoes are Aristotelian in the sense that the DEFENCE produces an impractical and farfetched offstage realm precisely through its circumscription of onstage representations, much as the *Poetics* does, though these echoes also call for a change in contemporary English theater practices, which try to depict the spatiotemporal scope of their subjects in too liberal a manner. More explicit than Aristotle, Sidney details the kind of irrationalities that he sees taxing the early modern English stage, at least as it had developed by the late 1570s:

> For where the Stage should always represent but one place, and the vttermoste time presupposed in it, should bee both by *Aristotles* precept, and common reason, but one day; there is both manie dayes and places, inartificially imagined. But if it bee so in *Gorboducke*, howe much more in all the the [*sic*] rest, where you shall haue *Asia* of the one side, and *Affricke* of the other, and so manie other vnder Kingdomes, that the Player when he comes in, must euer begin with telling where he is, or else the tale will not be conceiued.[36]

Redolent of Aristotle's remark that "it is necessary, right from the beginning, not to construct such [expansive] plots" (24.1460a33–34), Sidney's solution to this kind of gallivanting drama is to constrict the action of a play to only the most crucial events: "if they will represent an Historie, they must not (as *Horace* saith) beginne *ab ouo*, but they must come to the principall poynte of that one action which they will represent" (I1r). For the dramatic mode, Sidney wants the "conceived space" of the action to be isomorphic with the "perceived space" of the stage,[37] which allows playgoers to apprehend the performed activity itself without the added burden of having to imagine that the stage's actual space represents two or more posited locations, especially at the same time, with "*Asia* of the one side, and *Affricke* of the other."

Should prolix English playwrights happen to ask Sidney, "how then shall we set foorth a storie, which contains both many places, and many times?" he would reply, "do they not know that a Tragidie is tied to the lawes of *Poesie* and not of Historie: not bounde to follow the storie, but hauing libertie either to faine a quite new matter, or to frame the Historie to the most Tragicall conueniencie. Againe, many things may be told which cannot be shewed: if they know the difference betwixt reporting and representing" (H4v–I1r).[38] Such a "storie" comprises all of the events or episodes that contribute to a given fiction (*fabula*), which can nonetheless be abbreviated and concentrated into "the most Tragicall conueniencie" (*sjuzhet*), such as those concluding actions that befit the dramatic form. "By example this will be best expressed":

> I haue a storie of yoong *Polidorus*, deliuered for safeties sake with great riches, by his Father *Priamus*, to *Polminester* King of *Thrace*, in the *Troyan* warre time. He after some yeares, hearing the ouerthrowe of *Priamus*, for to make the treasure his owne, murthereth the Childe, the bodie of the Childe is taken vp [by], *Hecuba*, shee the same day, findeth a sleight to bee reuenged moste cruelly of the Tyrant. Where nowe would one of our Tragedie writers begin, but with the deliuerie of the Childe? Then should hee saile ouer into *Thrace*, and so spende I know not howe many yeares, and trauaile numbers of places. But where dooth *Euripides?* euen with the finding of the bodie, the rest leauing to be told by the spirite of *Polidorus*. (I1r)[39]

Though *Polidorus* is no Aristotelian god come to tell of events that have occurred offstage, he is at least a "spirite" or *daemon ex machina* who has lived and died the entirety of the "storie" that a theater audience would need to hear about in order to make its "most Tragicall conueniencie" intelligible.

The detrimental effects of trying to put onstage a comprehensive story such as Polidorus's include not only the implausible representation of "manie dayes and places, inartificially imagined," but also the adulteration of subject matter, which, through its capaciousness, brings high and serious occasions into contact with low and trivial ones. Sidney argues that by staging a tale's every episode, dramatic poets fail to exercise judgment and to discriminate between those events that give a "storie" gravity and substance to begin with—like Hecuba, who "findeth a sleight to bee reuenged moste cruelly of the Tyrant"—and other, more mundane events, which might be necessary conditions to the grave and substantial parts but which do not need to be put on theatrical display, such as the birth of Polidorus or his sailing over into Thrace. In the DEFENCE, the oratorical experience and the presentational style of theater hold sway over dramatic form, with the speakers personating only the most important figures in a fiction within the here and now, which may draw in the there and then through narrative but should not try to stage it in plain view. Of his contemporary English playwrights Sidney says, "their Playes bee neither right Tragedies, nor right Comedies, mingling Kinges and Clownes, not because the matter so carrieth it, but thrust in the Clowne by head and shoulders to play a part in maiesticall matters, with neither decencie nor discretion" (I1r–v). Both the mingling of "manie dayes and places" and the mingling of "Kinges and Clownes" are properly speaking vices of form or modality because, in the theater, it is the visual immediacy of these mixtures that defy reason and thus challenge the credibility of the representation itself. Rhetorically speaking, these minglings are unconvincing. Placed on a stage, a "mongrell Tragicomedie" (I1v) is quite a different beast than one narrated in a book, primarily because prose and epic forms offer virtually unlimited time and space, which the dramatic form simply cannot compass without sacrificing the audience's ability to believe in the fiction. As Sidney admits of such mingling, "I know *Apuleius* did somewhat so, but that is a thing recounted with space of time, not represented in one moment" (I1v), like a play.

If we understand poesy in the DEFENCE "as a mode of knowing through *formal representation*," as Turner argues, then the form or physical manifestation that dramatic stories take must be tethered not only to the physical space of the stage itself but also to the immediate perceptual experiences of the playgoers who come to knowledge through what they see and hear enacted there, which has the effect of putting the offstage far outside the audience's consciousness. In contrast to playgoers' immediate perceptions, the experience of narrative "as a mode of knowing" involves the creation of distance and the putting off of time through dilation, which Patricia Parker says "is frequently a synonym for temporality itself, or for the *mediate* as distinguished from the eternal, simultaneous or *immediate*," such as we might expect in theater.[40] In Sidney's view, the material limits of the stage should restrict the spatial reach of the dramatic action performed on it, just as the period that an audience spends watching a play should ideally define the temporal duration of that action—or, at the "vttermoste," "but one day" (H4r). To do otherwise is to confound the credibility of the dramatic imitation and to engage in what Sidney calls "grosse absurdities" (I1r), which seem here to be akin to Aristotle's "irrational elements." Further, the "mode of knowing" that Sidney promotes in the theater also resembles that of Horace's spectator, whose dramatic epistemology is constituted primarily by sight rather than hearing. Yet, also like Horace, Sidney affirms that onstage "many things may be told which cannot be shewed" (H4v). He writes, "for example, I may speake though I am here, of *Peru*, and in speech digresse from that, to the description of *Calecut:* But in action, I cannot represent it without *Pacolets* Horse. And so was the manner the Auncients tooke, by some *Nuntius*, to recount things done in former time or other place" (I1r). The DEFENCE views dramatic expanses offstage to be unrepresentable "in action," though they can be immediately traversed and conveyed through narrative "by some *Nuntius*," but only if absolutely necessary.

Not surprisingly, Sidney couches his pronouncements about the form and limits of onstage representations in a notion of space that privileges visual ways of knowing over those that are aural. He likewise differentiates the space of drama or theater from that of narrative or storytelling—spaces that are largely mappable as onstage and offstage, respectively—while at the same time granting that the two may be, and often need to be, combined, "else the tale will not be conceiued." This, he says, is "the difference betwixt reporting and representing." As Julie Stone Peters writes:

> If drama was made up of representing rather than reporting, and if representing meant representing on stage, it was the theatrical environment, then, that explained and helped interpret the formal rules for representational genres. That is, theatrical conditions determined dramatic form. Reworking Aristotle in the attempt to define the nature of the dramatic, Renaissance theorists may have been interested in the status of narrative form in and of itself, but their focus was on the relation of narrative form to medium.[41]

Thus, Turner observes, employing his "knowledge of geometry and the spatial arts," Sidney attempts in the DEFENCE to make contemporary English drama itself a "practical spatial art" by attuning it to its proper medium, by making it subject to "a distinct intellectual method," and by developing it into "an instrumental mode of knowledge with the power to transform nature, man, and society."[42] But Sidney encounters the same problem that Aristotle does in the *Poetics*: the recurrent inability to compress a unified dramatic action into the confined space of the stage without the admission of storytelling characters who bring offstage events with them. In tracing out the boundaries of the stage and its spatial arts, Sidney makes narrative a supplemental feature of the drama that is practical for providing exposition and background but entirely impractical for depicting individual episodes offstage because everything dramatically pertinent to the focused action should already be onstage to begin with.

The Stages of Our Storie

> Where our sceanes seemes to liue,
> I doe beseech you
> To learne of me who stand with gappes
> To teach you.
> The stages of our storie
>
> —Gower, in *Pericles, Prince of Tyre*

Both Aristotle and Sidney misrecognize, suppress, or diminish the fact that onstage "reporting" by *angeloi*, *nuntia*, and other more central dramatic characters inevitably occurs in the narrative mode, which gives rise to a contradiction in their categorical distinctions about the kinds of representation that are and are not suitable for the stage. If we were to view narration and enactment as always being locked in a hierarchical relationship, as Aristotle and Sidney appear to do, then we could go some way in resolving this contradiction. We must first of all accept that *diegesis*, or narration, is the mode of such genres as epic, while *mimesis*, or enactment, belongs to drama. As Lodovico Castelvetro explains, the dramatic mode

> represents words and things with words and things, whereas the narrative mode represents things with words only and represents direct utterances with indirect. It is more restricted in space, for it cannot represent places remote from one another, as the narrative mode may do, which in this respect need observe no restrictions of any kind. It is more restricted in time, for, unlike the narrative mode, it cannot represent actions that unfold over different periods of time. It may represent only things visible and audible, whereas the narrative deals with both the visible and the invisible, the audible and the inaudible.[43]

Because this understanding of modality has been axiomatic for millennia, it is an easy distinction to accept. Yet, however patently logical this division between narration and enactment may seem, we must also accept that such a prioritization—not to mention a purification—of modes predisposes us to subordinate one to the other whenever they appear in a mixed form. The conceptual payoff that Aristotle and Sidney achieve with this prioritization is that the primary mode can be seen to contain, control, and even neutralize the modal energies of the other, which is made to be a secondary or supplementary attribute of the first.[44]

The potential mixture of modes, then, is a chief concern or anxiety among these classical and early modern critics, not simply because they want poets to maintain representational integrity by matching modes to their proper generic forms—which is, after all, a performative dictum masquerading as a descriptive statement. More important, mixing modes is a concern because of the epistemological confusion that audiences can so easily experience, like that which Gower says he wants to try to alleviate in the epigraph that opens this section.

In book 3 of the *Republic*, for instance, Plato scrutinizes Homer's combination of modes within a larger discussion of the illusory or deceptive quality intrinsic to representational practices in general. Offering examples from the opening lines of the *Iliad*, where direct dialogue appears in the midst of narration, Plato's Socrates questions Homer's ethos and his manipulation of the reader into believing that the words that characters speak are not in fact Homer's own. Socrates says:

> "You know then that as far as these verses, 'And prayed unto all the Achaeans, / Chiefly to Atreus' sons, twin leaders who marshalled the people,' the poet himself is the speaker and does not even attempt to suggest to us that anyone but himself is speaking. But what follows he delivers as if he were himself Chryses and tries as far as may be to make us feel that not Homer is the speaker, but the priest, an old man. And in this manner he has carried on nearly all the rest of his narration about affairs in Ilion, all that happened in Ithaca, and the entire *Odyssey*." (3.393a–b)

Socrates determines, finally, that Homer "'and the other poets effect their narration through imitation' [i.e., dramatic dialogue; see *Poetics*, 4.1448b34–38]," "'But if the poet should conceal himself nowhere, then his entire poetizing and narration would have been accomplished without imitation'" (3.393c). Gerald F. Else notes that Plato becomes suspicious of Homer's combination of modes because "the poet impersonates the characters of his story—impersonates them not merely by putting speeches in their mouths but in the sense that he pretends to be the various characters, tries to make us think that he *is* Chryses or Agamemnon and all the rest in turn."[45]

To avoid such impersonation, which deludes and thus lies to the audience, poets might scatter verbal tags—"said Chryses," "Agamemnon replied"—that interrupt the illusion and prevent listeners from being deceived, which is William Gruber's sensitive reading of these passages:

> Plato sees conventional narrative markers as small but critical modifications to mimetic performance. They establish within the performer's imitation a steady rhythm of interruption and, more important, they show a conscious commitment to some cognitive frame beyond the imitation. To the extent that the poet frames showing with telling, Plato seems to be saying that spectators necessarily remain aware of the constructed nature of the performance.[46]

Such impersonation troubles Plato because the source and veracity of a poet's or character's utterances cannot be authenticated, but they nonetheless behave rhetorically as if the words were genuine and unmediated. This inability to authenticate indirect speech links intimately with the suspicion surrounding narrative and the preference for eyewitnessing. An epic poet who carefully differentiates his own words from those of his characters thus garners the audience's trust because, Plato suggests, his poeticizing is transparent and sincere. But on the stage, where the poet is altogether absent, characters *must* speak in their own persons for the dramatic fiction to be credible. Hence the concern that Aristotle, Sidney, and (much less so) Horace voice is that narration in the theater disastrously undermines the rhetorical assumptions of live performance, which are that the sights and sounds theater audiences witness are believable because they are plainly visible and immediate, arising from the scene as it unfolds.

Although I doubt that Aristotle, Horace, or Sidney would make this particular argument, their various anxieties coincide with Plato's in the detrimental effects that combined modes have upon their audiences. As we have seen, these effects can take the form of Horatian implausibility, Aristotelian irrationality, or Sidnean "grosse absurdities," but in all cases they create epistemological confusion for playgoers because the combined modes make distinct demands on their belief. Narration and enactment package their fictions differently, and they present their audiences with discrete configurations of knowledge, each with its own calculus for verifying facts about their representations and its own process for supporting the audience's trust in their fictions. When a poet combines these two modes, however, each of their rhetorical assumptions and energies makes the other's more conspicuous, causing an audience difficulty in discriminating between the forms of truth that narration and enactment portray. While Plato via Socrates censures modal combinations altogether, Horace, Aristotle, and Sidney are content simply to prioritize them whenever necessity asks that they be mixed, which allows one mode to envelop and constrain the energies of the other. I will be showing in the next chapter that such a prioritizing of narration and enactment is a theoretical move of abjection or purification that dramatic practice rarely warrants, but it is enough to say here that I actually agree with these critics about the epistemological confusion that results from the mixing of modes, only the effect, I believe, is a powerful dramatic strategy for prompting audiences to resolve that confusion through active interpretation.

To my knowledge, the only critic to give a technical name to this sort of mixed representation is Castelvetro, who calls it the "similitudinary" mode (*similitudinario*). Reliant in almost all cases on both narrative and dramatic forms, the similitudinary involves a narrator who simulates the direct speech of one or more characters by adapting his or her voice to theirs, much as the *Republic*'s Socrates describes Homer doing in the *Iliad*. Castelvetro writes that

> the similitudinary mode differs from the narrative and the dramatic in that it cannot rightly have an independent existence, but in so far as it quotes some one's words directly must be dependent on the narrative mode since it cannot dispense with the narrator, who is known to be so-and-so and different from the one whom he temporarily impersonates as he delivers the similitudinary utterance.[47]

He goes on to say that "the combination of the narrative and the dramatic modes in Cicero's *De Amicitia*, in some of Plato's dialogues, and in other works by other authors violates the nature of both modes" (35), which is a statement that avoids prioritizing one over the other, even if it still attempts to purify their formal qualities. And while Castelvetro lists seven "manners of representing spoken words"—"simple narrative, simple dramatic, simple similitudinary; narrative and dramatic combined, narrative and similitudinary combined, dramatic and similitudinary combined; narrative, dramatic, and similitudinary combined" (35)—he does not explore either the theoretical implications of these various compound modes or the practical effects that they might have on an audience, nor does he express the degree of concern that Sidney and especially Aristotle do about the very prospect of their combination.

"Similitudinary" is an apt term for a narrator's impersonation of a fictional character because such a representation is only "like" that which it impersonates, like a simile, as opposed to the way an actor might strive to assume the entire deportment of a character, like a metaphor.[48] But when a character who is already embedded in a dramatic fiction comes onstage and tells a story about action that playgoers have and will never witness for themselves, this compound representational activity exceeds questions of similitude and metaphoricity. This particular species of representation generates epistemological uncertainty through its mixture of narration and enactment, suggesting that something is potentially awry or askew between what playgoers see onstage and what they hear about from elsewhere. Such epistemological uncertainty, as we shall see, is not merely a lack or a muddling of playgoers' knowledge about dramatic action taking place offstage. It is instead the calculated deployment of certain forms of knowledge with corresponding forms of ignorance, on the one hand, and, on the other, the onstage intimation that there is pertinent knowledge to be had, which nevertheless remains either hidden or partial in its revelation. To adapt one of Gruber's formulations, the offstage is not simply hidden, but it is represented onstage in terms of its hiddenness.[49] Critics like Aristotle and Sidney might have tried to export such dramatic material from the stage, but the English Renaissance theater put this material to work to exploit the disjunctions between the knowledge and the ignorance that the stage delivered to its playgoers.

Epistemology of the Offstage

If the spectacles that a culture puts onstage happen to express the unspoken desires and anxieties of that culture's social body—or if, conversely, they offer a culture a way of articulating itself to itself—then perhaps those dramatic events that it keeps off the stage reflect a range of cultural or historical formations that it is not yet equipped to confront in so unmediated a fashion. Celia R. Daileader argues convincingly, for example, that although legal restrictions barred women from performing on the early modern English stage, many of the period's plays foreground the highly visible place of women in the culture's social, sexual, and political imaginary, paradoxically keeping them offstage while at once putting them at the center of its representations.[50] Viewing the offstage sphere as a kind of cultural subconsciousness has rich implications not only for the general study of drama but also for more specific forms of knowledge that plays may circulate between a performance and its audience. The kind of sexual issue or political configuration, say, that a given play precludes from being enacted on the stage, yet which it still allows to be narrated or revealed, may provide an index to gradations of legitimacy within certain cultural forms, just as it may reveal processes by which those cultural forms are mediated and indeed brought into existence through particular epistemologies. "It would be intriguing to consider," ponders Henry Turner,

> how the spatial distinctions operating on the early modern open stage could themselves be aligned with a variety of current theoretical paradigms: in this view onstage and offstage space might be correlated with (for example) conscious and unconscious, or discursive and non- or extra-discursive, and thus might begin to operate as a conceptual model for thinking through how some strands of early modern culture become explicit while others remain occluded or structurally "invisible."[51]

The so-called deposition scene in Shakespeare's *Richard the Second* comes to mind here since it was absent from the first three quartos, as does the censorship note in "The Booke of Sir Thomas Moore." Within the manuscript, the Master of the Revels Edmond Tyllney censors the staging of the "ill Maie daie" riots of 1517,[52] which involved craftsmen and other citizens rising up against diplomatically protected resident aliens, who had been infringing on the livelihoods of London merchants. In the margin next to the opening scene of the play, Tyllney subdues the rioters by writing:

⟨Le⟩aue o⟨ut ⟩
y^{e} ⟨i⟩nsur⟨rection⟩
   w⟨h⟩oly w^{t}
y$^{(e)}$ Cause ther off &
⟨b⟩egin w^{t} Sr Tho:
Moore att y^{e} mayors sessions
w^{t} A reportt afterwarde*e*
off his good servic‘
don being‘ Shriue off Londõ
vppõ a mutiny Agaynst y^{e}
Lũbard*e* only by A shortt
reportt & nott otherwise
att your own perrilles
Ed Tyllney[53]

For Tyllney it seems that the explicit enactment of the riot would be too immediate a depiction of the event, but its distancing by "A shortt | reportt" is a perfectly acceptable mode of representation.

The onstage visibility of a given issue, then, may say something about a culture's tendency to authenticate meaning visually, à la Horace's seeing-is-believing spectator. But it may just as easily employ spectacle inordinately to discredit the reliability of sight and/or to reinforce belief as a more strictly narrative- or language-based affair. As Jody Enders has said, drama's "special contribution to culture is its uncanny ability to ground belief in the sometimes dazzling, sometimes troublesome collision of the illusion of reality and the reality of illusion."[54]

Whether or not a culture's subconscious might be glimpsed through the onstage collisions of drama and narrative, the offstage may be said to act as a faculty of memory to the drama's immediate or present conscious awareness, which would be the stage itself. Drama's rhetorical premise is that the mode verifies itself by delivering action and dialogue directly and visibly to the conscious awareness of playgoers. But, as I will be suggesting in the next chapter, when characters verbally rehearse for playgoers their memories of absent, sometimes distant action and dialogue, the drama's epistemological ground shifts before their very eyes, causing playgoers themselves to shift between registers of belief. By insisting, therefore, that the verbal dimension of narrative is not simply a supplement to theatrical representation, we begin to restore onstage stories at least to the rhetorical conditions through which audiences acquire competing forms of knowledge in the theater, not just because spoken stories actually *do* portray dramatic action but, more significantly, because such a restoration offers a valuable way of situating theatricality as well as narrativity within a diachronic analysis of performance.[55] When drama and narrative come together onstage, they deliver to audiences bifocal forms of knowledge, which create the rhetorical conditions that invite audiences to contemplate and resolve the disparities.

Whenever it brings an absent offstage into the presence of performance, the drama effects what Plato would perhaps call a "fractioning of human faculty" (3.395b), which ostensibly occurs when an individual attempts to practice more than a single imitative art at once. Onstage narratives of offstage action likewise work to divide by "fractioning" representational forms and human epistemology. But unlike Plato, who finds this state of mind to be destructive, I believe that such a formal and epistemic fragmentation is a productive one because the analytical distance and cognitive dissonance that the offstage generates give the audience important interpretive work to perform.

Chapter 2

✦

The Narrative Economy of Social Commerce

> Telling is a responsible and commercial act [. . . .]
>
> —Roland Barthes, *S/Z*

> If we view narration and narrativity as the instruments by which the conflicting claims of the imaginary and the real are mediated, arbitrated, or resolved in a discourse, we begin to comprehend both the appeal of narrative and the grounds for refusing it.
>
> —Hayden White, "The Value of Narrativity in the Representation of Reality"

The "conflicting claims of the imaginary and the real," Hayden White suggests, "are mediated, arbitrated, or resolved" under the aegis of narrativity and through the act of storytelling. Because "our desire for the imaginary, the possible, must contest with the imperatives of the real, the actual,"[1] we tend to use narrative as one instrument for tailoring our desires to the constraints of living—to the demands of social and material realities—but also for bending those realities toward the heights of our imaginations. Narrative enables us, in other words, to script ourselves into lived situations that would otherwise seem to resist or refuse such social and material arrangements. Yet White also argues that, even before we project our most untried desires into novel livable forms, the structure of narrative mediates our relations with the world by organizing, often within a causal dynamic, the random and infinite perceptions our senses receive into manageable and communicable narremes: "far from being one code among many that a culture may utilize for endowing experience with meaning, narrative is a metacode [. . .]. Arising, as Barthes says, between our experience of the world and our efforts to describe that experience in language, narrative 'ceaselessly substitutes meaning for the straightforward copy of the events recounted.' "[2] If one way of rendering the world intelligible is by casting its dazzling contiguities into coherent narratable forms, then narrativity itself might be regarded as the force that bestows the impression that we exercise control over the meaning of our world—and that keeps chaos from coming again. As Roland Barthes has it, "Ultimately, the narrative has no *object*: the narrative concerns only itself: *the narrative tells itself*."[3]

The "story shall be chang'd."[4] In A MIDSOMMER *Nights Dreame*, Peter Quince, Nick Bottom, and their fellow artisans undertake the kind of scripting of futurity through narrative that White and Barthes describe, and they do so, appropriately enough, in the form of a script, "A tedious breefe Scene of yong *Piramus*, | And his loue *Thisby*" (TLN 1853–54). As they divvy up the parts "to con," or memorize (TLN 361), determine the time and location of their rehearsal, and "draw a bil of properties, such as our play wants" (TLN 365–66), the artisans reveal their reasons for turning their hard hands to this dramatic labor of the mind in the first place: "to play in our Enter- | lude before the Duke and the Dutches, on his wedding | day at night" (TLN 273–75). The projected performance may be motivated by the artisans' sense of duty to Duke Theseus, but such duty is itself caught up in a circuit of exchange that both affirms their mutual sociopolitical positions and enacts the nature of the relationship between them. Late in the play, Theseus tutors Hippolyta on this circuit of exchange:

> The kinder we, to giue them thanks for nothing[.]
> Our sport shall be, to take what they mistake;
> And what poore duty cannot doe, noble respect
> Takes it in might, not merit. (TLN 1886–89)

But the language of giving and taking—along with Hippolyta's misgivings about the artisans' mistakings—extends beyond the dutiful affirmation of class structure in Athenian society. The artisans dream that it might extend into the future and take the form of a royal pension, a dream where their "desire for the imaginary, the possible, must contest [*less*] with the imperatives of the real, the actual."[5] Motivating the artisans are the potential rewards that a winning performance may procure for them from their royal audience. In short, they want to be "made | men" (TLN 1764–65).

But, before the artisans have the opportunity to perform, the bottom of their play drops out, leaving them to agonize over the loss of their star player, which means that "the play is mar'd," as is their prospect of receiving pensions for it. Like the more financially secure futures they had hoped for, "It goes | not forward" (TLN 1751–52). Flute says with regret:

> *This*. O sweet bully *Bottome:* thus hath he lost sixe-
> pence a day, during his life; he could not haue scaped six-
> pence a day. And the Duke had not giuen him sixpence
> a day for playing *Piramus*, Ile be hang'd. He would haue
> deserued it. Sixpence a day in *Piramus*, or nothing.
> (TLN 1666–1770)

At this point in the play, it seems that the artisans' inability to script the future by projecting their imaginations into it will result in the story of their real lives remaining hopelessly unchanged: Flute-Thisby's reduplication of the words "sixpence a day" suggests that they are already stuck in a futureless moment. When all appears lost, however, the irrepressible Bottom returns, making it possible once again to give Duke Theseus and his conquered Amazon bride their interlude, which just might earn them sixpence a day after all. The social principle in which the artisans invest is one of narrative exchange, "a responsible and commercial act."[6] Banking on a financial payoff for their labor, they plan to perform the "Pyramus and Thisby" story so that Duke Theseus might see fit to underwrite their own more favorably plotted lives. *A MIDSOMMER Nights Dreame* leaves unstated whether they ever actually receive their desired pensions, which indicates that narrativizing the future in this way can be a rather risky venture. But, by the same token, narratives about the future are a way to theorize the practical consequences of new roles, of fresh social configurations, and of more ideal lives.

In the previous chapter we saw how narrative threatens dramatic integrity at the theoretical level because the two modes authenticate their representations according to different rhetorical assumptions. I argued there that most premodern theorists of the drama succeed in producing the stage's ideal conditions only by expelling narrative from the theater and by attempting to confine playgoers' knowledge solely to dramatic action that they can immediately see and hear. These writers contend that the two modes fail to synthesize when offstage events appear onstage through narration, causing audiences to experience confusion, incredulity, and/or contradiction, which jeopardizes their investment and belief in dramatic fictions. In this chapter I turn to practicing Renaissance playwrights to argue that they recognized the confusion, disbelief, and epistemic tensions surrounding the offstage, but that they took advantage of such narrative effects by depicting dramatic situations in which the plays' social conflicts themselves center on unseen events and on the forensic activities of determining the certainty of facts, of evaluating the credibility of stories, and of navigating the persuasive schemes and onslaughts of other characters. Lorna Hutson has recently shown, for example, how the teaching of *narratio* suffused educational institutions in Renaissance England, and as a result dramatists in the 1580s and '90s began more systematically to employ this core component of forensic rhetoric in the composition of their plays.[7] And Richard Meek, who discusses *Hamlet*'s use of unseen action, writes that "Shakespeare appears to have already realised that the way to create the most compelling illusion of reality is *not* to create a harmonious balance between narrative and drama, but rather to create a series of comparisons between the two modes. It is, then, the interplay between these two modes of mimesis that often creates the play's powerful illusion of immediacy."[8] The Renaissance theater's strategic substitutions of storytelling for direct enactment are, I want to suggest, representational exchanges that turn interpretive profits. To show those profits, this chapter examines how, why, and when characters exchange stories in the drama, using them as a kind of currency in bids for material goods, favor, or rewards—as Quince, Bottom, and the rest try to do—but, just as importantly, to gain their audiences' belief and trust.

I argue first of all that Renaissance playwrights modernized the stage by dilating it with verbal narrative. Patricia Parker observes that "the dilation of discourse is linked with the creation of spaciousness or intervening space," so when playwrights put stories into the mouths of their characters, they create new forms of dramatic space and time that exist elsewhere but that also intervene into the space and time of the stage.[9] Second, I argue that these narrative dilations and interventions function in plays to dramatize social cohesion through shared stories and a sense of communal experience, on the one hand, and to portray divisions between individuals and groups whose personal investments or master narratives are too dissimilar or incompatible to cohere, on the other hand. As a consequence, characters deploy stories about offstage events either to affirm or to refashion social bonds and configurations for self-interested reasons, which more often than not causes the dramatic action to change trajectories over the course of a given play. These narratives present truth-values that are independent of the immediate sights and sounds of the stage, which playwrights frame both as dramatic dilemmas for characters to negotiate and solve within their social worlds and as aesthetic dilemmas for playgoers to grapple with from their standings in the auditorium.

From much earlier in the sixteenth century, humanists had been promoting the interpretive expertise required to cope with these sorts of dilemmas. The humanist curricula in grammar schools, the universities, and the Inns of Court taught students how to contend with shifting rhetorical conditions by developing their verbal facilities as well as their aptitudes for understanding and responding to problems from multiple perspectives. Joel B. Altman demonstrates how the rhetorical pedagogy of debate *in utramque partem*, or arguing on both sides of the question, "permeated virtually all areas of intellectual life."[10] Teaching students to argue from contrary or even objectionable points of view ideally prepared them to defend their own morally upright positions more effectively, but in actuality it made one's ethical stance quite literally an arguable point.[11] Credible storytelling was a key component of such formal argumentation, which ultimately derived from ancient rhetoric and jurisprudence. The humanist cultivation of formal debate, oratorical proficiency, argumentation, and a responsive versatility in changing rhetorical circumstances made narrative a central preoccupation not only of strict literati but also of lawyers, courtiers, clergy, and others whose professional success depended on sophisticated skills of persuasion. I wish to add Renaissance playwrights to this list of professionals because their integration of these rhetorical strategies helped modernize the theater by significantly widening its representations to include intricate narratives about unseen sights within offstage spaces. The time-honored strategies for composing and delivering convincing narratives were to be found in the canons of classical oratory, which taught students how to make choices about what material to include (*inventio*), how to arrange that material into a believable chain of events (*dispositio*), and the ways to speak with great care and to assess an audiences' needs (*eloquentia*, *memoria*, *pronuntiatio*).[12]

In the *Institutio Oratoria*, furthermore, Quintilian details five elements that contribute to a well-told tale: lucidity, brevity, credibility, vividness, and (occasionally) grandeur. He begins by saying: "A Narrative is an exposition, designed to be persuasive, of an action done or deemed to be done."[13] Yet because "[t]here are many true things that are not very credible, and false things [that] are frequently plausible," he insists that "[w]e must therefore make just as much effort to make the judge believe the true things we say as to make him believe what we invent."[14] In constructing a persuasive narrative, Quintilian's orator must use lucidity (*dilucida*) to encourage the audience's understanding, brevity (*brevis*) to facilitate its memory, credibility (*credibilis*) to stir its belief, vividness (*evidentiam*) to enhance the story's lucid and credible appearance, and grandeur (*magnificentiam*) only in those cases that call "for a lofty tone."[15] These elements are rhetorically essential in narrative precisely because audience members, whether judicial or literary, have not seen the events with their own eyes, which requires that they be recounted with verbal dexterity. The effect of such dexterous *narratio* is the production of *enargeia*, which "makes the hearer forget the interposition of the aural or written medium, seeming to see the scene described before her mind's eye."[16]

In legal contexts, exquisitely constructed narratives were designed to meet the needs of evidential proof and "to overcome a certain scepticism, a certain anticipated judicial resistance to the way in which the narrator wants to present the events alleged to have taken place."[17] Skepticism of stories and storytellers, however, extended well beyond judicial settings in sixteenth- and seventeenth-century English culture. Hutson argues that a broader cultural familiarity with *narratio* and forensic rhetoric "became [. . .] part of a popular mental disposition,"[18] including within the popular theater:

> [T]his judicial pedagogy of narrative fostered an awareness of the "facts" as having been generated by the order and coherence of their telling. In other words, it fostered a tendency to represent dramatis personae as, on the one hand, forensically engaged in persuading one another of the truth of highly disputable "facts," and, on the other, as suspiciously testing and trying out the grounds for belief in one another.[19]

The important consideration that Hutson neglects in her otherwise shrewd discussion is the different ways that drama and narrative substantiate their representational claims. At a formal level, drama's rhetorical power rests in the openly visible actions and directly audible speeches of characters interacting in a fiction onstage, whereas narrative's rhetorical power resides entirely with a single speaker, whose credibility and persuasiveness depend on exercising the kind of oratorical skills that Cicero and Quintilian teach. We saw in the previous chapter how premodern theorists tend to view the modes of drama and of narrative as rhetorical oil and water. Horace says, for instance: "Actions that have been admitted to our consciousness through our having heard them have less of an impact on our minds than those that have been brought to our attention by our trusty vision and for which the spectator himself is an eyewitness."[20]

John D. Lyons likewise asserts, "The narrative of the offstage world has a much more tenuous claim to our belief than what is acted out before us, for such narratives depend either on the words of a single individual or on the often conflicting accounts of several characters."[21] Why, then, do playwrights combine narrative with drama in so wholesale a manner on the Renaissance stage? The reasons, I want to suggest, are aesthetic, critical, and rhetorical. First, working playwrights deliberately aimed to produce the aesthetic effect of *enargeia* through narrative's extraordinary ability to paint a scene's most vivid details within the listener's imagination. Second, while it is likely that few if any of these playwrights had classical dramatic theory in mind when they created their elaborate offstage scenes, their work represents a new counterdiscourse to the received critical consensus about the mixing of modes onstage. Finally and most important, offstage action and the narrative mode confront audiences with epistemic uncertainty that calls for interpretation. In these situations, new possibilities for dramatic meaning arise from a resolution of the ambivalence that offstage action creates. As Keith M. Botelho argues, "early modern dramatists contended that the path to truth and authority rested in careful listening with a discerning ear to all voices, distilling the truth [. . .] by aurally detecting the veracity of the information and the credibility of the teller."[22] In Renaissance theater, characters calculate their own self-interests against those of other characters by constructing rhetorically minded stories about unseen action, which dramatizes "highly disputable 'facts'" within "forensically engaged" social exchanges.[23] Exactly when a story's events supposedly took place and the actual point at which they are narrated influence the rhetorical tactics the teller employs to heighten credibility, which profoundly shapes listeners' epistemologies. This chapter therefore focuses on three temporal configurations between the onstage story and its offstage referents: prehistories, entr'actes, and simultaneous action.

Prehistories

In this section, I examine reported actions that take place before the opening lines of a play are even spoken, but an important distinction needs to be made at the outset between dramatic "exposition" and the narrative prehistories that I will be examining in Thomas Kyd's THE SPANISH TRAGE*die* and William Shakespeare's *The Life of Henry the Fift*. Characters frequently deliver "news," background to the plot, and other kinds of exposition from directly within the dramatic action, yet even such speeches are not always necessary for characters to communicate crucial offstage details. In Kyd's play, for example, Hieronimo enters "in his shirt &c." and finds the body of his son Horatio stabbed and hung up in the bower.[24] While the shirt in a sense "tells a story" about Hieronimo having been in bed asleep even before he delivers his line: "What outcries pluck me from my naked bed[?]" (D2v), the "meaning" of the shirt is not up for debate. Hieronimo's shirt possesses "iconic *identity*"—it is at once a nightshirt and a representation of a nightshirt on the stage—just as it is "indexical," pointing to the offstage bed from which he has been raised. But it offers a sign in the semiotic sense rather than an argument in the rhetorical sense.[25] Likewise, those dramatically embedded expositions that characters exchange and that merely bring the audience up to speed, as it were, are not of interest here, for despite the fact that they technically operate in the narrative mode, they rarely introduce disputable facts about the action.

In addition to these kinds of informal and embedded expositions, Renaissance playwrights used five formal techniques to convey a plot's necessary background: choruses, dumb shows, arguments, prologues, and inductions, which should be understood as liminal or nonorganic devices because they do not arise out of the dialogic structure of a play's fiction. These techniques differ from the prehistories I discuss in this chapter because they tend to put the audience into one of two interpretive positions with regard to their subject matter: the expositions are either rhetorically neutral and merely supply significant background that the play does not hold up to scrutiny, as I suggest above with Hieronimo's nightshirt, or they are tendentious and urge playgoers to take a specific stance on the play as a whole.

The chorus is a comparatively rare preliminary device in late Elizabethan and Stuart popular drama. The 1623 folio printing of Shakespeare's *Henry the Fift* furnishes the period's most recognizable example, though the play's opening uses it less for filling in narrative background than for metatheatrical commentary that places the audience firmly in the role of coproducer for the performance.[26] In THE TRAGICALL *History of D. Faustus*, on the other hand, the Chorus begins the play by relating in brief all of Faustus's life right up to the present, an exposition which the play simply offers at face value. It speaks

> for *Faustus* in his infancie:
> Now is he borne, his parents base of stocke,
> In *Germany*, within a towne calld *Rhodes*:
> Of riper yeeres to *Wertenberg* he went,
> Whereas his kinsmen chiefly brought him vp,

> So soone hee profites in Diuinitie,
> The fruitfull plot of Scholarisme grac't,
> That shortly he was grac't with Doctors name,
> . . . .
> And this the man that in his study sits.[27]

Like choruses, dumb shows seldom appear in the period's drama, but they are probably the most unique type of nonorganic device that playwrights used because in performance they dispense with language altogether while at once directing interpretations of the action that follows through their highly emblematic and sometimes telescopic tableaux. In *The Tragidie of Ferrex and Porrex* by Thomas Norton and Thomas Sackville, the undated octavo prints a "domme shew" before each act, along with a "signification therof," the aim of which is to diminish skepticism or ambivalence about the meaning of the ensuing action and to promote conclusive interpretations of it.[28]

As THE TRAGEDIE OF HAMLET, *Prince of Denmarke*, illustrates, however, dumb shows could also serve purely to crystallize a play's argument or plot. After "*The dumbe shew enters*" and performs, Ophelia asks, "Belike this shew imports the Argument of the | Play?"[29] In Ben Jonson's *SEIANVS HIS FALL*, the printed "*ARGVMENT*" gives the reader historical background as well as an implicit outline of what will follow in the play-text, though directly below "*THE ARGVMENT*" is a small section of text (set in larger type) on "*Traytors, &* | *Treasons*," which pulls the reader toward conclusive rather than deliberative interpretations of the argument and of the play itself, like Norton and Sackville's dumb shows.[30] In addition to the physical descriptions of its dumb shows, *Ferrex and Porrex* prints "The argument of the Tragedie" on the verso of the title page,[31] which consists of seven brief sentences that emphasize the main events in each of the play's five acts. Discussing the history of the dramatic "argument," Henry Turner explains that

> *Argumentum* was the term Terence, Donatus, Evanthius, and others had used to denote the "subject," "topic," or "story" of a play; along with *fabula* and *historia*, the term was used by Quintilian and others to describe the different kinds of narrations in oratory. Donatus and Diomedes had followed Terence in reserving the term *fabula* for plays in general and in using *argumentum* or *ficta argumenta* in reference to their fictional content.[32]

As for prologues and inductions, they too commonly introduce a play's "'subject,' 'topic,' or 'story,'" which may also contain essential narrative background. Unlike dumb shows and arguments, however, prologues, inductions, and even choruses are often lavish with customary modesty and apologia, as is the "*Prologus*" in *The Roaring Girle* by Thomas Middleton and Thomas Dekker:

> [A] *Play (expected long) makes the Audience looke*
> *For wonders:—-that each Scœne should be a booke,*
> *Compos'd to all perfection; each one comes*
> *And brings a play in's head with him: vp he summes,*
> *What he would of a Roaring Girle haue writ;*
> *If that he findes not here, he mewes at it.*
> *Onely we intreate you thinke our Scœne* [. . . .][33]

And, in Ben Jonson's *BARTHOLMEW FAYRE*, the lengthy "INDVCTION. ON THE *STAGE*" blends the conventional self-consciousness of inductions and prologues with an ostensibly unscripted confrontation at the newly built Hope playhouse between the "Stage-keeper," "Book-holder," and "Scrivener," who delivers to the audience "ARTICLES of Agreement, indented, between the | *Spectators* or *Hearers* [. . .] And the *Author of* | *Bartholmew Fayre*," articles which try to limit the audience's interpretive freedoms by aligning them with Jonson's intention.[34]

The collective point that these examples make is that either such formal devices are adamant about the specific meaning an audience takes from the play or they don't raise the question of interpretation at all because their subject matter isn't controversial. Moreover, these five techniques overlap and do not have discrete purposes. Both analeptic and proleptic, they summon narrative material for audiences from a play's past as well as from its future, presenting not just expositions but previews. In contrast to this kind of dramatic exposition, the narrative prehistories that I discuss in the rest of this chapter interject unverifiable, contingent, and/or contested knowledge into the unfolding dramatic action, which burdens audiences with problems of evidential uncertainty. When a character talks about an offstage event, his or her story overtly declares its subjective and biased point of view because the narration itself takes place within a dramatized social setting where conflicting interests are the sine qua non of the play's complication. The rhetorical choices that characters make when composing narratives about offstage events are especially evident when multiple versions of a story are told by a single character, or those told by several characters. With five independent accounts of its prehistory, Kyd's *THE SPANISH TRAGEdie* exemplifies in a profuse way how tales of unseen events shape dramatic characters and the alliances that they forge.[35]

The story that characters rehearse in the first act of Kyd's play centers on the battle between Spain and Portingale, with the Ghost of Don Andrea, the Spanish General, Prince Balthazar, Villuppo, and Horatio each offering accounts of the daylong conflict. When the Ghost of Don Andrea narrates his war experience to Revenge in the opening scene, he devotes only three lines to the battle: "in the late conflict with Portingale, | My valour drew me into dangers mouth, | Till life to death made passage through my wounds" (A2r). Moreover, he buries his bare-bones description of the battle among the remains of other stories. The Ghost obliquely mentions his "discent | Though not ignoble, yet inferiour far | To gratious fortunes of my tender youth" (A2r); he reveals that "In secret I possest a worthy dame, | Which hight sweet *Bel-imperia* by name" (A2r); and he finally expends much more breath recalling his epic journey through a classical underworld (A2r–A3r). Any one of these narrative strands may develop or become significant during the subsequent action, but for the audience at this particular juncture of the play, the meaning of each strand is uncertain.

Immediately in the next scene, the Spanish King and his entourage take the stage, wherein the onstage Ghost will relive the battle through its narration by the General. After the King requests him to "vnfolde in breefe discourse, | Your forme of battell and your warres successe" (A3v), the General delivers a sixty-three-line declamation, the most extensive of the testimonies in the play. He begins at the beginning: "Where Spaine and Portingale do ioyntly knit | Their frontiers, leaning on each others bound: | There met our armies in their proud aray" (A3v), and he ends with Spanish victory: "And our Carbines pursued them to the death, | Till *Phœbus* wauing to the western deepe, | Our Trumpeters were chargde to sound retreat" (A4v). Positioned between these lines, the General's commanding narration of the battle marshals the vividly descriptive powers of *enargeia*, for it moves from the general to the particular, from the battlefield's undifferentiated throng to the decisive single combat, balancing in every motion and phrase the ebb and flow of the opposing armies. The symmetry of the narrative's events is the symmetry of their narration, the structure of which George Puttenham calls "*Hypotiposis*, or the counterfait representation": "The matter and occasion leadeth vs many times to describe and set foorth many things, in such sort as it should appeare they were truly before our eyes though they were not present, which to do it requireth cunning: for nothing can be kindly counterfait or represented in his absence, but by great discretion in the doer."[36] The species of *enargeia* or *hypotiposis* that represents "actiuitie" Puttenham names "*Pragmatographia*": "But if such description be made to represent the handling of any busines with the circumstances belonging therevnto as the manner of a battell, a feast, a marriage, a buriall or any other matter that lieth in feat and actiuitie: we call it then the counterfait action [*Pragmatographia*]."[37] Utilizing "counterfait action," the General stylistically reproduces the mutual exchanges of a battle in which, for "three long hovres and more, | The victory to neither part inclinde" (A4r). His sententia encapsulates the poetic euphuism elegantly: "*Pede pes & cuspide cuspis, | Anni sonant annis vir petiturque viro*" (A4r), "foot to foot and lance to lance; arms clash against arms, and man is attacked by man."[38] At last Horatio, provoked by Andrea's death on the field, breaks the deadlock and defeats the Portingale prince Balthazar, the event that brings an end to the battle as well as to the General's story.

If we compare the General's account of the battle with the Ghost's and with the three others that will soon follow, it seems the most objective, probably because it offers such detail in its protracted and proportional style. His lengthy account also appears more objective when we consider how Hutson describes the persuasive power of *narratio* and *enargeia*:

> It is probable that its [*narratio*'s] contribution to the mimetic realism of Renaissance drama has been overlooked because of its very effectiveness. We are inclined to forget how much is not actually staged in a Renaissance play, because the *enargeia*, or vividness and presence, of various characters' narrations of events that take place elsewhere gives us the impression, especially as readers, of a reality as immediate as that which we imagine to take place on-stage.[39]

Confined to their own temporal experiences, however, playgoers at this instant have only the Ghost's description with which to compare it. The General's copious speech clearly fills a considerable epistemic gap about the recent conflict, a gap which the Ghost had lain open with his lean three lines in the previous scene. The brevity of Andrea's account might easily elicit the desire for a more comprehensive one, and the General's story certainly helps satisfy such a desire. But he also simply tells a pleasing tale in the sense that it is "good newes" (A4v) to the Spanish King, whose military forces, unpaid tribute, and imperial authority had been in jeopardy. The General furthermore aestheticizes his story, adopting an elevated style to reflect both the majesty of his primary audience and the occasion of Spanish victory. "List his discourse of Warre," to quote Shakespeare's Bishop of Canterbury, "and you shall heare | A fearefull Battaile rendred you in Musique."[40] The Spanish King is pleased not only by the good report or by the role his general has played in securing the victory, but also by the General's capacity to convey the battle's events as if, Puttenham says, "it should appeare they were truly before our eyes though they were not present." In recompense for the story, the king "Give[s] him his chaine" and tells him, "These words, these deeds, become thy person wel" (A4v).

Because "the two modes are theoretically opposed," says Francis Berry, narrative and drama interact in practice only by containing or framing each other.[41] Berry defines these two modes according to their generally fixed relations to space and time, particularly with regard to the activities of narrating a story, on the one hand, and of performing a play, on the other: "Reported events can be given as much space—or time—as an author wishes, depending on his evaluation of them; but events *shown*, or direct speech, can only take the space—or time—that they would in actuality take to be done or said."[42] Hence narrative takes "as its norm the past tense," and drama's "norm the present tense."[43] Yet the containment model that Berry uses to describe narrative's place onstage both neutralizes and underestimates its power to generate a representational surplus in the theater. While narrative always possesses a double-time structure—that is, the time of the events themselves and the time in which those events are told—an onstage narrative creates a triple-time structure because the narration itself occurs within a progressive dramatic fiction. It might be said, then, that *THE SPANISH TRAGEdie* actually begins in medias res, a nonlinear chronology that drama normally resists. By multiplying and dislocating the time and space of the stage through narrative, Renaissance playwrights harness diverse rhetorical energies to depict new kinds of conflicts within the drama, which changed the way playgoers experienced theater.

"These words, these deeds" that the General narrates arouse not just commendation from the King but anticipation to hear more: "Thanks good L. Generall for these good newes, | And for some argument of more to come" (A4v). For the Spanish King, the lengthy oration is but an "argument" that the General will later dilate more, offstage, as a royal entertainment, after national security and peace have been ratified by the Portingale Viceroy's tribute. To ensure receipt of this tribute, Spain holds prisoner the Viceroy's son, Prince Balthazar, who gives the play's third account of the battle and specifically of the conclusive single combat. As he had done with the General, the King bids Balthazar to speak, but he does so precisely because Lorenzo and Horatio tell contradictory stories about which one of them captured the prince. When they both claim Balthazar as a prize of battle, neither Lorenzo nor Horatio is entirely forthright about the details he uses to construct those claims. Moreover, they both try to seize Prince Balthazar's right to tell his own story:

> *King*. But tell me, for their holding makes me doubt,
> To which of these twaine art thou prisoner.
> *Lor*. To me my Liege.
> *Hor*. To me my Soueraigne.
> *Lor*. This hand first tooke his courser by the raines.
> *Hor*. But first my launce did put him from his horse.
> *Lor*. I ceaz'd his weapon and enioyde it first.
> *Hor*. But first I forc'd him lay his weapons downe[.] (B1v)

Their competing stories—manifested visibly onstage as Horatio and Lorenzo both hold onto their prisoner—make it difficult for playgoers to invest their belief fully into either one. Invoking "our priuiledge" (B1v), the King demands that Balthazar fill in the narrative gaps that Lorenzo and Horatio have consciously produced out of self-interest. Understandably more self-interested than his two captors, however, Balthazar remains cautious and says, "truth to say I yeeld my selfe to both" (B1v). The King soon resolves his own skepticism, which their contradictory reports have created, by brandishing his sovereign authority, "the censure of my doome," and he puts his own finishing touches on the story: "by my iudgement thus your strife shall end" (B1v).

Although the final two versions of *THE SPANISH TRAGEdie*'s prehistory take place in dissimilar contexts, they both foreground the art of persuasion and the personal stakes of the speakers who put the story to use: one in a scene of political conspiracy, and another in a scene of wooing. Villuppo, the Portingale courtier who gives the fourth account of the battle, manufactures a totally false description to gain preference over another courtier named Alexandro. Like the Spanish General had done for his sovereign, Villuppo responds to the Viceroy's command:

> Stand vp I say and tell thy tale at large. (seene.
> *Villup*. Then heare that truth which these mine eies haue
>
> . . . .
>
> *Alexandro* that heere counterfeits,
> Vnder the colour of a duteous freend,
> Discharged his Pistoll at the Princes back,
> As though he would haue slaine their Generall.
> But therwithall *Don Balthazar* fell downe. (B3r)

Having already seen and heard Prince Balthazar alive in the Spanish court, theatergoers would no doubt perceive the falsehood at once, but Villuppo still boasts of it in the scene's final soliloquy: "Thus haue I with an enuious forged tale, | Deceiued the King, betraid mine enemy, | And hope for guerdon of my villany" (B3v). When Horatio delivers the final version of the battle, it may not be "an enuious forged tale," but he nonetheless insinuates himself boldly with Bel-imperia as he tells of her dead lover's fate. The Spanish princess opens the scene with a now conventional request for narrative: "Signior *Horatio*, this is the place and houre, | Wherein I must intreat thee to relate, | The circumstance of *Don Andreas* death" (B3v). He first details "*Andreas* praise and worth" (B3v) in the hand-to-hand combat with Balthazar, including new information about a violation of the chivalric code-of-arms when Portingale halberdiers "pauncht his horse and dingd him to the ground" (B3v). Yet Horatio still manages to cast himself as the hero of this story: he singlehandedly defeats Balthazar; he recovers Andrea's corpse from the battlefield, "welding him vnto my priuate tent" (B4r); he laments over him with "sorrow, sighes [. . . and] teares" (B4r); and he performs Andrea's funeral rites, making it possible for him finally to cross the River Styx. And then Bel-imperia—in an act of self-possession that has irritated critics and editors for decades—falls in love straightaway with Horatio.

Because *THE SPANISH TRAGEdie* furnishes so many versions of the same prehistory, it never offers playgoers any stable or incontestable perspective from which to evaluate the action on the stage that they witness directly. The play provides a limited number of truths with regard to the battle's events, and it offers no fixed way of adjudicating between the various subjective truth-values that characters offer. By hailing theatergoers in different epistemic directions at the same time, the play asks them to negotiate the multiple versions of this offstage event within the context of the onstage representations. Discussing these five narratives from the opening act of Kyd's play, Frank R. Ardolino writes, "Each of these testimonies adds different information about the battle, in some cases amplifying what took place, but in most instances casting doubt on the veracity and accuracy of the previous assertions. Most of the descriptions are also rhetorical in the sense that the speaker adapts his testimony to suit what he determines to be the needs of the stage audience listening to him."[44] Ardolino's point about the descriptions being rhetorical reconstructions is key, for the question of which of these characters is being the most honest or objective is as inexhaustible as it is wearisome. Such a question would also be informed by an interpretive desire to know what *really* happened offstage when, theatrically speaking, the five narrative representations *are* the offstage battle. As they instrumentalize the play's prehistory, each of these five characters helps situate his own social, political, and/or romantic interests within the context of the action, revealing how those interests compete against or correspond with the interests of other characters.

If the first act of *THE SPANISH TRAGEdie* proliferates multiple versions of its prehistory for playgoers to weigh and evaluate for themselves, then Shakespeare's *The Life of Henry the Fift* concentrates its early scenes on a single account of its prehistory. As we will see, the account that *Henry the Fift* offers can sustain a variety of interpretations, but the king usurps hermeneutic authority over it by crowding out meanings that compete against his own political interests. To support his king, the Bishop of Canterbury tells a story about the origins of the French Salic law, a story which implicitly recognizes France's jurisdiction to write its own legal codes but which then displaces the country's authority to interpret them. I argue that King Henry V and the Bishop of Canterbury wield an absolutism over the founding story of Salic law and its interpretation, which shores up England's political establishment through war, bloodshed, the threat of rape, and terror. The dramatic action changes direction because of (and actually comes to mirror) their absolutist position. The play's resolve is remarkably singular: a war is planned, waged, and won, and even the ostensibly comic scenes of the subplot are noticeably tuned to the imperatives of the king's campaign against France. While Falstaff and his riotous debaucheries do make a narrative appearance in the play as promised, he "die[s] of a sweat" early in the action somewhere offstage.[45] Even if the play's final scene masquerades in the genre of comedy, the anticipated marriage between Henry and Princess Katharine essentially serves as the king's crowning achievement over King Charles VI of France. Further, in telling Charles and Isabel that their daughter Katharine "is our capitall Demand" (TLN 3084), Henry merely rehearses in a more diplomatic tone his earlier threat against the "pure Maydens" of Harfleur, who might have had the poor luck to "fall into the hand | Of hot and forcing Violation" (TLN 1279–80).

The force that England's Authorized Version of Salic law exercises over the play's trajectory also organizes the personnel whom the king conscripts to carry out his military action. As the plot develops in tandem with Henry's determination to pursue war, the king works to assemble a united front of multiple British identities and political interests. In other words, the unified movement of the plot into war is coincident with the issue of national and political solidarity, which both impels and endorses English militarism against France. "You are either with us or you are against us."[46] The play delivers a tour de force of various British accents, all pressed under the common banner of "*Harry*, England, and S. *George*" (TLN 1117): the Welsh Fluellen, the Irish MacMorris, the Scottish Jamy, and the underclass of England each speak the King's English with distinctive regional flair. Even the rather unique French-language scene with Katharine and Alice is entirely absorbed by the new lingua franca, as the princess learns to subject her body to the invasive English tongue. Most of the British characters seem to be of one mind, like Henry: "we haue now no thought in vs but France" (TLN 453).

In spite of the king's best efforts to unify, however, the divisions in the ranks are still visible. The infighting between Fluellen and Pistol; the "Sicknesse growing | Vpon our Souldiers" (TLN 1315–16); Michael Williams's indictment of the king on the eve of the battle of Agincourt; Westmoreland's wish to join to their forces "But one ten thousand of those men in England, | That doe no worke to day" (TLN 2260–61): the cracks appear like reflections in King Richard II's looking glass. And yet Henry is ultimately victorious, not least because he projects himself and his troops into a future of his own making, telling tales of what will be:

> This story shall the good man teach his sonne:
> And *Crispine Crispian* shall ne're goe by,
> From this day to the ending of the World,
> But we in it shall be remembred;
> We few, we happy few, we band of brothers[.] (TLN 2299–2303)

The king tends always to look forward in time, perhaps because the uncertainties of his future are less troubling than the disgraces of his past: his father's deposition of Richard II, the civil unrest that characterized Henry IV's reign, and his own "wilder dayes" (TLN 417) are all remarked on at various points in the play, only to be replaced by stories of a better—not to mention a geographically more expansive—England. But if Henry would rather forget those recent events that contribute to his and his family's disgrace, he consciously promotes other events from the distant past, ones which he uses to justify his war against France. Centering on the institution of Salic law, not only are these distant events diffuse and complex, but it is their very diffusion and complexity, their almost impenetrability, that make them an appealing tale to be told for the king's cause.

"*In terram Salicam Mulieres ne succedaul*, | No Woman shall succeed in *Salike* Land" (TLN 185–86). At Henry's behest, the Bishop of Canterbury presents to the court a rival interpretation of the French law of royal succession:

> the *Salike* Law
> Was not deuised for the Realme of France:
> Nor did the French possesse the *Salike* Land,
> Vntill foure hundred one and twentie yeeres
> After defunction of King *Pharamond*,
> Idly suppos'd the founder of this Law,
> Who died within the yeere of our Redemption,
> Foure hundred twentie six[.] (TLN 201–8)

Canterbury goes on to explain that it was not the French Pharamond but the Frankish Charlemagne who helped institute the Salic law when he "Subdu'd the Saxons, and did seat the French | Beyond the Riuer Sala, in the yeere | Eight hundred fiue" (TLN 209–11). Surely French political historians are mistaken, he suggests, and not just about chronology. For, despite the fact that some French would "vniustly gloze ['Salic'] | To be the Realme of France," "their owne Authors faithfully affirme, | That the Land *Salike* is in Germanie, | Betweene the Flouds of Sala and of Elue" (TLN 187–88, 190–92). Proceeding all the way up to "the Kings of France vnto this day" (TLN 237), he delivers a veritable laundry list of the French royal line, which has itself sullied the Salic law, he claims. Before Canterbury gives his speech, which compresses nearly a millennium of history into sixty-three densely packed lines, the king had pledged that "we will heare, note, and beleeue in heart, | That what you speake, is in your Conscience washt, | As pure as sinne with Baptisme" (TLN 177–79). Canterbury therefore launders France's sloppy historiography, "So, that as cleare as is the Summers Sunne" (TLN 233), Henry is justified in claiming the throne of France through his great-grandfather King Edward III, who had claimed it himself through his mother, Isabella.

That Henry responds to the lengthy speech with a single, largely monosyllabic question—"May I with right and conscience make this claim?"—suggests that the clarity of Canterbury's scholastic historiography could itself use a little laundering, and so he stretches his story even further back into the ancient past:

> The sinne vpon my head, dread Soueraigne:
> For in the Booke of *Numbers* is it writ,
> When the man dyes, let the Inheritance
> Descend vnto the Daughter. (TLN 243–47)

By enlisting the book of Numbers—which, like Canterbury himself, is fond of recollecting family histories so that other peoples' lands can be divvied up more equitably—he underscores how the construction of a narrative necessarily relies on a selective use of details, or *dispositio*. But he also shows that the more selective the details, the more vulnerable their rhetorical power is to dispute. For instance, if "the *Salike* Law | Was not deuised for the Realme of France," then Judaic pronouncements in the book of Numbers were not exactly devisèd for the realm of England. Moreover, when he "subdu'd the Saxons [and], | There left behind and settled certaine French" (TLN 193–94), Charlemagne was a conqueror, not a reclaimer, of foreign lands. In seeking solid ground for his historical and genealogical claims that current English borders should actually reside within France, Henry instead discovers that sovereign borders are perpetually in flux. Contemporary France suddenly bears an uncanny resemblance to the Salic lands themselves, which were once Saxon, then Frankish, and now German. Thus, after listening to Canterbury tell his version of history, Henry does not so much secure his genealogical rights to claim French lands as obtain historical precedents for invading and taking those lands for himself. In fact, the king's first concern once he resolves to wage war is that such historical precedents for invasion are available to anyone with the appropriate military resources. Henry says:

> We must not onely arme t'inuade the French,
> But lay downe our proportions, to defend
> Against the Scot, who will make roade vpon vs,
> With all aduantages. (TLN 283–86)

English borders would seem to fluctuate, too. One of the ways that Henry manages to "defend | Against the Scot" is by recruiting them, which helps generate the united military front that he needs and which also fortifies the unified dramatic action that he compels toward war.

Compared to the civil discord that had characterized his father's divided, two-part history, King Henry V's theater of war moves geographically outward and temporally forward. As I have suggested, *Henry the Fift* has a tendency to want to leave the past behind: the king even asks his God to "thinke not vpon the fault | My Father made, in compassing the Crowne" (TLN 2145–46). But Canterbury's story about Salic law is not the only prehistory that Henry instrumentalizes to move the action into France. When the Bishops of Canterbury and Ely meet in the play's opening scene, we learn that Henry has just recommenced a parliamentary bill, one his father had introduced and gotten passed some three years earlier. If reenacted, the bill would seize much of the church's property, "the better halfe of our Possession," Canterbury fears, "For all the Temporall Lands, which men deuout | By Testament haue giuen to the Church, | Would they strip from vs" (TLN 47–49). The concerns that Canterbury and Ely express about this bill in fact consume the play's opening lines:

> [M]Y Lord, Ile tell you, that selfe Bill is vrg'd,
> Which in th'eleuēth yere of [ye] last Kings reign
> Was like, and had indeed against vs past,
> But that the scambling and vnquiet time
> Did push it out of farther question. (TLN 39–43)

The "scambling and vnquiet time" refers to the domestic rebellions that had occupied Henry IV for most of his reign. Faced with the prospect of losing his own sovereign lands (which his cousin King Richard II had so generously handed over to him), Henry IV had had to make the confiscation of church "Lands" a much lower priority in his domestic policy.

Yet Henry V is trying not to replay his father's story—or, rather, he is trying to arrange the same political and legal circumstances into a different, more powerful narrative. He uses the same parliamentary bill, in other words, not to enlarge his own coffers and lands by plundering England's resources, as his father had tried to do, but to persuade the church to contribute funds to a greater enterprise, which will plunder the resources of France instead. Canterbury tells Ely:

> I haue made an offer to his Maiestie,
> Vpon our Spirituall Conuocation,
> And in regard of Causes now in hand,
> Which I haue open'd to his Grace at large,
> As touching France, to giue a greater Summe,
> Then euer at one time the Clergie yet
> Did to his Predecessors part withall. (TLN 118–24)

Canterbury's circuitous, sixty-three-line historical narrative about Salic law and French royal history is thus anything but disinterested, and, like the Welsh, Irish, Scottish, and English soldiers whom the king tries to unite behind a common national cause, Henry also manages to leverage the church to contribute substantial funds as well as historical and biblical precedents to his military campaign. Whether or not Canterbury has been accurate in his interpretation of Salic law is really beside the point, for the intricacy and density of his story overtake the substance of what he actually says, making his interpretation almost incomprehensible without both an intimate awareness of the history and a delicate parsing of his words. The speech does not convey to theatergoers transparent knowledge about past events through an understanding of the narrative sequence. It conveys, rather, two differential knowledges at the same time, one that is restricted by the audience's imperfect understanding of the history and another that is constituted by an impression (and the impressiveness) of the story's construction, which seems at once both learned and periphrastic. Attached to the knowledge that playgoers acquire is the additional knowledge that they are ignorant about a great deal of other, inaccessible knowledge.

On the one hand, what playgoers have learned about the individual political motivations of Canterbury and Henry, and, on the other, what they are unable to comprehend about Canterbury's story of Salic law open up epistemological disparities that establish prime conditions for playgoers to have to judge how each character appropriates the events of the past to manipulate those of the present and future. Whether recent, remote, or even biblical, the offstage material that characters put on the stage through their storytelling ends up situating and directing the dramatic action that follows in *THE SPANISH TRAGEdie* and *Henry the Fift*. In Kyd's play, the five separate accounts of the Spanish battle with Portingale give rise to and orient the events of the first act, but to a large extent these accounts *are* the first act, whereas the opening of Shakespeare's play uses narrative both to unite political divisions throughout Britain and to initiate conflicts with France that were previously dormant. Any character who tells a story onstage, however, inevitably adopts the burden of persuading the audience of its veracity, requiring him or her to package and market both its details and its supposed benefits in a way that convinces its hearers to buy the story. Audiences can therefore index the competing social and political interests of dramatic characters on the degree to which their various narratives inspire trust and belief.

Entr'actes

When Roland Barthes says that "Telling is a responsible and commercial act," he adds that the "outcome" of that act is "(the virtuality of transformation)."[47] By this he seems to mean the virtuality or *enargeia* of a story and its changing arc that a hearer experiences as opposed to the actuality of the context in which it is narrated, but he also seems to mean the potential that exists to transform that actuality through the virtual representation of the narrative itself. We have seen how characters capitalize on the absence or nonvisibility of offstage events to transform their own social and political positions as well as the courses of action that they inhabit. The last section demonstrated that dramatic prehistories function not as expositions that make the ensuing action more intelligible to theatergoers but instead as motivated reconstructions of those past events, which both comprise and unsettle the audience's and other characters' knowledge, making intelligibility itself a contested notion. Holding intelligibility up to scrutiny is a key way that Renaissance playwrights modernize their theater. In this section, the offstage events that characters narrate also intensify and dilate dramatic action by stressing the self-interested and often rival perspectives that characters promote for themselves onstage. These offstage events, however, occur either during or between staged scenes and, compared to prehistories, often create a greater sense of urgency or force within a play's unfolding action. That urgency or force derives from the spatiotemporal proximity between the onstage scene and the offstage events, which puts into explicit tension the visible and the nonvisible, the direct and the mediated, the known and the unknown.

Unlike most earlier dramatists, Renaissance playwrights compose and emplot multiple threads of action that do not merely converge at some point onstage for audiences to witness firsthand. If we understand dramatic "emplotment" to be "the selection of episodes from out of a larger potential continuum of events and their arrangement so as to produce probability, complexity, and interest,"[48] then multiple threads of action in Renaissance drama often simultaneously develop their own logics, velocities, trajectories, and timetables off the stage, which is to say that these plays exercise control over not only the audience's knowledge but also their awareness of knowledge that has not yet been fully disclosed. For example, after Gloucester reveals to Edmund his secret letter from Cordelia, six separate factions begin to move toward Dover at different rates and through different routes: the French military, mad Lear and disguised Kent, blind Gloucester and disguised Edgar, time-serving Oswald, Regan's defensive army led by Edmund, and Albany's halfhearted forces. How and when these groups will converge are questions that *KING LEAR* raises in order to heighten the intensity and anticipation of a clash whose circumstances and outcome theatergoers may think they know, based on every other earlier version of the story, but which Shakespeare's version wrenches toward a new catastrophe. At the level of the dramatic fiction, *KING LEAR* sets a series of offstage actions in motion while modulating our knowledge about their details. Yet Shakespeare undermined his original audience's epistemology even further by radically altering the conclusion of this culturally familiar story of King Lear and his daughters.[49]

Renaissance playwrights' modern strategies for emplotting scenes on and off the stage have the effect of circumscribing audiences within a succession of epistemological phases as a given performance unfolds. To be sure, all fictions progressively divulge their characters, actions, and so forth "to produce probability, complexity, and interest" for the audience.[50] But the difference between this common unfolding of a fiction and the phases of knowledge that interest me here is that Renaissance drama's nonvisible events offstage possess an epistemological weight that is both defined by its absence and overtly juxtaposed with the immediately visible action upon the stage. The tension or conflict between the visible and the nonvisible, between surface and depth, and between signifier and signified is the problem that will occupy us in this section, in Shakespeare's *Much adoe about Nothing* and John Ford's *THE CHRONICLE HISTORIE OF PERKIN VVARBECK*. In both plays, "blood" is the nonvisible depth to which external signs must refer. Blood itself acts as a metonym for "genealogy"—itself a curiously wrought tale—which will be either noble or base and which ostensibly determines one's behavior. On the other hand, the visible surface that signifies the difficult-to-see blood will include one's clothes, deportment, speech, actions, and complexion, as well as the narratives that can be stitched together from these signs to denote either nobility or baseness, along with their many forms of expression.

In *Much adoe about Nothing* and in PERKIN VVARBECK, characters employ complex narratives about offstage action to insinuate themselves into social and political positions that they would not otherwise be able to enjoy. PERKIN VVARBECK offers a forceful counterpoint to *Henry the Fift* insofar as the characters in Shakespeare's play exploit their verbal stories with more success than does the title character of Ford's play. Like Perkin Warbeck, Don John in *Much adoe about Nothing* ultimately fails with the narrative that he presents, but it is significant, first, that his story inspires belief so readily among many of the play's noble characters and, second, that the entire crisis that prevents the main plot from hastening to its nuptial conclusion centers on an incident that playgoers never actually see staged. Taking place the night before Hero and Claudio are to marry, the offstage playlet features Borachio courting Margaret—who stands at Hero's window, wears Hero's clothes, and responds to Hero's name—all while Don Pedro, Don John, and Claudio himself secretly look on. Although Borachio is the one who tells the most extensive version of the story about this offstage encounter, Don John orchestrates it by tailoring the aristocratic materials of fashionable clothing to suit his own political ambitions, not to mention his revenge on his brother's legitimate blood.

This offstage action dramatizes the social problem of boundary crossing because Borachio and Margaret-as-Hero appear to change their class-defined roles as easily as one might a garment. Because "clothes are detachable [. . . and] can move from body to body," write Ann Rosalind Jones and Peter Stallybrass, "That is precisely their danger and their value: they are bearers of identity, ritual, and social memory, even as they confuse social categories."[51] To curb this sort of confusion of social categories, sumptuary laws in the period were designed to make visible an individual's place (usually defined by blood) within the social hierarchy, but since *Much adoe about Nothing* links a transgressive mobility through that hierarchy with a false narrative of female inconstancy, the offstage scene demonstrates the culture's blinding overinvestment in the power of clothing as a signifier for social status. In the late sixteenth-century culture in which this play first appeared onstage, the mercantile class was acquiring unprecedented and disposable wealth just as new goods and markets were becoming economically viable, and so individuals began to blur social categories through the medium of clothing, wearing colors, cuts, yardage, and styles that the sumptuary laws reserved for higher classes. During her reign, Queen Elizabeth issued eight separate proclamations to enforce the country's last sumptuary law (1 and 2 Philip and Mary, cap. 2), which reveals not that English citizens were obeying it but rather that their clothes repeatedly violated its orders. As Wilfrid Hooper shows, another major motivation for Elizabeth's proclamations was the economic protection of native textile industries against competitive imports from the Continent.

Both motivations for the sumptuary laws therefore aimed to restrict the flow of socioeconomic and geographical boundary crossing.[52]

That fashion and narrative are both shapeable and changeable—like taffeta, or the story of Lear—not only suggests how gainful it must have been to produce, and how popular to consume, textiles and texts in early modern England but also indicates how vulnerable both media were to being cut with inferior materials. When Borachio tells Conrad about his conversation with Margaret at Hero's window, he prefaces it with a commentary on "fashion," arguing that the entire system by which clothing signifies social rank is a fundamentally unstable and deceptive one. He seems to recognize the multivalency that the word "fashion" conveyed in the period, critiquing the power of "fashion-as-change" precisely because of its adverse effects on fashion as "'deep' making,"[53] which is the cultural belief "that clothes permeate the wearer, fashioning him or her within. This notion undoes the opposition of inside and outside, surface and depth. Clothes, like sorrow, inscribe themselves upon a person who comes into being through that inscription."[54] Clothing possessed more than symbolic value in the period because of this "'deep' making," which Ann Rosalind Jones and Peter Stallybrass explain through the practice of livery:

> Livery acted as the medium through which the social system marked bodies so as to associate them with particular institutions. The power to give that marking to subordinates affirmed social hierarchy: lords dressed retainers, masters dressed apprentices, husbands dressed their wives. But livery, as it dignified the institutions to which it identified people as belonging, also dignified the participants in such institutions. This mutually supportive interplay of loyalties is what was seen as being at risk by writers attacking sartorial anarchy, the tendency of modern Englishmen (and women) to dress as free-floating individuals rather than as representatives of groups defined by shared labors or loyalties.[55]

As an underclass character in *Much adoe about Nothing*, Borachio is far less concerned in his speech to Conrad with how "sartorial anarchy" disrupts the integrity of social categories than with how the instability of fashion actually reconstitutes individuals into grotesque and outlandish figures who shift and change with every new popular trend.

Before Borachio enters with Conrad and recounts to him the offstage affair at Hero's window, Dogberry and Verges set the scene by charging several night watchmen to "comprehend all | vagrom men," after which Dogberry and Verges exeunt, the watchmen sit, and Borachio and Conrad enter.[56] Unaware that others are in earshot, else Borachio would not incriminate himself, Conrad urges him (somewhat obscenely), "forward with thy tale" (TLN 1430), which he begins by telling about the profit he has made for wooing Margaret-as-Hero:

> *Bor.* Therefore know, I haue earned of *Don Iohn* a thousand Ducates.
> *Con.* Is it possible that anie villanie should be so deare?
> *Bor.* Thou should'st rather aske if it were possible anie villanie should be so rich? for when rich villains haue neede of poore ones, poore ones may make what price they will. (TLN 1435–41)

Considering the criticism that he will in a moment level against underclass devotees of "giddie [. . .] fashion" (TLN 1466), Borachio makes the argument here that getting paid by "rich villains [who] haue | neede of poore ones" is much more rewarding than the profit from simply dressing fashionably and thus appearing to be rich. He says to Conrad:

> thou knowest that the fashion of a doublet, or a hat, or a cloake, is nothing to a man.
> *Con.* Yes, it is apparell.
> *Bor.* I meane the fashion.
> *Con.* Yes the fashion is the fashion.
> *Bor.* Tush, I may as well say the foole's the foole, but seest thou not what a deformed theefe this fashion is?
> (TLN 1443–50)

Fashion is deformed because it continually alters its shape, but fashion is also a thief because every time it changes, it steals its own former value from those who wear it so devoutly. "Seest thou not," Borachio insists once again, "what a deformed thiefe | this fashion is?" and continues:

> how giddily a turnes about all the Hotblouds betweene foureteene & fiue & thirtie, sometimes fashioning them like *Pharaoes* souldiours in the rechie painting, sometime like god Bels priests in the old Church window, sometime like the shauen *Hercules* in the smircht worm eaten tapestrie, where his cod-peece seemes as massie as his club. (TLN 1456–63)

John A. Allen observes, "Like a 'deformed thief' (l.115), fashion steals from men their knowledge of themselves, reducing them to posturing automatons who nourish the illusion of their individuality while actually possessing none, because they do not even choose the fashions they will wear but, whether they will or no, are fashioned to them."[57] When contemporary gallants dress themselves like "*Pharaoes* souldiours," "god Bels priests," and "shauen *Hercules*," they refabricate these exotic figures and their stories into the guise of modern fashion, and the virtuality of such stories transforms the wearers within—though they are probably disappointed to learn that a massive codpiece gives only the appearance of male enhancement.

Critiquing the theater and its visual extravagance in 1580, one antitheatricalist blasts, "None delight in those spectacles, but such as would be made spectacles."[58] Although Borachio's condemnation of underclass fashionmongers is identical to that of this and other antitheatrical writers, his motivation differs substantially. He implies, for instance, that aristocratic fashion first robs social inferiors of fine clothes, and then it deludes them into the belief that the fashion alone can confer on them a higher social status, which reveals how fully they have invested into the exclusionary system itself. And if those who happen to indulge in such a delusion can actually afford to purchase whatever fashion is current, then they are soon robbed even of that luxury since "the fashion weares out | more apparrell then the man" (TLN 1464–65). But Conrad is confused about why Borachio seems to be following a different plotline than the one he began about Don John and the "thousand Ducates," and so he asks, "art not thou thy selfe | giddie with the fashion too that thou hast shifted out of | thy tale into telling me of the fashion?" (TLN 1465–67). Conrad is unable to read more deeply, in other words, and see that his companion's discussion of fashion serves not a decorative but a heuristic function in the story, so Borachio narrates the offstage encounter:

> Not so neither, but know that I haue to night wooed *Margaret* the Lady *Heroes* gentle-woman, by the name of *Hero*, she leanes me out at her mistris chamber-vvindow, bids me a thousand times good night: I tell this tale vildly. I should first tell thee how the Prince[,] *Claudio*[,] and my Master planted, and placed, and possessed by my Master *Don Iohn*, saw a far off in the Orchard this amiable incounter.
>
> *Con.* And thought thy *Margaret* was *Hero*?
>
> *Bor.* Two of them did, the Prince and *Claudio*, but the diuell my Master knew she was *Margaret* and partly by his oathes, which first possest them, partly by the darke night which did deceiue them, but chiefely, by my villanie, which did confirme any slander that *Don Iohn* had made, away vvent *Claudio* enraged, swore hee vvould meete her as he was apointed next morning at the Temple, and there, before the whole congregation shame her with vvhat he saw o're night, and send her home againe vvithout a husbaud. (TLN 1468–86)[59]

With the unwitting assistance of Margaret—who becomes as much of a stage prop as the borrowed clothes she wears—Don John and Borachio have dramatized a scenario that is both rhetorically and visually persuasive enough to influence Don Pedro's and Claudio's belief, which confounds the nuptial conclusion toward which the play's action has been moving.

Despite Conrad's confusion about it, Borachio's excursus on fashion highlights exactly the reasons why the offstage action at Hero's window has been so effective at gulling Don Pedro and Claudio. By critiquing the conspicuous consumption of gallants, who mistake the worn sign for the referent, Borachio also implicitly censures Claudio and Don Pedro, who inspire such behavior in the first place and who unhesitatingly accept that Hero is "but the signe and semblance of her honour" (TLN 1690). Investing in the misogynistic innuendo of Hero's inconstancy, in other words, Don Pedro and Claudio accept the threadbare story of woman's "seeming" (TLN 1713). The misogynistic narrative governs their interpretation of the signs, and not the signs their narrative, which shows in how quickly they reverse the value of Hero's surface and substance. For example, after Claudio tells her father, Leonato, "Giue not this rotten Orenge to your friend," he addresses the wedding party and throws the signs of her innocence and purity into doubt:

> Behold how like a maid she blushes heere!
> O what authoritie and shew of truth
> Can cunning sinne couer it selfe withall!
> Comes not that bloud, as modest euidence,
> To witnesse simple Vertue? would you not sweare
> All you that see her, that she were a maide,
> By these exterior shewes? But she is none:
> She knowes the heate of a luxurious bed:
> Her blush is guiltinesse, not modestie. (TLN 1691–99)

Not surprisingly, Hero has little control over who gets to tell her story, and for every objection that she voices, Claudio manages to weave it back into his own account as yet more evidence of her inconstancy. Much like Borachio's detested fashionmongers who mimic the likes of "shauen *Hercules*," Hero, too, gets cast into classical roles through Claudio's allegations:

> Out on thee seeming, I will write against it,
> You seeme to me as *Diane* in her Orbe,
> As chaste as is the budde ere it be blowne:
> But you are more intemperate in your blood,
> Than *Venus*, or those pampred animalls,
> That rage in sauage sensualitie. (TLN 1713–18)

Visible in Hero's blush, the blood that Claudio repeatedly mentions might be read as shamefastness, but he reads it both as a sign of guilt and as evidence of a hot disposition, which uncontrolled leads to lust. Claudio and Don

Pedro ratify their reading of Hero through the strength of their nobility, and they are confident in the knowledge of their reading because what they "saw a far off in the Orchard" (TLN 1474) their honor would never allow them to mistake.

It is true that Don John and Borachio are responsible for engineering this illusion and causing havoc in Messina, but Claudio and Don Pedro are themselves responsible not only for jumping so quickly to false conclusions about Hero but also for being injudicious readers of the evidence, which gives others the power to script those actions that Claudio and Don Pedro think are their own. The affair at Hero's window is all the more persuasive to these two aristocratic men because Don John and Borachio have provided the materials from which their victims can construct their own story about her immodest behavior. The details arrange themselves into a narrative of inconstancy that is always a necessary adjunct to that of female fidelity, the double-edge of which Claudio signals in his second line of the play, which regards Hero's honor: "Is she not a modest yong Ladie?" (TLN 161), he asks Benedick. Jean E. Howard asserts, "The more a fiction draws on conventional schemata, the more it appears true to life," and Don John has certainly conventionalized the characters and props that he stages at Hero's window.[60] Yet I would disagree with Howard that "This action is not dramatized" and that it is "assigned to the unreality of the unseen."[61] For, although the scene is clearly not staged in plain view of theatergoers, it *is* dramatized for Claudio and Don Pedro, who take the virtuality for the actuality itself and therewith alter the play's trajectory. In fact the offstaging of the scene at Hero's window is epistemologically crucial to the play's action because the event is based as much on unconfirmed hearsay for theatergoers as it is for the wedding party that hears the story onstage.

While they may believe that they are outside of the events they report, objective observers of plain facts, Claudio and Don Pedro are in fact caught up by the story itself. Indeed, the story writes them. And as a marketable product for which the Messinese community will pay dearly, not only is this story successful in humiliating the honor of Claudio and Don Pedro, or in exposing the vulnerability of aristocratic and patriarchal integrity, but also dramatically, the offstage event at Hero's window serves as the communal crisis that most of the characters first invest in, which initially blocks the orderly progression of the comedy, and then disinvest from, which enables them finally to achieve marriage and social reintegration. Even if they are ultimately foiled, by play's end Don John and Borachio have wooed the community into buying and living a story that they have fashioned out of their own experiences as second-class citizens. Harry Berger Jr. notes, "The ease, indeed the alacrity, with which Leonato, Claudio, and the Prince seize on Hero's guilt confirms what they already suspect,"[62] which is to say that the aristocracy already owns this story that surfaces as an anxious fear of class miscegenation and bastardy, a specter that materializes from the shadows of Hero's window. This bastard narrative produced by Don John—who, let us not forget, is himself socially marked as adulterated—is therefore a counter-narrative that is forever immanent in the aristocratic one trying to work itself out through the male alliances that virginal marriage partners guarantee. As Howard argues, who controls the power of telling and staging stories is a major preoccupation of *Much adoe about Nothing*, which "seems to engender in readers fears about never getting to 'the real,' but of being trapped in competing and manipulative discursive constructions of it."[63] By making the offstage scene at Hero's window the play's central conflict, Don John and Borachio stain the social fabric with the seed of illegitimacy. They propagate themselves in the imaginations of aristocratic men, who believe that they see in Hero those infidelities that would jeopardize their own power and privilege: "The storie that is printed in her blood" (TLN 1785).

The authority with which Claudio protests—"Her blush is guiltinesse, not modestie"—demonstrates the interpretive latitude that a respected aristocratic man enjoys over such signs, though to be credited his audience must still assent to his word, much like any audience listening to a character's narration of offstage action. Because it is unseen and subject to labile signs, the exact vintage or constitution of one's blood or the credibility of characters' stories acquires currency from its "signe and semblance," the "exterior shewes" of a social or narrative rhetoric from which characters endlessly fashion their personal histories. In John Ford's *THE CHRONICLE HISTORIE OF PERKIN VVARBECK. A Strange Truth*, the bloodline and the story line that Warbeck imparts to his protector King James IV of Scotland are one and the same, and James credits both of them because they so befit his notions of royal comportment:

> How like a' King a lookes? Lords, but obserue
> The confidence of his aspect? Drosse cannot
> Cleaue to so pure a mettall; royall youth!
> *Plantaginett* vndoubted![64]

Perkin Warbeck is of course no king, nor does he manage to become one. But, for a time, he does manage to convince some very powerful people that he is King Edward IV's youngest son, Richard, Duke of York, who (unlike his unfortunate brother Edward V) allegedly escaped the assassins sent by his uncle, Richard, Duke of Gloucester, after to be King Richard III. In the end, only a small force of disaffected English subjects seems to want to "Cleaue" to Warbeck and the personal history he tells, but the play's intermediate action shows that his professed genealogy resonates in appealing ways to a relatively large audience, which is at least willing to accept that the crown worn by the current Tudor monarch, Henry VII, actually belongs de jure to Warbeck. However secure the Tudor dynasty had made itself in history by the time Ford's play was performed, its action depicts one way of building the narrative groundwork for a coup d'état.

PERKIN VVARBECK is a play that utilizes onstage narrative in subtle but compelling ways. As in *Henry the Fift*, the action of Ford's play is entirely dependent on competing versions of its prehistory, but whereas Shakespeare's king succeeds in invoking a selective and manipulable past only to move beyond it, Warbeck's project tends to stall at the invocation stage. Notably, Warbeck's vision of a royal Yorkist future for himself and for England falters not at the conspicuous point at which he tells his story of captivity, escape, and long European exile. Rather, it falters in the interstitial spaces offstage in which a majority of the English people get belated access to his story, weigh the meandering narrative against their present political situation, and then simply decide not to buy it. The contrast with *Henry the Fift* is revealing, for if "*Warlike* Harry" (TLN 6) single-mindedly unites the English, Welsh, Irish, and Scottish in a war against an external enemy, then it is the English people in PERKIN VVARBECK who make a popular and communal choice to unite behind the pacific King Henry VII to cultivate a national peace. The play's political resolution comes about through an unofficial form of collective decision making, even though this collectivity ultimately assembles itself in support of Henry VII's sovereignty. In other words, faced with the prospect of yet another civil war—which could very well settle the crown on one who has persuaded several European rulers that he is a stronger claimant than Henry VII—much of England's populace opts for the status quo.

Along with occasional reports of battles and civil uprisings, the main entr'acte event in Ford's play is the public response to a joint proclamation issued to the English people by the Scottish James IV and Warbeck. This proclamation is itself based on the lengthy prehistory that Warbeck tells when he first arrives on the stage at James's court (C4v–D1r). Once Warbeck proclaims his history publicly and makes known his pretensions to the English crown, Henry VII's Bishop of Durham delivers onstage the English response to the proclamation, which denies Warbeck's claim unequivocally. Like Warbeck's history, however, Durham's story cannot entirely conceal the seams of its construction, which omits the network of both noble and common citizens who support Warbeck and have been conspiring against Henry VII since the beginning. The English conspirators even include Sir William Stanley, "My Chamberlaine," the king grieves,

> my Counsellor, the loue,
> The pleasure of my Court, my bosome friend,
> The Charge, and the Controulement of my person;
> The keyes and secrets of my treasurie;
> The *all* of *all* I am: I am vnhappie:
> Miserie of confidence,——let mee turne traytor
> To mine owne person, yeeld my Scepter vp
> To *Edwards Sister*, and her *bastard Duke*! [C3v, italics in original][65]

Although Henry VII had earlier recognized that "Forraigne attempts against a State and Kingdome | Are seldome without some great friends at home" (B2r), he only gradually realizes just how much ground Warbeck's story has gained among his English subjects. To add strength to his cause, Warbeck petitions help from James IV, who trusts him because "King *Charles of Fraunce*, | And *Maximilian of Bohemia* both, | Haue ratified his Credit by their Letters" (C4r–v). As with the story that Claudio tells with Don Pedro at his side, the word of trusted noblemen lends proof to a story's rhetorical armor.

"The vulgar storie of *a Princes* ruine" (C4v). One of the ways that Warbeck makes his story plausible is by furnishing specific details about Richard of Gloucester's plot to murder his young nephews in the Tower of London, which was a familiar historical event in the late fifteenth century but which was also carried out in secrecy and therefore subject to speculative and fabricated reports. Even Shakespeare's treatment of the murders in *The Tragedy of Richard the Third* is a narrative of a narrative. In that play, Richard's hired assassin Sir James Tyrrell soliloquizes on the report given to him by the two men whom he had suborned to carry out the murders, Dighton and Forrest, who "Wept like to Children, in their deaths sad Story."[66] In Ford's play, Warbeck need hardly tell the familiar circumstances of the story since

E V R O P E knowes,
And all the Westerne World what persecution
Hath ragd in malice, against *Vs*, sole heire
To the great throne, of old *Plantaginetts*.
How from our Nursery, wee haue beene hurried
Vnto the Sanctuarie, from the Sanctuarie
Forc'd to the Prison, from the Prison hald
By cruell hands, to the tormentors furie;
Is registred alreadie in the Volume
Of all mens tongues, whose true relation drawes
Compassion, melted into weeping eyes,
And bleeding soules: but our misfortunes since
Haue rang'd a larger progresse through strange Lands,
Protected in our Innocence by Heaven. (C4v)[67]

After affirming what "E V R O P E knowes" already, Warbeck adopts the royal plural and transports his sovereign audience from the safety of the "Nursery" to the threatened security of the "Sanctuarie" and then to the peril of the "Prison," the guilty associations of which stand in opposition to the innocence of the nursery, which he attaches to himself in the present through divine intervention: "Protected in our Innocence by Heaven." Along with increasingly urgent verbs—"hurried," "Forc'd," "hald"—his use of anadiplosis (in the repetition of "Sanctuarie" and "Prison") builds tension toward the climax of "the tormentors furie," a tension that he momentarily releases by reiterating that "the Volume | Of all mens tongues" has told this story countless times before.

The physical movements he recounts from "Nursery" to "Sanctuarie" to "Prison" "to the tormentors furie" prepare the narrative ground thematically for his own "larger progresse through strange Lands." Yet just as he offers to enlarge on his "misfortunes," the magnitude of which he links with an expansive Continental geography, Warbeck catches his audience off guard by suddenly jumping backward in the story and refocusing James's attention on the scene of pathos in the Tower:

> *Edward the Fift* our brother, in his Tragedie
> Quenchd their hot thirst of bloud, whose hire to murther
> Paid them their wages, of despaire and horrour;
> The softnesse of *my childe-hood* smild vpon
> The roughnesse of their taske, and rob'd them farther
> Of hearts to dare, or hands to execute.
> Great King *they* spard my life, *the butchers* spard it;
> Returnd the tyrant, my vnnaturall Vncle,
> A truth of my dispatch[.] (C4v–D1r, italics in original)

Warbeck's rhetorical tactic here is to insinuate that if even the tyrannical and distrustful Richard of Gloucester can be convinced that his two young and royal nephews have been duly dispatched by some hired hands of a hired hand, then surely James IV should be able to swallow his tale whole.

The strength of his narrative rests in the meshing of familiar information with unfamiliar, which enhances its lucidity, credibility, and vividness. Moreover, Warbeck creates a dialectic between what "EVROPE knowes" about the murders in the Tower and the falsified "truth of my dispatch" delivered to and trusted by Richard of Gloucester. The logical conclusion of the dialectic is for James IV to believe neither "The vulgar storie of *a Princes* ruine" nor the falsehood that Richard thought to be true, but rather the version that transports the past into the present at the moment of its recounting: "Great King *they* spard my life, *the butchers* spard it." If Edward V "Quenchd their hot thirst of bloud," then Warbeck's preserved blood is precious indeed. Nevertheless Warbeck cannot control all the details of his life, and the one that threatens his narrative the most is that he actually hails from Tournai in Flanders, a fact on which his enemies have capitalized to disprove his royal pretentions. Earlier in the play, Henry VII had given his own account of Warbeck's "larger progresse through strange Lands," describing how he "first discradled | From *Tournay* into *Portugall*," went to the "superstitious *Irish*," was "Conjur'd into *Fraunce*," "Stole into Flaunders," and was finally "beaten backe with shame and scorne" from Kent (C2v). So when Warbeck comes to relate his prehistory to James IV, he shrewdly confronts his enemy's account not by dismissing it but by detailing his reasons for having been in Tournai in the first place:

I was conveyd
With secresie and speede to *Tournay*; fosterd
By obscure meanes, taught to vnlearne my selfe:
But as I grew in yeares, I grew in sence
Of feare, and of disdaine; feare, of the tyrant
Whose power swaide the throne then, when disdaine
Of living so vnknowne, in such a servile
And abject lownesse, prompted mee to thoughts
Of recollecting who I was; I shooke off
My bondage, and made hast to let my *Aunt*
Of Burgundie acknowledge mee her kinsman;
Heire to the Crowne of *England*, snatch'd by *Henry*
From *Richards* head; a thing scarce knowne ith world. (D1r)

Warbeck first exploits the credibility of his enemies' reports by appropriating and retelling some of their most damning evidence against him; then he makes Margaret, Duchess of Burgundy, his blood relative; and he concludes with an ingenious substitution: everyone knows that at the Battle of Bosworth Field Henry of Richmond "snatch'd" the English crown from "*Richards* head." But, since Warbeck claims to be Richard, Duke of York, "*Richards* head" here is not Richard III's but his own. The "thing scarce knowne ith world" is the ease with which one king can verbally supplant another.

In the world of the play, the ability to control how the details of Warbeck's story either coalesce with or diverge from England's recent political history will determine the truth-value that audiences grant to it, and thus whether the action will escalate into civil war. At first, James IV endorses him confidently, such as when he responds to Warbeck's account of the prehistory:

if you can
Make this apparent what you haue discourst
In every Circumstance, wee will not studie
An answer, but are ready in your Cause (D1r)

which the king soon makes good, risking much more than his political reputation by deploying Scottish troops into English territory to aid Warbeck's campaign. Eager to solidify his factions in England and to drum up broader English support for his "Cause," he publishes his story in the form of a joint proclamation with the Scottish king. "Good: the Proclamations readie," James tells Warbeck, "By that it will appeare, how the *English* stand | Affected to your title" (F2v). The readings of the proclamation as well as the public reactions to them both reside offstage in the play, and the only information that playgoers receive about the proclamation's reception is in a report that Henry VII's Bishop of Durham delivers from the walls of Norham Castle, which is under siege by the Scottish army. After James demands of the bishop, "Set ope the portes, and to your lawfull Soveraigne | *Richard of Yorke* surrender vp this Castle" (F4v), Durham denigrates Warbeck, calling him "a vagabond, a straggler, | Not noted in the world by birth or name" (G1r). Here, Durham begins to drive a wedge between James and Warbeck as he gives an account of how their joint proclamation has fared on English soil:

> What Nobleman? what common man of note?
> What ordinary subject hath come in,
> Since first you footed on our Territories,
> To onely faine a wellcome? children laugh at
> Your Proclamations, and the wiser pittie,
> So great a Potentates abuse, by one
> Who juggles meerly with the fawnes and youth
> Of an instructed complement[.] (G1r)

Whether or not Durham portrays the proclamation's reception by the English people in anything like an accurate or full manner, his speech compels James to reconsider his own political alliances and the consequent health of his royal standing among fellow European heads of state.

In other words, whether Durham tells James the truth or not, his story generates in the play a powerful truth-effect, one which so irrevocably alters the conditions under which Warbeck seeks the English crown that his odds of succeeding plummet almost on the instant. After Durham and Warbeck verbally compete for James's favor at Norham Castle, the Scottish king falls silent, prompting the Earl of Crawford to remark, "The King is serious, | Deepe in his meditation" (G1r). Several scenes after the siege at Norham, James calculates all the resources that he has ventured in Warbeck's cause, weighing the costs and risks against the historical trajectory that seems to be taking shape before him, and decides to give up the fight altogether:

> *K. Ia.* Cosen, our bountie, favours, gentlenesse,
> Our benefits, the hazard of our person,
> Our peoples liues, our Land hath evidenc't,
> How much wee haue engag'd on your behalfe:
> How triviall, and how dangerous our hopes
> Appeare, how fruitlesse our attempts in warre,
> How windie rather smokie your assurance
> Of partie shewes, wee might in vaine repeate! (H2r)

James plots a different course because the conclusion of the one that Warbeck pursues is stalled irremediably in the past—a past that has replayed itself "For ninetie yeares," during which time

ten English Kings and Princes,
Threescore great Dukes and Earles, a thousand Lords
And valiant Knights, two hundred fiftie thousand
Of English Subiects haue in Ciuill Warres,
Beene sacrificd to an vnciuill thirst
Of *discord* and *ambition*[.] (B1v, italics in original)

Instead of helping to perpetuate the "vnciuill" past of the Wars of the Roses, as Warbeck tries to do, James IV looks to the future with Henry VII and the English people, electing "To seale an oath of peace through Christendome" (H2r).

It might have been otherwise, however, both dramatically in Ford's play as well as on the stage of history.[68] And, even if Tudor absolutism mythologized the inevitability of its rule, we must recognize that "inevitability" is a teleological narrative form that overdetermines de facto power by delegitimizing other political narratives that compete for a hearing. In *Perkin VVarbeck*, Henry VII must fight to quell a variety of rebellions and conspiracies, which for the most part occur offstage but which also end up dominating much of the play's onstage dialogue. When characters report these acts of sedition, the insurrections take over the stage verbally the way that Warbeck wants to take over the English crown in actuality, and sometimes they even threaten to engulf the stage with violence. The possibility and even probability of the play following another course of action and coming to a different conclusion must remain feasible for it to retain the audience's attention and interest, *even when the audience already knows the details of English history or how the play will end*. To read Warbeck throughout as being doomed to fail, or to construe his story simply as an utter fabrication, forecloses the limited phases of knowledge that we experience as the play unfolds; it ignores the real power that his story exercises over many English citizens and European heads of state; and it homogenizes the play's multiple meanings in a way that, not coincidentally, bears a striking resemblance to Tudor absolutism itself. "It has often been remarked," says Lisa Hopkins, "that Ford's depiction of the character of the Pretender differs radically from his sources by never having Perkin confess to his true identity, and also by representing him as a figure of innate dignity who appears utterly convinced of the justice of his own claims."[69] Perhaps the statement "A Strange Truth" that sits prominently on the play's title page should not be read as a comment on the strangeness of Warbeck's story but as a recognition of just how much truth some listeners had granted to it.

The stories that characters tell onstage hold out the promise of alternate horizons of possibility. For whether they draw such stories from nonvisible, offstage events in the past or simply make them up and project them there, characters use narratives onstage as ploys to escape their current circumstances and to change their lives in self-interested ways, which usually requires changing other characters' circumstances in the process. Such stories may be good investments or bad, and their tellers may either profit a community or bring adversity to it, but neither case has any direct bearing on whether those stories are marketable to others or whether narrators can garner belief, raise support, or find an audience to listen to them. Stories may be false but plausible, true but unlikely, false and doubtful, or true and probable, so the distance between "truth" and "truth-value" may be wide indeed. To dramatize this distance, Renaissance playwrights model for theatergoers the processes of both skepticism and belief by showcasing, on the one hand, characters who try to persuade their audiences to trust their versions of unseen events offstage, and, on the other, characters who forensically weigh and evaluate evidence about incidents that they have not seen with their own eyes. Because the truth-values that characters ascribe to stories might seem wise at first but turn out poorly, or they may appear to be foolish decisions that end up concluding well, characters' forensic modeling also highlights the provisionality of their convictions and teaches the benefits of reserving or revising one's judgments.

The Offstage and Its Double

> so bestow our selues, that seeing vnseene
> We may of their encounter frankely iudge
>
> —Claudius, in *THE TRAGEDIE OF HAMLET*

We began this chapter with Athenian artisans in *A MIDSOMMER Nights Dreame* trying to escape their current circumstances by scripting themselves into a more lucrative and comfortable future. While their success at such narrative projection remains forever uncertain, characters in *THE SPANISH TRAGEdie* and in *Henry the Fift* manage to transform individual and national destinies by telling selective stories about the recent and the distant past. These transformations tend to benefit only a privileged few: the Spanish General wins greater favor from his king, for instance, and Horatio (temporarily) achieves the love of Bel-Imperia, whereas Henry V conquers France and takes Princess Katharine as his war bride. And although many others fail to profit—and occasionally even suffer—at the material level as a result of these transformations, some of them nonetheless invest in and become part of larger, collective narratives, especially if we believe Henry's promise at Agincourt: "This story shall the good man teach his sonne."[70] When characters construct stories from dramatic prehistories as well as from offstage episodes occurring entr'acte, they use them to reconfigure social and political relations on both large and small scales. In fact, the dramatic crises in *Much adoe about Nothing* and in *PERKIN VVARBECK* arise from strategically delivered narratives, and the trajectories of their action alter course when characters and communities either believe or reject the stories that they hear. We have witnessed new narratives projected into the future, old histories and laws appropriated and narrativized to provoke a plan of action in the present, and recent incidents contrived to bring about changes in sociopolitical and interpersonal relationships.

In this last section, I turn to offstage events that happen simultaneously with the stage's visible performance. As suggested earlier, Renaissance plays often feature multiple threads of action that occur at the same moment in time but in different locations either on or off the stage. Schemes are set in motion, armies are deployed, love letters are dispatched, royal orders are sent down, journeys are embarked on, and whole worlds seem to rise and fall behind the scenes, "Euen now, now, very now."[71] Discussing this dramatic phenomenon, Pierre Corneille explains:

> When I say that it is not necessary to account for what the actors do when they are not on stage, I do not mean that it is not sometimes very useful to give such an accounting, but only that one is not forced to do it, and that one ought to take the trouble to do so only when what happens behind the scenes is necessary for the understanding of what is to take place before the spectators.[72]

Thus, just after Bolingbroke closes a scene to depart on his expedition to Wales—"come Lords away, | To fight with *Glendoure*, and his Complices; | A while to worke, and after holliday"—Richard II enters and asks, "Barkloughly Castle call you this at hand?" indicating the king's arrival on the Welsh coast from his Irish wars.[73] The mere sequencing of the two scenes conveys that Bolingbroke and Richard will soon encounter one another face-to-face, but in the meantime the rebel forces march their offstage route to the king's location in Wales.

In contrast to this common sort of simultaneous action in *Richard the Second*, a scene in part 1 of Christopher Marlowe's *Tamburlaine the Great* and another scene in Thomas Middleton's *Women Beware Women* take place just outside of playgoers' sight, and yet the audience is still able to perceive these scenes by reading the characters' interactions onstage as a metaphor for the action offstage. This unseen action does not take the form of verbal narrative, however, but must rather be composed as a scenic story by playgoers within their imaginations. Although they continue to be separated spatially, the onstage and offstage in these linked scenes coincide in a temporal sense because they occur in unison. In a representational sense, moreover, the onstage action signifies literally for itself (as all scenes do), but it also signifies on a figurative level, which provides playgoers with the narrative material to create the offstage action in their minds. If stories about offstage events give rise to a triple-time structure in live performance, as I have suggested, then these scenes in Marlowe's and Middleton's plays produce narrative's double-time structure entirely through drama's visibility and immediacy. Each of these two onstage scenes is conventionally "dramatic" by presenting directly visible action and dialogue for audiences to experience. But the onstage scenes also take the narratorial position of relaying offstage action, which is not narrated in a strict sense but which manifests instead through a secondary, metaphoric reading of the visible action and dialogue. These two intriguing scenes therefore double the stage's scenographic meanings, which challenge playgoers to register, process, and interpret at least twice the dramatic material at the same time.

In THE DEFENCE OF *Poesie*, Philip Sidney catalogs incredible dramatic situations that tax the stage, which has the unhappy effect of alienating the sympathies of even generous audiences. He objects especially to the playwrights of his day taking liberties with place and time. In fact, "*Gorboducke*," the best Elizabethan dramatic model in Sidney's estimation, does not scape whipping: "For it is faultie," he says, "both in place and time, the two necessarie Companions of all corporall actions."[74] Had Sidney not written the DEFENCE about a decade earlier than *Tamburlaine* stormed the stage, some of his critical objections might easily have been leveled at Marlowe's play, "where you shall haue *Asia* of the one side, and *Affricke* of the other."[75] Among the many other "grosse absurdities" afflicting contemporary plays, representations of battle onstage Sidney finds unusually preposterous: "two Armies flie in, represented with foure swords & bucklers, and thẽ what hard hart wil not receiue it for a pitched field[?]"[76] Whether Marlowe's *Tamburlaine* suffered in performance from such anemic battle scenes is difficult to say, though the play's printed stage directions imply that most of the physical fighting took place offstage, accompanied by conventional alarums and frenzied entrances and exits to suggest the melee of warfare.

During one of the play's offstage battles, however, the stage is occupied by an analogous verbal battle, which metaphorically stands in for, while also physically standing in front of, the unseen combat between Tamburlaine and Bajazeth. Furthermore, the concurrent incidence of the military and verbal battles both affirms and reverses conventional representations of gender by absenting the masculine physical combat and making it available to playgoers only through the more feminine exchange taking place onstage. Spoken by Bajazeth's wife Zabina and Tamburlaine's captive Zenocrate, the verbal battle spans fewer than 50 lines of dialogue, which rest within a much longer scene of 274 spoken lines. Prior to exiting for the battle, Bajazeth, Tamburlaine, and their respective followers engage in a highly structured parley, one filled predictably with masculine bravado and the kind of escalatory rhetoric that made Marlowe's two-part drama such a sensation in the 1580s and '90s. Following a tight locutionary pattern, the alternating speeches suggest that the men are observing a sort of martial protocol of verbal engagement. Both groups of adversaries respond to and echo their opponents in an increasingly hyperbolic manner, which Zabina and Zenocrate come to imitate after the men leave the stage to do battle.[77]

In succession, Bajazeth and Tamburlaine first call on their men to prepare for the field (C6v); they then each complain at the other's "presumption" (C6v); both swear to be victorious, one "By *Mahomet*" (C6v) and "the holy *Alcaron*" (C7r), the other "By this my sword that conquer'd *Persea*" (C7r); each of Bajazeth's three followers makes vaunting contributions to the exchange, which their emperor applauds, followed by similar remarks from Tamburlaine's three men, whom he also commends (C7r); Bajazeth and Tamburlaine then speak to their paramours, who both wish them success (C7r–v); and finally each delivers a rousing speech before exiting to the field (C7v–C8r). When all the men have left the stage, both women likewise protest at the other's presumption (C8r–v); Zabina insults "*tamburlaine* the great Tartarian thiefe," and Zenocrate insults the "great Bassoe" Bajazeth (C8v); in turn, each speaks to her maid, Ebea and Anippe, both of whom respond in kind (C8v). But suddenly, after the stage direction "*They sound the battell within, and stay*" (C8v), Zenocrate conspicuously breaks the pattern of balanced alternating dialogue by praying to "Ye Gods and powers that gouerne Persea," followed by Zabina, who calls on "*Mahomet*, [to] solicit God himselfe" (C8v). Zenocrate comes to dominate Zabina rhetorically, in other words, insinuating herself at a point in the verbal battle (and into the textual space) where we would actually expect Zabina to speak next. In response to the offstage business "*To the battell againe*" (C8v s.d.), Zenocrate makes the offensive claim that "By this the Turks lie weltring in their blood | And *tamburlaine* is Lord of Affrica," to which Zabina can only reply weakly and defensively: "Thou art deceiu'd" (D1r). Just before the offstage battle ends and Tamburlaine returns victorious, Zenocrate auspiciously speaks the last lines, declaring that Tamburlaine "liues and will be Conquerour" (D1r), leaving Zabina no chance to respond.

The dialogic blows that the women exchange appear at first to be conventionally feminine, particularly compared to that which the men exchange before exiting to the battle. Tamburlaine, Bajazeth, and their men are more active in their speeches, focusing on the palpable consequences of combat and bloodshed, while Zenocrate, Zabina, and their maids are more passive, concerned with disgracing their rivals by making their "daintie fingers fall to woorke" (C8v). On the one hand, the masculine heft of the dialogue between Tamburlaine and Bajazeth is evident both in the proportion of their speeches, which fill more than twice the textual space as the women's, and in the threats of physical violence with which they load their words. On the other hand, the exchange between Zenocrate and Zabina is less physically dominating both in the text and in the substance of their threats, which involve humiliation and the subjugation of each woman to the other's maid. When Zabina tells Zenocrate, "Thou shalt be Landresse to my waiting maid," Zenocrate rejoins that both Zabina and her maid Ebea "for their sausinesse shall be employed,

| To dresse the common souldiers meat and drink" (C8v). The women's verbal engagement also proceeds from that of the men's, in the sense of coming after as well as being a feminine imitation of their speeches. Before exiting, the men essentially deputize their paramours, seating them next to each other and bestowing on them their crowns. Tamburlaine makes Zenocrate his surrogate by ordering her: "manage words with her as we will armes" (C7v), which tends to stress the feminine passivity of the women's onstage dialogue and the masculine activity of the impending offstage combat.

Compared to the live physical activity of theater, the oratorical practice of narration might be regarded as a rather passive undertaking for storytellers and listeners alike. This is not to say that narration is unburdened by oral and aural labors: characters necessarily select the material for their stories, they arrange that material into plausible sequences, and they consciously perform them with verbal eloquence to accommodate the dispositions of specific audiences. And listening, too, demands of audiences physical and mental exertion. But the bodily inactivity of the narrative mode is in fact what grants it access to an unrestricted scope of space and time. In contrast, dramatic performance is relatively animated, which customarily limits the time and space of a play to that of its enactment because of its "corporall actions,"[78] as most premodern critics of the drama maintain. For example, one way that Aristotle distinguishes between drama and epic is by describing their formal relations to time and space:

> For the purpose of extending its length, epic poetry has a very great capacity that is specifically its own, since it is not possible in tragedy to imitate many simultaneous lines of action but only that performed by the actors on the stage. But because of the narrative quality of epic it is possible to depict many simultaneous lines of action that, if appropriate, become the means of increasing the poem's scope.[79]

Yet, in *Tamburlaine the Great*, Marlowe actually manages to construct "simultaneous lines of action" by doubling the representational value of the onstage scene between Zenocrate and Zabina. Because the women's verbal confrontation is framed as a battle—"manage words with her as we will armes," Tamburlaine says—playgoers witness both an argument on the stage and a metaphorical representation of physical combat that occurs simultaneously just beyond their view. By contracting the immediacy of two battles into the theatrics of one, the scene also doubles the perceptual and interpretive work that playgoers perform. The staged action is at once theater as theater and theater as narrative, and the masculine activity of warfare is thus visible only through the Levantine veil of femininity seated on the stage.

As it simultaneously depicts both itself and an unseen battle, this onstage scene at first, and paradoxically, masculinizes Zenocrate and Zabina and feminizes Tamburlaine and Bajazeth. Although Zenocrate and Zabina appear more passive in their verbal rather than physical combat, they inhabit the more active mode of theater, whereas the visually obscured Tamburlaine and Bajazeth become narrative subjects through the embodiment and substitution of their paramours. That is to say, the women dominate playgoers' physical senses because they are immediately visible, unlike the men. Yet, when she speaks out of turn, Zenocrate administers a convulsion to the prevailing dialogic balance, which has two effects: it indicates that Tamburlaine has begun to overwhelm Bajazeth on the field, and it shifts the axis of masculine power from the two women onstage to Zenocrate and Tamburlaine, as they each begin to prevail in their conflicts. Zenocrate not only asserts her belief in Tamburlaine's offstage success through her words, but she portrays that success by breaking the rhetorical symmetry of the dialogue and by dictating its new structure, which enacts Tamburlaine's imminent victory. Likewise, Zabina verbally falters and, unable to match Zenocrate's spoken daggers, her own disequilibrium becomes both the signal and the narrative of Bajazeth's capitulation. Zenocrate tells Zabina:

> If *Mahomet* should come from heauen and
> My royall Lord is slaine or conquered. (sweare,
> Yet should he not perswade me otherwise.
> But that he liues and will be Conquerour.
> *Baiazeth flies, and he pursues him.*
> *The battell short, and they enter,*
> *Baiazeth is ouercome.* (D1r)

Another victim of Tamburlaine's performative rhetoric and bloodlusty sword, Bajazeth succumbs and is caged with Zabina like a Turkish curiosity. But in this particular battle Zenocrate seems to play a tangible role in the victory, as if by deputizing her Tamburlaine had actually endowed her with his ability to effect conquests by first saying it will be so.

If, as Sidney believes, it is a poetical vice to populate the stage with "manie dayes and places, inartificially imagined" (H4r), then Marlowe's *Tamburlaine* is surely a reprobate dramatic poem, strutting from continent to continent with the kind of blithe respect that Tamburlaine himself shows toward others' sovereign borders. In this pair of scenes, however, Marlowe has not depicted "*Asia* of the one side, and *Affricke* of the other," but he has managed to compress the men's physical battle offstage into the figurative meaning of the action that playgoers witness onstage. As theatrical substitutes for Tamburlaine and Bajazeth, Zenocrate and Zabina offer the audience two dramatic stories at the same time: a literal verbal battle characterized as a feminine version of male warfare as well as a figurative enactment of that warfare, which momentarily gives the women greater mimetic power than the men who fight unseen offstage. In WOMEN BEWARE WOMEN, Thomas Middleton endows an onstage game of chess with a similar mimetic power, making the various moves on the chessboard an elaborate double entendre, which signifies for the Duke of Florence's rape of Brancha offstage. Compared to Marlowe's scene of verbal battle, Middleton's action multiplies the analogical connections between the onstage and offstage scenes not only by turning the individual chess moves into details about the rape but also by making the game itself emblematic of Florence's prevailing climate of politico-sexual scheming.

After the Florentine Leantio secretly marries the beautiful Venetian Brancha, a woman above his social station who has willingly but naively forfeited her wealth to wed, he plans to keep her out of public sight because, unlike his new bride, he fully knows the underhanded lengths to which others will go to obtain beauty, wealth, and status. At the end of the play's first scene, he muses about her to himself: "Who could imagine now a Gem were kept, | Of that great value under this plain roof?"[80] As a "Factor" (G3v) or mercantile agent, Leantio must frequently be away from home, so he commissions his mother (named only "Mother" in the text) to watch over Brancha in his absence. Only moments after he leaves for business, however, Florentine citizens enter and proclaim the Duke's approach, which reminds Mother of the "yearly custom and solemnity | Religiously observ'd by th'Duke and State | To St. *Marks* Temple, the fifteenth of *April*" (H5r). Mother and Brancha watch this procession pass from their gallery window and, several scenes later, we learn from the courtiers Livia and Guardiano that the Duke has seen and become infatuated with Brancha. Guardiano tells Livia:

> The Duke himself first spi'd her at the window ;
> Then in a rapture, as if admiration
> Were poor when it were single, beck'ned me,
> And pointed to the wonder warily
> As one that fear'd she would draw in her splendor
> Too soon, if too much gaz'd at[.] (I2r)

The two courtiers thus devise a stratagem to procure Brancha for the Duke's sexual indulgence, since "'Twould prove but too much worth in wealth and fa- | vor | To those should work his peace" (I2r), which puns on the working of the Duke's peace/piece, both penis and chess piece. Eventually persuading Mother to bring her secret guest to her home for a friendly and innocuous visit, Livia arranges for the Duke to wait upstairs until Guardiano can deliver Brancha to him.

Once Brancha arrives, Guardiano obligingly takes her on a tour of the household to see the "rooms and pictures," while Livia and Mother pass the time "till evening" by playing chess (I7v). The women discuss their game for some lines, when Guardiano and Brancha "*Enter above*" (I8r) in the theater's gallery. Impressed with Livia's furnishings, Brancha assures Guardiano:

"Trust me Sir, | Mine eye nev'r met with fairer Ornaments," to which he replies:

> There's a better peece
> Yet then all these: —*Duke above*
> *Bran*. Not possible Sir !
> *Guard*. Believe it
> You'll say so when you see't: Turn but your eye
> now
> Y'are upon't presently. *Exit*.
>
> (I8r)

Guardiano exits here, handing Brancha over to the Duke, who for some seventy lines tries unsuccessfully to seduce her with "wealth, | honor" (K1r), until he eventually conveys her out of sight to another room of the house. The conversation that Livia and Mother immediately strike up about their game does double duty as the Duke begins to rape Brancha offstage, when Guardiano reenters and delivers a long aside that relishes in his pandering:

> Yet to prepare her stomach by degrees
> To *Cupids* feast, because I saw 'twas quezy,
> I shew'd her naked pictures by the way ;
> A bit to stay the appetite. Well, Advancement ! (K2r)

The conclusion of the chess match coincides with the conclusion of the rape, and Brancha reenters to lament in an aside that "mine honors Leprous," as she curses the Duke, Guardiano, and Livia for their "smooth brow'd treachery, | That wore the fair vail of a friendly welcome" (K2v).

Like Marlowe's scene in *Tamburlaine*, Middleton's chess match doubles the stage's representational labor by depicting both itself and an unseen offstage event. Yet, unlike *Tamburlaine*, this doubling of representational labor takes place both on the physical level of their maneuvering of chess pieces and on the discursive level of their dialogue through double entendre. That opponents playing chess are by definition adversarial makes the game a powerful but troubling visual substitute for the rape, which likewise involves one person's deprivation of another's power. The primary way that Livia's conversation with Mother represents the offstage rape is through the language she uses to describe her opponent's obliviousness and vulnerability to her aggressive chess moves. Celia R. Daileader notes how Livia's "*double entendres* throughout the game keep the audience alert to the unseen act," providing a verbal substitute onstage for the sexual violence that happens off it.[81] When Guardiano and Brancha initially exit to see the household's furnishings, Livia tells Mother:

Alas poor Widow, I shall be too hard for
thee.
Moth. Y'are cunning at the game, I'll be sworn
(Madam*)*.
Liv. It will be found so, ere I give you over: [I7v]
She that can place her man well,
Moth. As you do (Madam).
Liv. As I shall (Wench) can never lose her
game;
Nay, nay, the black King's mine.
Moth. Cry you mercy (Madam).
Liv. And this my Queen.
Moth. I see't now.
Liv. Here's a Duke
Will strike a sure stroke for the game anon;
Your pawn cannot come back to relieve it self.
Moth. I know that *(*Madam.*)*
Liv. You play well the whilst;
How she belies her skill ! I hold two duckats,
I give you Check and Mate to your white King.
Simplicity it self, your Saintish King there.
Moth. Well, ere now Lady
I have seen the fall of Subtilty: Jest on.
Liv. I but Simplicitie receives two for one.
Moth. What remedy but patience! (I8r)

It is at this point that Guardiano and Brancha "*Enter above*," leaving Livia and Mother to fall silent while the Duke enters and attempts to seduce Brancha visibly in the gallery. The "ironically named Guardiano"[82] thence abandons his domestic sightseer to the concupiscent Duke, who immediately tells her, "He's gone Beauty ! | Pish, look not after him : He's but a vapor, | That when the Sun appears, is seen no more" (I8v).

Livia's language in the match so far is mainly in the future tense: "I shall be too hard for | thee," "It will be found so," "Here's a Duke | Will strike a sure stroke for the game anon." Like Guardiano showing Brancha "naked pictures" "to prepare her stomach by degrees | To *Cupids* feast," her aggression toward Mother (and the offstage rape that it will figuratively represent) is only anticipatory, which prepares theatergoers' stomachs, too, for the attack that will soon follow. Livia cues both the sexual nature and the asymmetry of power in the attack with the language: "too hard," "give you over," and "strike a sure stroke." When she insists that "the black King's mine," Livia identifies Guardiano as her most valuable and villainous player, just as she predicts that her rook, which was commonly called a "duke," "Will strike a sure stroke."[83] This onstage scene confronts theatergoers with two radically different perspectives at once. The first is a relatively harmless conversation about the chess match that the two women play, which confines the scene's signifying power to the immediacy and visual openness of the stage. The other perspective breaks free of the stage's visible space and extends outside of Mother's knowledge to point up the stratagem by which Guardiano is—at that very moment—moving and positioning Brancha, a mere "pawn," to be assaulted by the Duke. By understanding that Mother *mis*understands her double meanings, the audience comes to share the same epistemology as Livia, who calls Mother "Simplicity it self." As Mother "receives two for one" without realizing it, playgoers receive "two for one" scenes by shuttling between the literal and figurative action that plays out before them.

As soon as the Duke and Brancha "*Exit above*," Livia and Mother resume their conversation about the chess match:

> *Liv*. Did not I say my Duke would fetch you
> over (Widow) ?
> *Moth*. I think you spoke in earnest when you said
> it (Madam).
> *Liv*. And my black King makes all the haste he
> can too.
> *Moth*. Well (Madam) we may meet with him in
> time yet.
> *Liv*. I have given thee blinde mate twice.
> *Moth*. You may see (Madam)
> My eyes begin to fail.
> *Liv*. I'll swear they do, Wench. (K1v)

If "my Duke" is the rapacious Duke, here, and if "my black King" is Guardiano, then should we read Livia's remark: "my black King makes all the haste he | can too" as an indication that Guardiano is voyeuristically masturbating offstage? A consummate offstage moment, if so. In any event, Livia reveals to Mother that "I have given thee blinde mate twice," a technical term for the checkmating of an opponent that goes unnoticed by the aggressor. The language of seeing and blindness that governs the end of this exchange once again aligns playgoers with Livia's knowledge while distancing them from Mother's. But the knowledge that the scene produces for playgoers does not simply stand in opposition to Mother's ignorance, for even Livia is blind to the details of the scene offstage, although she and the audience can surmise that Brancha is being raped there. The distribution of knowledge about the rape begins with the least-informed Mother, whose "eyes begin to fail"; it broadens with Livia and the audience, who must still rely on the narrativized chess match to gain access to it; it increases significantly with Guardiano, who seems to be at hand (so to speak) for the event itself; and it ends with the Duke and Brancha, who are at the center of this scene's meaningful action even though physically farthest from the stage.

Livia now brings the chess match to its obscene climax:

> *Liv*. The game's ev'n at the best now ; you may see Widow
> How all things draw to an end.
> *Moth*. Ev'n so do I Madam.
> . . . .
> *Liv*. Has not my Duke bestir'd himself?
> *Moth*. Yes faith Madam ; h'as done me all the mischief in this Game.
> *Liv*. H'as shew'd himself in's kind. (K2r)

Through Livia's decisive endgame against Mother, the Duke's rape of Brancha "draw[s] to an end" as "all things" must, which puns of course on the phallic meaning of "things" and their orgasms.[84] While spectators only witness this sexual violence indirectly through the narration of the chess match, Daileader notes that in another Middleton play, *A Mad World, My Masters*, "an amorous couple can be heard panting and grunting offstage"[85]—which is certainly not to say that Brancha's rape is "amorous." But is it not suggestive, then, to consider how an actor playing Guardiano might pause at the textual line break when he says, "Hark, list, there's some body coming | down; 'tis she" (K2r), as Brancha reenters to curse them all?[86]

Ania Loomba writes that "what is especially important in the case of [the chess game in] *Women Beware Women* is that he employs it to desensationalise the rape. Violence on the female body has become a sort of courtly game in which those outside the royal circle are pawns."[87] I would agree with Loomba that the chess match indeed mediates the rape and thereby blunts the full force for the audience of the sexual violence against Brancha. But it also serves as a figurative representation of the rape, giving playgoers an even more immediate knowledge of the event than if it was recounted after the fact, as in most other offstage episodes. In addition to metaphorizing the rape, the women's maneuvering of pieces on the chessboard also emblematizes the broader "courtly game" that Loomba observes. Although *WOMEN BEWARE WOMEN* depicts a social system in which one's possible moves may seem like relatively free choices between black and white, those moves are for the most part predetermined by the political game that characters like Brancha and Mother are compelled to play. This game is not one of strategic moves on a flat, square playing field but one that is largely conducted outside of rival players' visibility and knowledge. That Brancha and Mother are initially blind to their own participation in this game makes them easier targets for players like the Duke, Livia, and Guardiano, who comport themselves not directly and openly but rather in ways that are askew and oblique, like the multidirectional moves that rooks, queens, and kings can make on a chessboard, while pawns may move only unidirectionally.

The distribution of sight and blindness in this scene is not perfectly mappable as a distribution of knowledge and ignorance among its characters and spectators, for some know more than they see, others see but cannot understand, while still others understand but do not fully know.[88] Nevertheless, the pleasure that the Duke, Livia, and Guardiano seem to take from seeing and knowing is matched by their delight in others' lack of sight and knowledge, which is an economy that imbues both the court and this dramatic scene with immense power. One adjunct to this economy is that concealing a desirable object from the sight of others serves to fetishize it, which adds pleasure and value both to its concealment and to its discovery. In an earlier scene, Leantio had wanted to keep Brancha out of sight, hoarding her like the "matchless Jewel" to which he likens her, to prevent her beauty from provoking desire in others. He had said to himself:

> 'tis great policy
> To keep choice treasures in obscurest places :
> Should we shew Theeves our wealth, 'twould make
> 'em bolder ;
> . . . .
> The Jewel is cas'd up from all mens eyes. (G7r)

Yet Leantio has himself stolen Brancha from her wealthy Venetian family, calling her "the best peece of theft | That ever was committed" (G5r). So, when the Duke spies Brancha at her window during the procession, the series of events that ensues from his lust for her completes the circuit of desire that Leantio had already set in motion in the play's earlier scenes. While avarice might prompt an individual "To keep choice treasures in obscurest places," the discovery of such treasures inevitably spurs an appetite to possess them. The desire to get and the fear to lose are but two sides of the same Florentine coin.

By making these enacted scenes signify metaphorically for simultaneous action occurring off the stage, Marlowe and Middleton devise an intricate dramaturgy that capitalizes on the necessary interdependence of seeing and not-seeing as well as of knowing and not-knowing, which generates the space for interpretation. These onstage scenes, in other words, do not present self-evident representations or transparent meanings. They rather demand that playgoers actively interpret the stage's visible scenes as doubly embodied narratives, which stand in figuratively for the offstage action that they do not directly witness. Playgoers engage in such interpretive acts because the simultaneous scenes are both radically distinct from and analogically linked to each other, creating disjunctions in meaning that are structurally parallel to those produced when characters narrate offstage events from the past within the presence of performance. For instance, while the General's narrative in THE SPANISH TRAGEdie stylistically imports a recent battle for the listening pleasure of the Spanish King, Zenocrate and Zabina in *Tamburlaine the Great* offer a real-time representation of another offstage combat through their verbal sparring. Likewise, the sexual corruption of Hero in *Much adoe about Nothing* is portrayed on the stage through the indirection of report, but in WOMEN BEWARE WOMEN the Duke's nonvisible rape of Brancha acquires palpable force through the literal manhandling of chess pieces and Livia's figurative narration of the offstage violence. During such moments, the theater doubles playgoers' perceptual and interpretive labors, but they are amply rewarded with twice the drama for an equivalent investment of their time.

The Commercial Theater

In the final pages of *S/Z*, Roland Barthes writes that

> narration (object) modifies narration (action): the message is parametrically linked with its performance; there is no question of an utterance on the one hand and on the other its uttering. Telling is a responsible and commercial act (are these not the same thing? in both cases, a matter of *weighing*?) whose outcome (the virtuality of transformation) is "indexed" on the price of the merchandise, on the object of the narrative. This object, therefore, is not final, it is not the goal, the term, the end of the narration [. . .]: as meaning, the subject of the anecdote harbors a recurrent force which reacts on language and demystifies, ravages the innocence of its utterance: what is told is the "telling." Ultimately, the narrative has no *object*: the narrative concerns only itself: *the narrative tells itself*.[89]

Narration modifies narration, Barthes says, a statement whose perfect reversibility would tautologize its meaning, "the 'genius' of the language (subject, verb, complement),"[90] were it not for the statement's virtual subject and predicate, held intact by the bulging integrity of their parentheses: (object) modifies (action). What he seems to mean is that the narrative object—its "message" or subject matter—modifies the action of narrating it, but since the statement reverses itself so readily, we might also understand it to mean that the act of narrating also transforms the story being told. While the context of telling may exhibit an "innocence" or autonomy undisturbed by the narrative event that occurs within it, the story "demystifies, ravages the innocence of its utterance," making the retailing of a story between teller and recipient the actual object/ive of the narrative: "what is told is the 'telling.'" As such, narrative comes to modify its narration, turning the scene of storytelling into a representational space and time where the verbal performance becomes the story's own parameter and duration.

When dramatic characters tell others about action off the stage, they likewise alter the parameters of the stage and of the scene. Such stories take listeners on imaginative journeys to places and events that cannot be immediately authenticated within the theater's representational economy. Since the tangible details of offstage action must be quite literally re-presented through rhetorical practices, characters inevitably market their stories to audiences and fashion them as creditable objects of social commerce. Not all listeners buy the stories that other characters tell or sell, and, as we have seen, the relative accuracy with which characters represent offstage events has no essential relationship with the truth-values that their tellers or audiences might ascribe to them. Such truth-values function in the drama as rhetorical effects that storytellers have calibrated and that their audiences have weighed either to affirm or to reorganize existing personal, social, or political relations. Stories from the offstage sphere, in other words, transform the context of their performance—"narration (object) modifies narration (action)"—which in the drama encompasses both the specific scene of storytelling and the more comprehensive dramatic plot within which the narrator and audience take part. If "Telling is a responsible and commercial act," as Barthes maintains, then the narrative commerce that characters transact on the stage comes to constitute the social relations depicted there. Sitting or standing in the offstage space of the theater's auditorium (another offstage site that we will examine in the next chapter), playgoers take up interpretive positions analogous to characters on the stage, who must work to reconcile the stories they only hear about with those events that play out before their very eyes.

Part II

The Offstage in Amphitheaters and Texts

Chapter 3

✦

Cleaving the General Ear

> A ring is the natural form in which the maximum number of spectators can press about an object of interest.
>
> —E. K. Chambers, *The Elizabethan Stage*

> In theory if not in practice, the business of hearing, as "audience" (from the Latin *audire*, "to hear"), was more important than the business of seeing, as "spectators" (from the Latin *spectare*, "to see").
>
> —Andrew Gurr, "The Shakespearean Stage"

> *Pyra*. I see a voyce ; now vvill I to the chinke,
> To spy and I can heare my *Thisbies* face.
>
> —Bottom as Pyramus, in William Shakespeare, *A MIDSOMMER Nights Dreame*

In the previous chapter we saw onstage storytellers using an array of rhetorical tactics to persuade audiences of the veracity of their narratives. There, I emphasized that stories about offstage episodes are rhetorical in form and function because characters consciously select the material for their narratives (*inventio*), they arrange that material into a credible series of events (*dispositio*), and they transform the social relations within the drama through their eloquence, presence of mind, and verbal performances (*eloquentia*, *memoria*, *pronuntiatio*).[1] I have argued that the power that stories exert over their audiences on these dramatic occasions rests in the rhetorical and narratological savvy of characters who construct and promote unseen sights to others and thereby ask their listeners to trust their ears more than their very eyes.

In the two most influential classical authorities on rhetoric in the period, Cicero's *De Oratore* and Quintilian's *Institutio Oratoria*, early modern writers could mine potent methods of constructing logical arguments for oratory as well as convincing sequences of events for narratives, with Horace's *Ars Poetica* speaking to literary considerations unaddressed by the two rhetors. "Taken together," Bruce R. Smith remarks,

> Cicero, Quintilian, and Horace offered Renaissance readers a self-consistent, fully realized system for interpreting playscripts. Fundamental to that system was a sense of those scripts as plans for a rhetorical event, an exchange between an actor speaking *in loco poetae* and using all the devices of persuasion to convince his listeners of a moral argument, often one with political implications.[2]

For early modern humanists advocating a regimented curriculum and moral programme for educating talented young men, the political implications that Smith refers to involve the weighty matters of state on which they might someday have the chance to counsel their prince, a situation we observe, for example, in both the action and the second performance context of *Gorboduc*, which was staged for Queen Elizabeth on January 18, 1561/2.[3] On the other hand, for dramatic characters narrating offstage events to audiences who have not witnessed them, those political implications are seldom moored to the kind of objective "moral argument" that humanists tended to idealize. The politics are more frequently scripted according to characters' personal motivations and the social shift in power, privilege, or opportunity that they try to bring about through the telling of story. Some characters certainly seek to convey offstage events with accuracy in their fullness and detail, while others exploit the persuasive power of narrative for personal gain. But, in every instance, characters who tell stories onstage fashion them to the context and audience of their telling so that they might achieve calculated results with their rhetoric.

This chapter therefore proceeds from our earlier considerations of the offstage as a formal problem—particularly as dramatic theory frames the boundary between onstage and offstage as a divide between knowledge and ignorance, and as dramatic practice employs distinct modes of representation to create discrete epistemologies—by examining how the material forms of early modern amphitheaters shaped the representational energies of drama and narrative. Glynne Wickham begins volume 1 of his *Early English Stages 1300 to 1660* by asserting that the actor–audience relation "is conditioned by the physical structure of the building that contains them both."[4] One of the fundamental ways that all theaters condition performance involves imposing a "definitional constraint" on each side of the stage's physical boundaries in an effort to achieve an ideal relationship between its performers and its playgoers. Keir Elam elaborates:

> This definitional constraint, whereby the actors' and spectators' roles are distinguished and the levels of reality (dramatic versus theatrical) are conventionally established, is the crucial axiom in the theatrical frame. It is on the basis of this understanding that the performers are able to interact on stage apparently oblivious to the audience and its

> doings, just as the spectators themselves find no difficulty in identifying which elements belong to the representation and which to the excluded theatrical context, and so do not expect to impinge directly on the interaction. This firm cognitive division is usually reinforced by symbolic spatial or temporal boundary markers or "brackets."[5]

Elam's description of the actors being "apparently oblivious to the audience and its doings" indicates that he has a more "representational" or at least modern theater in mind here, but such "definitional constraint" between the stage and the auditorium likewise obtains in the "presentational" or nonillusionistic amphitheaters of Renaissance England. On the one hand, "representational" performance posits a fictional dramatic situation that aims to suspend or erase the theatrical context in which it takes place in order to create a kind of voyeuristic illusion for spectators—the theater of Henrik Ibsen and Anton Chekhov, for instance. "Presentational" performance, on the other hand, posits a fictional dramatic situation that does not renounce its own "positedness," but rather "bring[s] attention to bear on the theatrical and dramatic realities in play, on the fictional status of the characters, on the very theatrical transaction" between stage and auditorium.[6]

S. L. Bethell describes these performance conditions in terms of the Renaissance audience's "double consciousness," which preserved an awareness of

> the essential artificiality of the play-world, [. . .] thus holding play-world and real world before the mind simultaneously yet without confusion. Such an attitude has the advantage of accepting and exploiting the situation as it really is, whereas naturalism must engage in a constant effort to delude the audience into taking for actuality what they are bound to know, in their moments of critical alertness, to be only a stage performance.[7]

The language of "representational" and "presentational" usefully historicizes the mentality of Renaissance playgoers, for whom the expectation of a naturalistic theatrical illusion would have been impossible. Yet it is just as important to observe that even in a presentational setting performances can, and often do, engross the audience without any pretense to naturalism. In *Pierce Penilesse*, for example, Thomas Nashe recalls how when the player enacted John Talbot's death onstage he had "his bones newe embalmed with the teares of ten thousand spectators at least, (at seuerall times) who in the Tragedian that represents his person, imagine they behold him fresh bleeding."[8] Producing dramatic presence without illusion, presentational theater creates a "Flexible Dramaturgy," to borrow Robert Weimann's phrase, which can move between a performance's "dramatic" and "theatrical" registers with ease, just as actors might move between the more fictionalized space of the *locus* and the more unlocalized space of the *platea*.[9] In the context of the "definitional constraints" that the stage and the auditorium construct through their material conditions, I investigate playgoers' conscious fixation on or absorption into the stage's activities, as opposed to an amnesiac experience of theater that trades self-awareness for voyeurism. In addition to the amphitheaters' material conditions, we will also consider how the many goings-on within the auditorium disrupt and distract the audience, not by "breaking the dramatic illusion," since there was none, but rather by competing for playgoers' attention.

That a theatrical performance requires an attentive audience to become anything more than just a rehearsal is hardly surprising. But the less evident point here is that the stage must efface the auditorium and its inhabitants to accomplish its work. Such effacement hinges, first of all, on heightening playgoers' attention to the stage's visible and audible representations and, second, on diminishing playgoers' attention to the contrived theatrical "frame" in which the performance takes place. "Disattention" is Erving Goffman's term to describe the performance's successful eliding of the theatrical "frame" and the audience's temporary distraction from it.[10] A conscious break in this kind of "disattention" we might call "alienation," which interrupts and intervenes in the stage's dramatic presence whenever a playgoer concentrates more on the theatrical frame, the spectatorial environs, or the self. I wish to activate the Brechtian language of alienation because the architectural and playgoing conditions that will occupy us in this chapter function as alienation devices. Bertolt Brecht famously developed alienation effects to counter the anesthetic effects that he saw naturalistic theater promoting within its audiences. The goal of the Brechtian A-effect is to highlight not just the artifice of the theatrical frame but ultimately the constructedness of the social circumstances represented in the dramatic fiction, which is designed to encourage playgoers to critique and analyze.[11] In contrast, the kind of alienation we will see in Renaissance amphitheaters entails a competition between the onstage activity of performance and the offstage space of the auditorium.

This chapter, then, examines both the material conditions of Renaissance amphitheaters and what I will describe as "microcultures" of playgoing. With the term "microcultures," I intend to avoid the somewhat blunt instrument of "playgoing culture" and to mark instead particular material practices within the auditorium, which will help differentiate and diversify not just early modern playgoers and their many sensibilities but specifically the varied activities in which they engaged during—and sometimes over and against—performances. As we shall see, both the amphitheaters' material conditions and their spectatorial microcultures gave physical shape to the rhetorical circumstances of live performance on the stage, which strove to engross playgoers' concentration precisely by disattending their focus from themselves. I want to argue that if theater, by convention, tries to persuade its playgoers to disregard themselves and to disattend to the spectatorial space they occupy, then dramatic fictions only achieve their power, immediacy, and "presence" onstage through the disappearance of the offstage. Put another way, it is the fictional absence of the real auditorium that transforms the fiction onstage into a real presence. Because the offstage space of the auditorium is always a necessary but disavowed condition of the theater, its effacement makes theater "an 'uncomfortable' artform because its symbolic register [i.e., the dramatic fiction] is continually threatened by another, one in which theatre's fictionality, its meaning-*making*, remains overt."[12] Renaissance amphitheaters in particular keep the constructedness of their fictionality on display even as they ask playgoers to disregard it, which means that the presence of a directly visible fiction is always vulnerable to intrusions by the frame offstage.

As one of the two primary media that delivered drama to audiences in the period, amphitheaters reproduce on physical and perceptual levels the competitive dynamic that we witness between enactment and narration on the stage. I will turn to the medium of printed dramatic texts in the final chapter, but here I address the geometrical configuration of the amphitheaters and analyze how the centrality of their stages positions playgoers physically within the offstage space of the auditorium. Like the discourses of drama and narrative, the auditoria of the open-air playhouses are fundamentally rhetorical in design because they distribute and locate playgoers in relation to the stage's discourse of debate and dispute, which by dramatic definition portrays political, social, and interpersonal conflicts among its characters. The auditoria offer up to playgoers a certain number of bodily and sensory freedoms without exactly making them free, and they place limitations on playgoers' participatory options without dictating how they should engage. The internal geometry of early modern amphitheaters, I argue, situates playgoers within a sensory-perceptive field that is both centripetal and centrifugal by focalizing spectators on the central thrust stage while at the same time gravitating their aural-visual awareness into the offstage circuit of the auditorium. Within this sensory-perceptive field, both stage and auditorium vie for playgoers' attention.

That the various goings-on within the interiors of amphitheaters contended for playgoers' conscious attention is an implicit assumption of scholars working on the performance conditions and audience phenomenologies of early modern theater. One of the prevailing challenges that these scholars have faced has been denaturalizing the cultural dominance of the visual—which we as modern theatergoers have inherited from proscenium-arch stages, perspective scenery, and naturalistic theater, not to mention the media of film, television, and video—and then supplanting it with an oral/aural heuristic, which some scholars argue was more culturally pervasive in England during the sixteenth and seventeenth centuries. Andrew Gurr, for example, opens his classic *Playgoing in Shakespeare's London* with an emphatic distinction between the activities of hearing and seeing:

> The strongest way of registering the essential difference between playgoing in Shakespeare's time and now is to register the etymological difference of an audience from a spectator. "Audience" is a collective term for a group of listeners. A "spectator" is an individual, seeing for him or herself. Modern playgoers are set up, by their physical and mental conditioning, to be solitary spectators, sitting comfortably in the dark watching a moving picture, eavesdroppers privileged by the camera's hidden eye. In fundamental contrast the early modern playgoers were audiences, people gathered as crowds, forming what they called assemblies, gatherings, or companies. They sat or stood in a circle round the speakers who were enacting what they came to hear and see. An audience comes to hear, and therefore it clusters as closely as possible round the speaker. Spectators come to see, and so they position themselves where they can confront the spectacle. The Elizabethan stage, being the centre of a circle, had no front.[13]

Gurr is of course setting up this opposition to estrange our modern sensibilities—and rightly so. Yet, essential as it is to historicize the playgoing experience in early modern England, this now critical orthodoxy can easily reverse the polarity of our modern scopophilia to the neglect of the visual dimension of playgoing in the period. Gabriel Egan demonstrates that early modern writers actually spoke of going to "see a play" far more frequently than they went to "hear" one—"the preponderance of visual over aural phrasing is more than twelve to one," he writes—though of course tastes or demands could certainly shift midaction.[14] The PROLOGUE in Thomas Middleton's *NO WIT [NO] HELP LIKE A VVOMANS* asks:

> [H]*Ow is't possible to suffice*
> *So many Ears, so many Eyes ?*
> *Some in wit, some in shows*
> *Take delight, and some in Clothes ;*
> *Some for mirth they cheifly come,*
> *Some for passion, for both some*[.][15]

Unless a playgoer was physically disabled in vision or hearing, both eyes and ears continued to function simultaneously during performances. Indeed, the very premise of such arguments for prioritizing one sense over the other requires both of them to be operative, which means that either one might take precedence while they appeal to the conscious attention of playgoers.

Judging from the less colloquial discourse of apologetic in the period, live drama seems to have given theatergoers visual as well as aural pleasure. In *A Discourse of English Poetrie*, William Webbe asserts, "Those on stages haue speciall respect to the motions of the minde, that they may stirre bothe the eyes and eares of their beholders."[16] Although objecting to the lack of critical distance among "the common people, who reioyse much to be at playes and enterludes," George Puttenham nevertheless observes that they "haue at all such times their eares so attentiue to the matter , and their eyes vpon the shewes of the stage."[17] Philip Sidney had insisted that, in the fields of philosophy and history, "the one giueth the precept, & the other the example," whereas "the peerlesse Poet performe[s] both."[18] Hence Thomas Heywood in *AN APOLOGY For Actors* argues that theater marries the virtues of oratory and painting while supplementing their weaknesses: "A Description is only a shadow receiued by the eare but not perceiued by the eye: so liuely portrature is meerely a forme seene by the eye, but can neither shew action, passion, motion, or any other gesture, to mooue the spirits of the beholder to admiration."[19] A gifted stage actor, Heywood concludes, can do all of these things by playing on the combined visual and aural cues that engender emotional responses in theatergoers.

Simply giving precedence, then, to either hearing or seeing fails to account for how some early modern writers conceived of the experience of popular theatergoing. It likewise overlooks the ways that sight and hearing mutually enhance and even direct each other in the theater, especially because both senses have the effect of positioning the playgoer's body in space. In *The Acoustic World of Early Modern England*, Bruce Smith notes, "Ordinarily, listening is an intensely *situated* experience. The listener stands at the center of a sphere that extends in all directions. Just how far he is able to hear depends on all sorts of contingencies, as does the degree to which his range of hearing and his range of vision happen to coincide."[20] In an amphitheater, the interior faces of the building's outermost walls comprise one of these "contingencies," putting a limit on how far occupants can see while at the same time severely restricting how far they can hear beyond that perimeter. Further, if each playgoer looks and listens from "the center of a sphere" wherein successive aural visual stimuli communicate spatiotemporal coordinates, then Gurr's collective audience is also (and unsurprisingly) a gathering of individual spectators and auditors, not one of whom shares the same perspective on the stage. By considering this double labor of the playgoing experience—a labor performed by eyes and ears, which are subject to the inclinations of communal as well as individual bodies, all distributed within a circular configuration—we can delineate the rhetorical conditions of the auditorium and thus the sensorial demands placed on its inhabitants. That is to say, we perceive how attending a performance at an early modern amphitheater exercised playgoers' visual and aural attention not just with activity on the stage, as is to be expected, but also with offstage commotion in the equally visible and audible space of the auditorium.

When we think of the internal geometry of amphitheaters as a rhetorical instrument that directs its playgoers' senses by persuading them to take a literal stance to see and hear, then the sheer scope and volume of the auditorium become conspicuous and inexorable elements of each and every playgoer's aural-visual field. What were the actual physical positions from which early modern theatergoers watched and listened to stage plays? What did it mean to have a "standing" at a performance? Was the stage always capable of arresting and retaining playgoers' attention? What sort of offstage distractions might the auditorium have provided in competition with the action and dialogue onstage? Heywood's talented actor, who combines rhetorical gestures and body language, can "shew action, passion, motion, or any other gesture, to mooue the spirits of the beholder to admiration," but what opportunities did playgoers have to "mooue" themselves around the auditorium at will? To answer these questions we must examine exactly what we know about the geometry and auditoria of amphitheaters like the Rose and the Globe. Reviewing the archeological work that began in 1989 and that is still ongoing will provide a firm basis not only for analyzing the physical conditions of these versatile rhetorical instruments, but also for understanding the site-specific nature of much of our knowledge.

Playhouse Digs

On January 31, 1989, an archeological team from the Museum of London unearthed the first chalky remains of foundations belonging to the Rose playhouse at the corner of Park Street and Rose Alley in the Borough of Southwark (figure 3.1). In October of that year and only a short distance down Park Street to the southeast of the Rose site, the team exposed and then evaluated roughly 10 percent of the surviving groundwork of the two Globe playhouses (figure 3.2). "What they found embedded in the mud," reports Russ McDonald about the vestiges of the Rose,

> was not much to look at: the foundations of pillarlike corner supports for the polygonal building's sides, the foundational outline of the original and the redesigned stage[s], a narrow trench or drip line made by rainwater falling off the thatched roof, bits of mortar and hazelnut shells that served as flooring in the yard in front of the stage, and evidence of a major reconstruction project [. . .].[21]

What they found of the remains of the second Globe was quantitatively even less than that of the Rose—if culturally more profound because of its deeper associations with Shakespeare. Julian Bowsher and Pat Miller detail the few surviving remnants that were examined for the first Globe:

> Phase 1 of the Globe was represented only by a disturbed chalk and ragstone footing, interpreted as the outer gallery wall of the first Globe playhouse [. . .]. The main, central, foundation survived to

Figure 3.1. Photograph of the Rose playhouse remains, oriented north, May 13, 1989. Courtesy of Andrew Fulgoni, © Fulgoni Copyrights Ltd. 1989–2017.

> *c* 6.30m long and varied in width from 0.40m at the southern end to a maximum of 0.80m. This foundation consisted, at its northern end, of chalk rubble set around timber stakes [. . .]. Part of the foundation [. . .], a sandy mortar interspersed with chalk lumps and brick fragments, was partially overlain by a dark brown to black deposit that included lenses of charcoal, crushed brick, and clay [. . .] and also lay to either side of the outer gallery wall. This has been interpreted as possible evidence of the 1613 fire.[22]

For the second Globe playhouse that opened in 1614, an outer gallery wall was also evaluated: "This brick wall was 0.38m wide, and three courses of brick remained to a height of 1.63m OD. Only 2.50m of this wall remained."[23] While other Southwark excavations by the Museum of London have revealed significant portions of the last of the purpose-built amphitheaters, the Hope, this dual-purpose playhouse and bear-baiting house was fraught with

Figure 3.2. Photograph of the Globe playhouse remains, oriented southeast, 1989. Courtesy of Museum of London Archaeology.

infighting and was rather short-lived as a theatrical venue.[24] During excavations in 2008, 2010, and 2011 in Shoreditch, the Theater site exposed a small percentage of its foundations consisting of brick, ragstone, and chalk blocks, which largely define the inner wall of a gallery to the north, as well as "a short section of brick and tile floor projecting into the yard" and "a slightly south-sloping gravel yard surface" (figure 3.3).[25]

Compared to the documentary and pictorial evidence on which theater historians had had to rely prior to 1989, these few material remains of the Rose and the Globe on Bankside and of the Theater in Shoreditch might appear remarkably unspectacular. Except for "fragments of a brick superstructure" at the Rose[26] and a couple meters of outer brick wall at the Globe,[27] no other part of the superstructures has survived. Moreover, some of the foundations have been subjected to destructive intrusions from modern building activities, and the Rose's foundations are to a great extent "robbed out,"

Figure 3.3. Photograph of the Theater playhouse remains, oriented southeast. Courtesy of Museum of London Archaeology.

meaning that virtually all that exists "is the trace left behind by a feature which has long since disappeared or been destroyed; the footprint not the foot itself."[28] Yet, in spite of appearances, these remains have advanced and continue to advance our knowledge in significant ways about many facets of the early English amphitheaters, they have literally altered the shape of the reconstructed Globe on Bankside, and they have furnished physical data that Bowsher notes "immediately belied the tired documentary evidence hitherto used to create the image of a 'typical Shakespearian theatre.'"[29]

The discovery of the Curtain playhouse has since confirmed Bowsher's sentiment in remarkable ways. In 2011, just two hundred yards from the Theater dig, archeologists from the Museum of London, led by Chris Thomas, exposed small sections of the Curtain, which included not only a gravel yard surface and foundations of limestone blocks and bricks but also portions of the inner gallery wall that "still stand to their full height," some brick flooring beneath the lower gallery, and "piers that would have supported tiers of wooden seats" (figure 3.4).[30] "'At one of the entrances into the yard from the galleries we found that part of the brick floor had been replaced with sheep knucklebones,' Chris Thomas said. 'These have been seen covering open spaces at other 16th- and 17th-century sites in London.'"[31] During a three-month excavation that commenced in April 2016, a MOLA team, led by senior archeologist Heather Knight, made the surprising revelation

Figure 3.4. Photograph of the Curtain playhouse remains, oriented south. Courtesy of Museum of London Archaeology.

that the Curtain had been rectangular in shape, not polygonal, as had long been assumed. Speaking to Scott Simon on NPR's *Weekend Edition*, Knight says that the playhouse had made "use of an existing building at the front of the site" and also made "use of a garden wall at the back of the site. And so [. . .] they've just filled in the space between the existing building and the garden wall with two long galleries."[32] In addition to unearthing segments of "brick walls up to 1.5 metres (4ft 9in) high,"[33] the team has found that the stage was "about 14 metres long and five metres deep,"[34] which is much shallower than expected. Perhaps most exciting of all, "Archaeologists have discovered traces of a tunnel structure, accessed by doors on either end of the stage, which would have allowed actors to exit from one side and come on again from the other without being seen by the audience."[35] What was once one of the most underdocumented playhouses from the period is turning out to be the most well-preserved.

Bowsher has said that "there was no 'typical Shakespearian theatre,' "[36] which is a point that theater historians have been rehearsing more and more insistently as evidence mounts about the notable differences among playhouses in the period. As early as 1972, Glynne Wickham had stressed that "all discussion of *the* Globe and *the* Fortune is of its very nature inaccurate and misleading since in both cases we are dealing with two buildings and not one, and since in both cases a substantial time-gap separates the first from the second."[37] Although the Rose (1587) did not suffer accidental incineration like the first Globe (1599) and first Fortune (1600), the extensive remodeling it underwent in 1592 means that that building, too, was not self-identical throughout its life span. Moreover, both Fortune playhouses were uniquely square in shape, the timbers from the Theater (1576) were disassembled and reused in framing the first Globe, and the Hope (1614) was originally purposed as a "Plaiehouse fitt & convenient in all thinges, bothe for players to playe in, and for the game of Beares and Bulls to be bayted in the same."[38] With so little uniformity among early modern amphitheaters, I am cautious in making any generalizations about them here, particularly whenever evidence for specific playhouses diverges or is entirely absent. Because all of these amphitheaters are structurally dissimilar from the rectilinear hall theaters like the Blackfriars (1576, 1599, 1608) and the Cockpit (1616; which, incidentally, also burned to the ground and was rebuilt/reborn as the Phoenix [1617]), I restrict my discussion to those purpose-built playhouses that, for all their many differences, share four identifiable characteristics. In the pages that follow, we will move from the outside inward to detail these shared characteristics, which include the amphitheaters' polygonal shapes; their accommodations for playgoers in multilevel, roofed galleries; their standing room in the yard, open to the sky; and their thrust stages.

Early modern panoramas of London that offer representations of the amphitheaters depict their shapes as either circular or polygonal, shapes which often seem to be stylized and influenced by the amount of detail in the engraving. In Jhon Norden's "the moste Famous Citty LONDON" (1600), the Rose, the Swan, and the Globe all exhibit hexagonal or octagonal forms, whereas Jodocus Hondius's "*LONDON*" (1611) makes what is either the Rose or the Beargarden a ten- or twelve-sided building while turning the Globe's into a smooth circular shape. Conversely, Wenceslaus Hollar's *Long View of London*, the most topographically accurate panorama from the period, represents the "Beere bayting h[ouse]" and "The Globe" with no visible angles at all in their exterior walls, and it also famously reverses their names (figure 3.5).[39] Following the excavation of the Rose and the evaluation of the Globe sites in 1989, Bowsher and Blatherwick asserted, "Despite the common view of the 'circular' shape of these playhouses, Elizabethan carpenters did not possess the technology to bend timbers, and a polygon in some form was to be expected."[40] The evidence from the excavation has shown that the Rose was originally built as a fourteen-sided polygon, whose symmetry was made elliptical apparently during its 1592 renovations, which the archeologists called "Phase Two." The shape of the Rose's 1587 ground plan, "Phase One," was at first "thought to be an irregular one, albeit of fourteen sides. It has now been seen that this was based on faulty measurements and that it was entirely regular."[41] The evaluation of the Globe remains, on the other hand, revealed a single angle of 162 degrees in the outer wall, which suggests that the second playhouse built on that ground, if symmetrical, had been twenty-sided.[42] The twenty-four-sided shape that made more geometric sense

Figure 3.5. Wenceslaus Hollar, *Long View of London* (1647) (detail). Folger Shakespeare Library Shelfmark: Map L85c no. 29. Used by permission of the Folger Shakespeare Library.

to modern scholars and that had already been adopted for the building of the new Globe was thus modified to reflect the icosagonal structure. Jon Greenfield, the chief architect of the new Globe, explains that this archeological "evidence could not be ignored and the revisions had to be made."[43]

To locate the origins of the playhouses' shapes, Frances A. Yates and Richard C. Kohler have each argued that Vitruvius Pollio's *De Architectura* profoundly influenced their geometrical designs, but John Orrell, S. P. Cerasano, and others insist that builders would have relied instead on vernacular techniques for their design methods. For instance, Orrell writes that the builder's "skill is more likely to be traditional than newfangled and book-fed. It may be that he has heard of Vitruvius, but it is extremely unlikely that he has read the *De Architectura*, or that he would design and build a Vitruvian theatre on the antique model. What he knows of design geometry will be what the generations have known."[44] Orrell goes on to explain that the planning of an amphitheater would begin with a survey of the land and calculations using the traditional *ad triangulum* or *ad quadratum* methods, which are frequently "met in sixteenth- and early seventeenth-century architectural design, especially in centrally planned buildings."[45] The amphitheater's maximum width would then be established by marking out a square on the ground using one of the early modern builder's primary measuring tools, a statute "rod" or "perch" that is 16.5 feet in length, or perhaps by using the more versatile "line," which the surveyor Valentine Leigh describes: "Your line being foure perches of length, and euery perch ende a knot, would be well searced [i.e., seared] with hotte waxe or rosen, to auoyde the stretching thereof in the weete, and shrinking in the drought."[46] After the playhouse's outer limits had been determined, builders would "run diagonals across their [. . .] square to find its centre, and then describe a circle round it, touching its corners. It is simply a matter of one man taking a line in a ring about the site like a pony on a lunge."[47] Finally, the builder would inscribe a polygonal shape into the circle. Although no line of influence can be demonstrated to extend from Vitruvius or other classical models, the builder's physical line radiating from the center to the amphitheater's perimeter will become our geometrical exemplar as we examine the auditorium's rhetorical conditions.

Hollar's *Long View of London* suggests that there is always a possibility builders plastered or "rendered" the outer walls of playhouses to give the buildings a round appearance, although this was not a common practice in the period. Had builders given the exteriors of the amphitheaters cladding to offer an impression of perfect roundness, however, the interiors of the timber structures would have remained polygonal in shape and thereby dictated the geometrical organization of the galleries within. As we move from the building's polygonal exterior into the galleries, we see that all the available documentary evidence and the one pictorial representation of an amphitheater's interior indicate that early modern playgoers could occupy one of three separate gallery levels. Based on the position and depth of what is generally agreed to be a rainwater drip line from the Rose's thatched and unguttered roof, Greenfield has recently made the highly provisional suggestion that this playhouse might have possessed only two galleries.[48] Be that as it may, whether two or three stories in height, the amphitheaters' galleries would have been framed in vertical segments called "bays," which "collect the structural loads at certain points where main columns are placed. In timber-framed buildings the bay divisions are also points at which the building is tied together across its span."[49] The vertical load of each bay would rest on sleeper beams or groundsills jointed into a trapezoidal shape, which would be mimicked in the structure of all the galleries above it.[50]

A single bay, then, would form an outer face in the building's polygon, it would be jointed to neighboring bays on either side, and it would taper toward the yard to define the inner perimeter of the galleries (figure 3.6). When framed, the circling galleries formed by the individual bays would have been fitted with what were often called "degrees," which are simply graduated rows of seating that rise away from the stage to enhance spectators' sight lines. Historians of the early modern theater have frequently interpreted the playhouses' exterior windows that are visible in some of the panoramas as providing natural light to otherwise darkened walkways, which, they deduce, must have been built behind the backmost degrees to facilitate ingress and egress. But the number of degrees that each gallery might have held is still

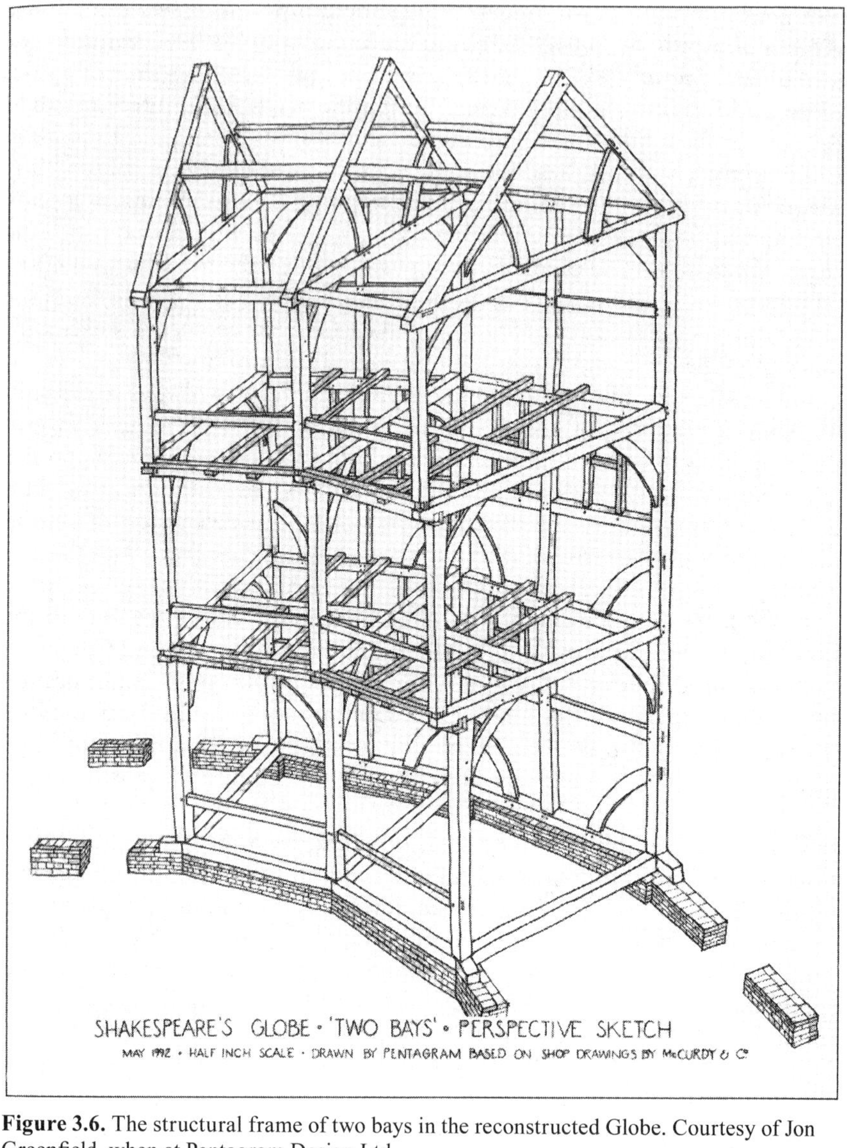

Figure 3.6. The structural frame of two bays in the reconstructed Globe. Courtesy of Jon Greenfield, when at Pentagram Design Ltd.

not known for any of the playhouses, though much scholarship draws on "analogical evidence," which involves "the great mass of documentation accounting for the preparation of various royal houses for masques and plays enrolled in the Pipe Office accounts of the Works," now at the National Archives.[51] For many of these royal performance occasions, the number that recurs in these Works accounts is eighteen inches square to accommodate the hindquarters of each nonaristocratic audience member—a number that theater historians have used to approximate how many degrees amphitheater galleries may have contained and to calculate the maximum audience capacity for such a theater.

Whatever the exact figures and details might have been, it is essentially inarguable that the amphitheaters' galleries were unequipped with rows of seating, which ascended toward the back wall of each auditorium bay and which were situated, in all likelihood, at three gallery levels. The recent dig at the Curtain, which revealed "piers that would have supported tiers of wooden seats,"[52] would seem to confirm the presence of such degrees. In his revised edition of *A Perambulation of Kent*, William Lambarde explains, "No more than such as goe to *Parisgardein*, the *Bell Sauage*, or *Theatre*, to beholde Bear baiting, Enterludes, or Fence play, can account of any pleasant spectacle, vnlesse they first pay one pennie at the gate, another at the entrie of the Scaffolde, and the thirde for a quiet standing."[53] Andrew Gurr interprets this passage to mean: "To enter the yard cost a penny, to enter the galleries cost another, and to sit in comfort in the gentlemen's rooms cost another," but he adds that "'to get a standing' meant to find a viewing-place, whether standing or sitting."[54] Regardless of the location they achieved with their price of admission and no matter what posture they assumed, all playgoers would therefore take up a "standing" during the performance of a play. Tiffany Stern makes a persuasive case that "members of the audience had freedom of movement in the galleries as well as in the yard; that at least some of them stood to watch plays; and that all felt free to walk about during performances."[55] Further, both Stern and Orrell hypothesize that the highest galleries in the amphitheaters were perhaps mixed-use spaces wherein playgoers could either sit, stand, or stroll at their leisure.[56]

Hence the seating and standing configuration offered by the amphitheaters' galleries wraps playgoers around a central, open area while banking upward those who are seated in each successive degree. The number of bays that would have been devoted to the auditorium depends on two factors: first, the exact polygonal shape of the individual amphitheater, and second, the number of bays occupied by the tiring-house. For Phase One of the Rose, the offset location of the stage would have allowed nine full bays (with a possibility of two other partial bays, out of a total of fourteen) to be used for spectating, whereas Phase Two's elongation in the northern portion of the building would extend that total to ten bays (figures 3.7 and 3.8). The new Globe, in contrast, devotes fifteen of its twenty bays to gallery seating.

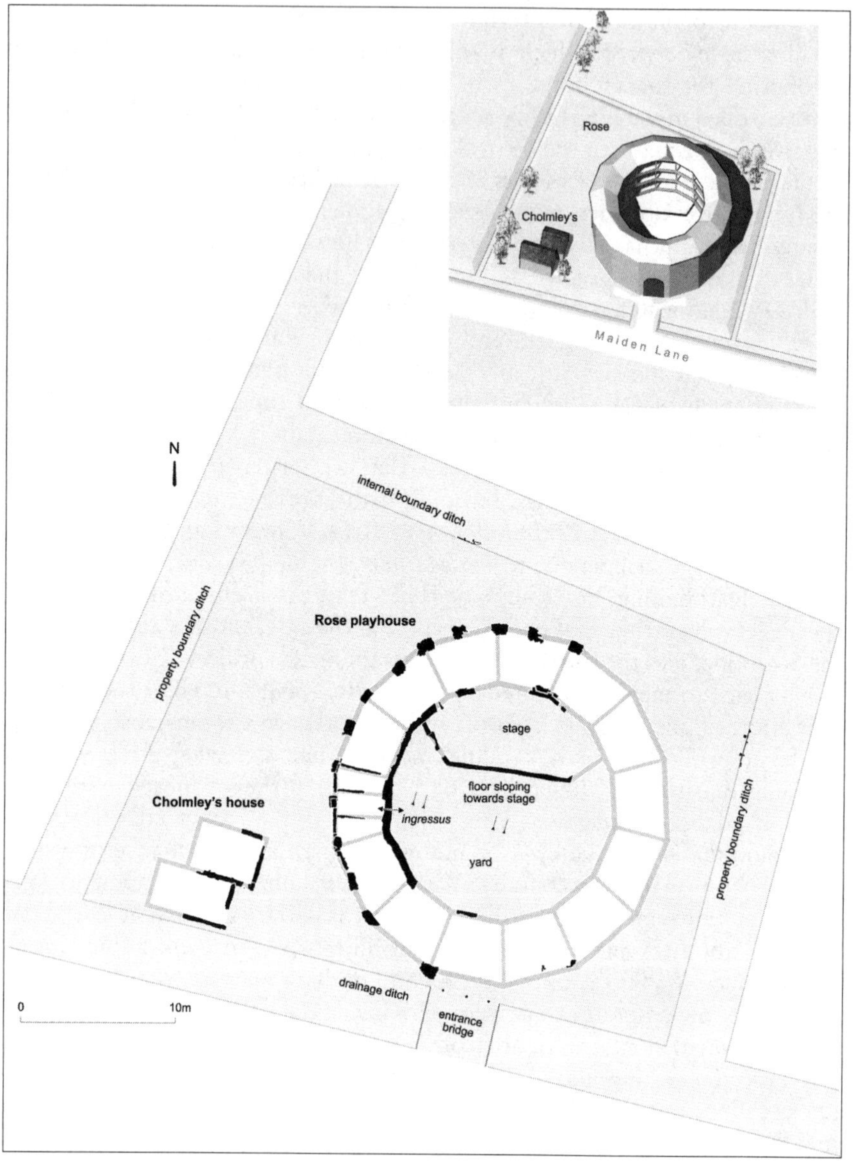

Figure 3.7. Drawing of Phase One of the Rose playhouse remains, including reconstructed element. Courtesy of Museum of London Archaeology.

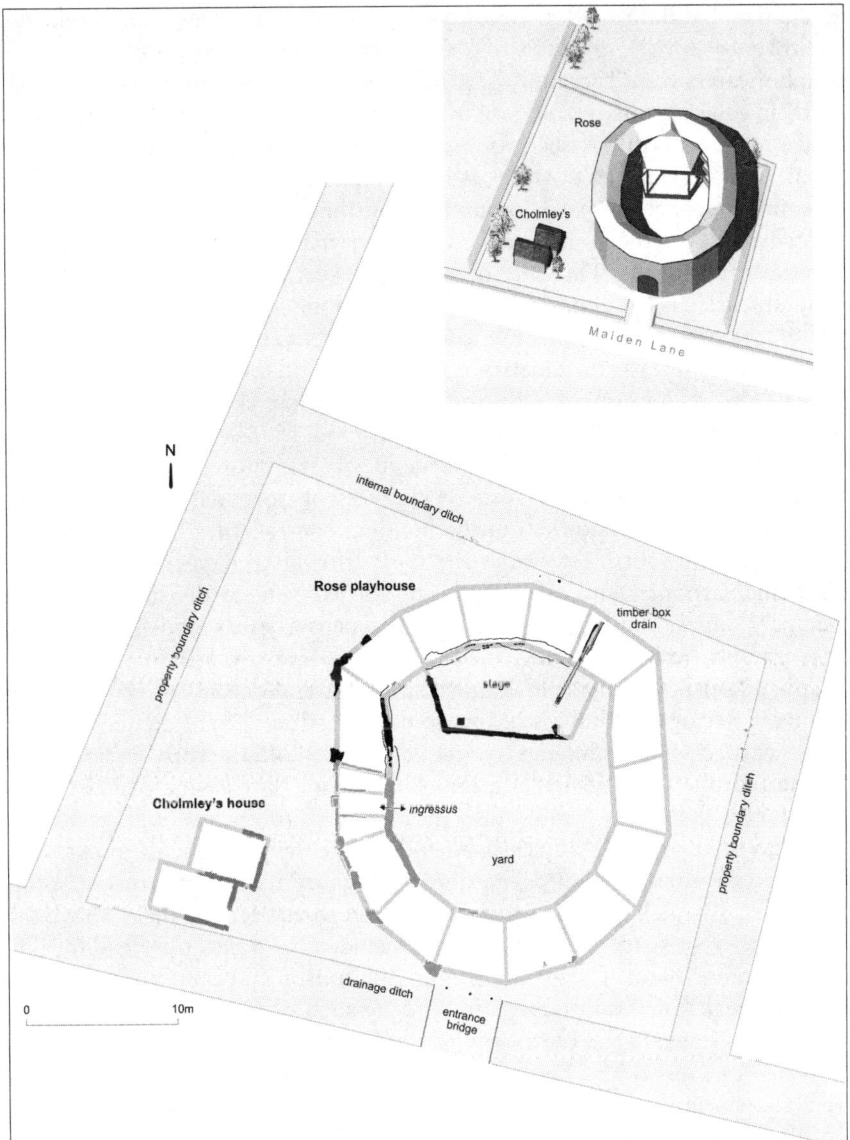

Figure 3.8. Drawing of Phase Two of the Rose playhouse remains, including reconstructed element. Courtesy of Museum of London Archaeology.

Excluding the data from the Rose excavation, no other evidence from the period exists for the ratio of auditorium to tiring-house bays, and the various amphitheaters would certainly have differed based on the number and heights of their galleries, the overall size of the polygonal structure, the dimensions of the stage, and the presence of a canopy or stage roof. In the absence of a great deal of evidence, however, it is not unreasonable to assume that most amphitheaters would have committed two-thirds to three-quarters of their roofed space to their audiences, with the remaining space being reserved for the tiring-house. The only other gallery seating left to consider in the amphitheaters is the gentlemen's and lords' rooms, which seem to have been private, partitioned sections immediately adjacent to the stage and possibly even located in separate galleries above and behind the stage.

Aside from Aernout van Buchel's copy of a lost sketch by Johannes de Witt depicting the interior of the Swan around 1596—which shows in the stage gallery figures who may be playgoers, actors, musicians, or some combination thereof (figure 3.9)—the best pieces of documentary evidence we possess about these rooms is in the building contracts for the Fortune and the Hope. The Fortune contract specifies: "ffower convenient divisions for gentlemens roomes and other sufficient and convenient divisions for Twoe pennie roomes," and also for "the gentlemens roomes and Twoe pennie roomes to be seeled wth lathe lyme & haire," whereas the Hope contract stipulates: "Two Boxes in the lowermost storie fitt and decent for gentlemen to sitt in."[57] Because theater historians do not regard the "Twoe pennie roomes" or general-admission galleries to have been walled off, the verb "to be seeled" in the Fortune contract likely means "to provide 'lathe lyme & haire' ceilings for," but "to ceil" could also mean either "to enclose with walls" or "to clad or cover."[58] In any case, assuming that the gentlemen's rooms were designed to isolate higher-paying theatergoers from other patrons, it seems doubtful that such measures would be taken to enclose a gallery above the stage since that space would already be secluded from the larger auditorium. On the other hand, Carlo Buffone in Ben Jonson's *EVERY MAN OVT OF HIS HVMOR* speaks of the intimacy afforded by such partitioned spaces located "ouer the | stage, in the Lords roome"; here, "ouer" might mean not directly "above" but rather "higher up than" and adjacent to the stage.[59] All these references seem to suggest that, at least in some amphitheaters, playgoers could purchase seating in what would be prototypes of Restoration-era boxes that flanked the stage—which Thomas Dekker describes as "now but the Stages Suburbs" and "those boxes"[60]—but conceivably in the stage gallery, too, where action "above" or "aloft" would also have taken place.

Moving from the periphery of the auditorium into the central area of the yard, we would find ourselves noticeably less comfortable than in the galleries, where we could have the option to sit for the two or three hours of a performance instead of standing for the duration on our feet. One advantage

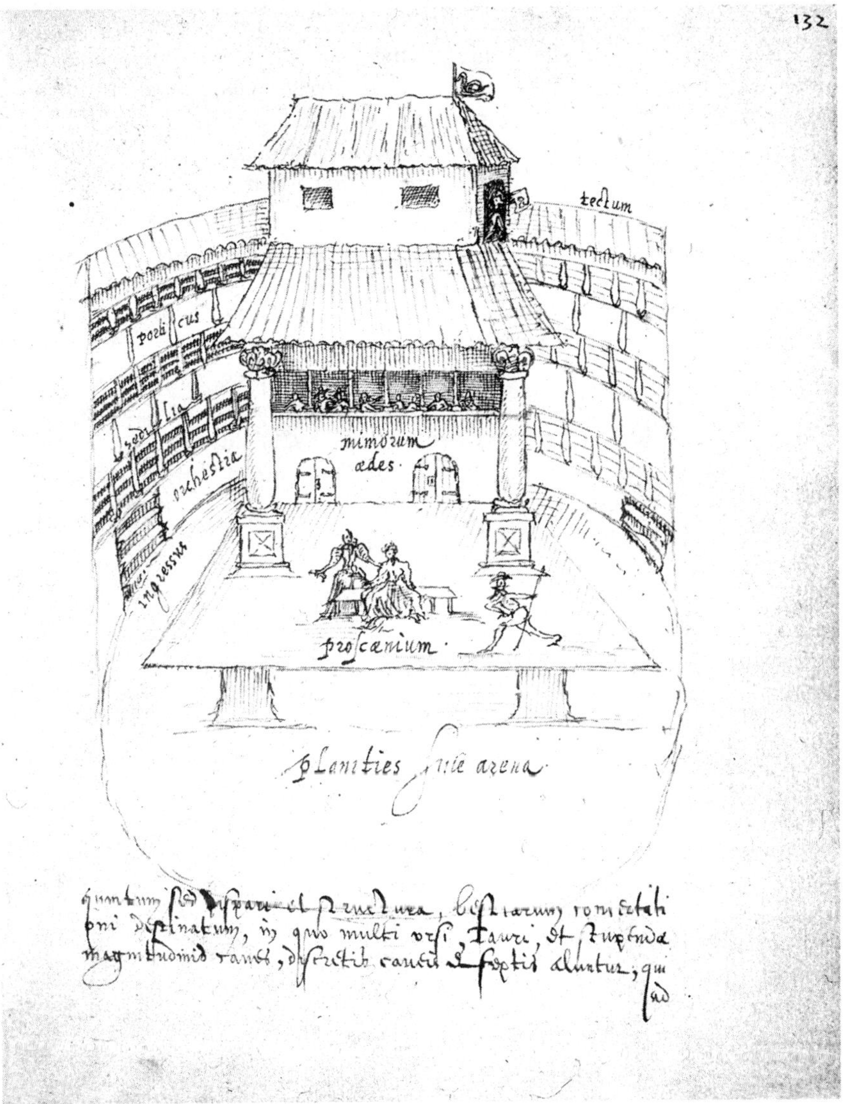

Figure 3.9. Aernout van Buchel, sketch of the interior of the Swan about 1596, copied from a lost sketch by Johannes de Witt. Courtesy of the Utrecht University Library, Ms. 842, fol. 132r.

that the yard would have offered over those playgoers sitting at ease in the galleries is greater maneuverability, which an individual could use to shift weight, to move away from or toward other individuals, and to change one's literal standpoint on the whole perceptual field, whether directed toward the stage or off it. Those in the yard would still be limited by the number and compression of fellow groundlings, a situation that would be enhanced for seated gallery patrons, who would certainly have had some range of motion in their upper bodies even if they found their lower halves hemmed in by others'. Yet, as Stern argues, "even where fixed benches were provided, walking to new seats or opting to stand for a while was still acceptable."[61] Despite "not a single reference in the entire seventy-five years of playgoing to the deterrent effect of rain or snow,"[62] some surely took refuge in the eavesdrop, a narrow stretch of space between the inner wall of the lower gallery and the drip line from the roof.[63] Finally, at the Rose site archeologists discovered that the floor of the Phase One yard had been raked rather steeply toward the stage at an angle of about fourteen degrees,[64] which presumably helped improve sight lines much as the pitched benches in the galleries did.

The sizes and shapes of the amphitheaters' yards are known for only the first Fortune and Phases One and Two of the Rose, though we can extrapolate rough figures for the second Globe. While possessing no measurements, we also know that the Hope was to be built with "suche large compasse, fforme, widenes, and height as the Plaie house called the Swan."[65] The Fortune contract stipulates "The frame of the saide howse to be sett square and to conteine ffowerscore foote of lawfull assize everye waie square w^th^oute and fiftie fiue foote of like assize square everye waie w^th^in."[66] Subtracting the space of the Fortune "Stadge [which] shall conteine in length ffortie and Three foote of lawfull assize and in breadth to extende to the middle of the yarde,"[67] standing room in the first Fortune's yard would have contained about 1,842.5 square feet—that is, assuming the stage was rectangular. Bowsher and Blatherwick calculate the volume of the Rose's Phase One yard as 1,239.3 square feet and that of Phase Two as 1,719 square feet,[68] whereas the second Globe's yard would have been about 3,012.5 square feet—a figure that requires many assumptions for which we have only analogical evidence. Although they give impressions of exactitude, such figures are by their very nature abstract, saying little about the range of physical dispositions that these spectatorial areas accommodated and even encouraged by their geometrical configurations. What we can say is that the central standing room in the amphitheaters was defined by the inner perimeter of their lower galleries, stretching from about two-thirds to three-quarters of the way around the polygonal shape and then interrupted by the extension of the stage from the tiring-house into the yard.

As we finish mapping out the material conditions within which the amphitheaters arranged their audiences, our final consideration is the stage. Since our concern is with the physical disposition of playgoers, however, and not with the representational engine of the stage as such, we can confine our discussion to its placement in relation to the variety of spectatorial spaces established earlier in this chapter. But we move quickly into the realm of conjecture here because, aside from the archeological remains of the two stages at the Rose, the van Buchel/de Witt rendition of the Swan's interior, a 1568/9 legal dispute that describes the Red Lion's stage, the limited details in the contracts for the Fortune and the Hope, and the newly revealed shallow stage at the rectilinear Curtain playhouse, there is no other hard evidence to be had. The foundations for the Rose's two stages clearly indicate that they tapered toward their fronts while the tiring-house wall defined a taper toward their backs (see again figures 3.7 and 3.8). During the court proceedings regarding the building of the Red Lion, the construction "obligation" was read aloud and describes "one Skaffolde or stage for enterludes or playes," which was to be built

> of good newe and well seasoned Tymber and boords whyche shall conteyne in height from the grounde fyve foote of assyse and shalbe in lengthe Northe and South fortye [word deliberately blanked out] foote of assyse and in bredthe East and West thyrty foot of assyse Well and sufficientlye stayed bounden and nayled wyth a certayne space or voyde parte of the same stage left unborded in such conveyent place of the same stage.[69]

As for the other available evidence, R. A. Foakes writes:

> The Swan drawing shows a rectangular stage, and it has been generally assumed that other public theatres likewise had rectangular stages. The contract for the Fortune specifies that the stage should be 43 feet "in length" (i.e., measured at its widest point where it met the inner frame of the theatre?), and extend to the middle of the yard, but it is not clear that it would have been rectangular; it was to have been "placed & sett" as indicated in a plan now lost. The contract for the Hope calls simply for a "stage to be carryed or taken awaie," and gives no indication of its shape.[70]

Challenging the assumption that most amphitheater stages were rectangular in the period, Foakes concludes that "It is conceivable therefore that a number of theatres had stages tapering into the auditorium."[71] Nevertheless, the one fact to which all the evidence points is that these were thrust stages. None of them seems to have been recessed into a frame, as popular theaters would develop after the Restoration. Rather, the stages projected in various degrees, shapes, and sizes into the amphitheaters' central yards, where playgoers could surround them on their open sides.

Ut rhetorica architectura

> [. . .] being cannot be otherwise than round.
> —Gaston Bachelard, *The Poetics of Space*

> [. . .] architecture presents a convergence of all the arts—including rhetoric.
> —Bruce R. Smith, *The Acoustic World of Early Modern England*

Looking at the internal design of amphitheaters, we immediately discern a series of geometrical strategies that focuses playgoers' eyes and ears toward the centrally placed stage. The polygonal shapes of the playhouses; the storied galleries that follow the buildings' inner contours around by as much as 270 degrees, and which also bank seated patrons upward; and the standing room in the yards, which are raked and embrace on at least three sides acting platforms extending toward the middle of the auditoria: each of these architectural features points playgoers in the direction of the stage's performance. The word "theater" ultimately derives from the ancient Greek θέα, "sight," which becomes *θέᾱτρον* (> Latin *theātrum*), signifying "a place for viewing." William N. West observes that "*Theater* first appears in English in a Wycliffite Bible manuscript of 1382, transliterating the Latin *theatrum* or, less likely, the original Greek *theatron*, and is glossed as a 'comune biholdiyng place.' "[72] As places built expressly for the common viewing and hearing of dramatic stories, early modern amphitheaters maximized audience capacities while giving everyone a unique standing and perspective on the play. By situating the audience within such perceptual dynamics, the auditorium's geometrical configuration performs work on the bodies of playgoers, obliging them to adopt a variety of physical positions. "A ring is the natural form in which the maximum number of spectators can press about an object of interest," as E. K. Chambers says.[73] But, true as this may be, there is nothing especially natural or unconditioned about an amphitheater, which constructs space—and, more precisely, constructs distinct spatial relationships—by producing subjects to inhabit it. Such subjects cannot be said to preexist their entry into this space, but are rather inscribed by it with playgoing subjectivities, which are shaped by architectural forces no less than they are by the individual temperaments and cultural meanings that accompany the act of theatergoing. The amphitheaters create these playgoing subjectivities in part through the social and economic categories with which they name their various spectatorial spaces: the yard for the houseless heads of undifferentiated groundlings and understanders, the two-penny rooms, the gentlemen's rooms, the lords' rooms.[74]

The work that the auditorium performs on theatergoers ultimately consists of turning their bodies toward the dramatic action, making them amenable to seeing and hearing a play from just about any vantage point with relatively little obstruction. Just as the art of rhetoric attempts to persuade an audience to accept and adopt a position on a disputed subject being argued, so the geometry of the auditorium invites playgoers to take up a standing and a perspective on the stage's subject matter. The power that this spatial configuration exercises on the bodies of playgoers is certainly not a violent one: those in the audience presumably come to the theater because they want to be there to enjoy a performance, and of course they always reserve the freedom to look away or leave. Even so, the architecture *compels* theatergoers to assume a range of physical postures, and because those postures are in direct relation to the performance of a dramatic discourse filled with its own disputations, the compulsion is a rhetorical one that encourages and rewards their bodily, sensory, and mental compliance.[75] We will conclude this chapter by examining how this particular disposition of physical postures and sight lines at once focalizes spectators on the performance while diverting their attention into the offstage space of the auditorium, but if we turn now to the ways that spoken rhetoric was depicted visually in the period, we find that the art of persuasion enters in not just at the ears. We discover instead that graphic illustrations of this persuasive force operate through a complex interaction between hearing and seeing, much like theater. Moreover, these illustrations of rhetoric-at-work highlight geometrical relationships that are increasingly sensitive to the dispositions and needs of the individual listeners being addressed.

In the first and also unauthorized edition of Andreae Alciati's *Emblematum liber* appears an emblem titled "ELOQVENTIA FORTITV*dine præstantior*," "Eloquence, surpassing strength" (figure 3.10).[76] After noting in the woodcut the "bow," the "rough club," and the "Nemean lion [that] cloaks his naked body," the text asks: "Is this therefore the likeness of Hercules?" The figure's age and hoary temples, it suggests, might convince us to think otherwise. But "What of his tongue, pierced with light chains, by which he cleaves the ears of men and draws them to him without difficulty?" (*Quid q[uod] lingua illi leuibus traiecta cathenis, | Quîs fissa facili allicit aure uiros*).[77] The answer the emblem gives is the stuff of legend and no less than the origins of the rule of law, whose institution is not through a founding violence but instead through the power of words: "Don't the Gauls say that with his tongue, not with his might, Alcides excelled in providing nations with laws? Arms yield to the toga, and he who is powerful in speech draws to his wishes even the most resistant hearts." Although the bow- and club-toting Hercules could surely subdue his followers without much difficulty, it is "with his tongue, not with his might" that he binds others to him. In this deceptively simple woodcut, the single chain that represents Hercules's rhetoric does not strike his audience's ears as it extends from his tongue. Rather, it falls across the groins of the naked men who trail behind, ostensibly covering their shame through the civilizing process of law, in which bare, outstretched "Arms yield to the toga."[78]

Figure 3.10. "ELOQVENTIA FORTITV*dine præstantior*," in Andree Alciati, *Emblematum liber* (Augsburg: by Heinrich Steyner, 1531), E6r (detail). By permission of the University of Glasgow Library, Special Collections, Sp Coll S.M. 18.

Later incarnations of this image become even subtler in their depictions of Hercules's spoken rhetoric, the earliest of which appears in Alciati's first authorized volume *EMBLEMATVM LIBELLUS* in 1534 and is then reprinted throughout Europe in the 1530s and '40s. In a French edition titled *LES EMBLEMES*, the "*Eloquentia fortitudine præstantior*" woodcut offers a composition with far greater detail than in the earlier image, and there are many more people visibly captivated by the "light chains" (*leuibus* [. . .] *cathenis*),[79] which now stretch explicitly from Hercules's tongue to their ears (figure 3.11).[80] Furthermore, compared to the 1531 woodcut, this one enhances the depth perspective and scope of the scene, disclosing an elaborate landscape where a line of followers recedes into the distance behind a rising hill. The civilizing influence has also shifted from the covering of primal nakedness to the leading of fully clothed bodies out of a wilderness, in which even a lion looks on peacefully as if tamed by the sound of Hercules's voice—or perhaps by the visual warning of the lion skin he wears. That the men disappear into the landscape's distance, where they become almost indistinguishable from it, also makes thematic sense, but as the law-giving figure in the image Hercules illogically blends in with the foliage as well. A different woodcut in *DIVERSE IMPRESE*—an Italian-language reprint of several 1540s and '50s Latin-French

Eloquentia fortitudine præstantior.

Figure 3.11. "*Eloquentia fortitudine præstantior*," in Andre Alciat, *LES EMBLEMES* (Paris: by Christian Wechel, 1540), N4v (detail). Photograph courtesy of The Newberry Library, Chicago, Case *W 1025 .019.

editions—shows a landscape that is even more expansive, extending to a valley, a mountain, and a mass of clouds in the background (figure 3.12).[81] In contrast to earlier versions, this image puts a greater geographical space under the controlling gaze of the viewer. The cohort that follows Hercules seems fewer in number, but this difference is offset by their crowding and by the sense of motion with which they are depicted as their leader strides toward the far left of the frame, his bow already partly out of view.

Look specifically now at his *eloquentia* in the three woodcuts. What is described in each text as "light chains" appears in the first image to be stout enough to moor a small sea vessel. Visually, this is some heavy rhetoric. The chains have become comparatively lighter in the second emblem: stemming more explicitly from Hercules' mouth, at some distance from him the chains splay outward, making clear contact with many of the listeners' ears. In the *DIVERSE IMPRESE* image, finally, the light chains have transmuted into delicate threads that divide at the point at which they leave his tongue. Once uttered, the threads in this image reach backward separately, each one securing itself to the ear of one of Hercules's adherents. Pulling the men along like slaves in a chain gang, the single heavy vinculum that we see in the earliest emblem gradually gives way to lighter, plural chains and then to an array of mere

Figure 3.12. "Che la eloquenza vince la Fortezza," in Alciato, *DIVERSE IMPRESE* (Lyons: by Gvlielmo Rovillio, 1564), L4v (detail). Photograph courtesy of The Newberry Library, Chicago, Case W 1025.01692.

threads, which mildly urge the people to follow. By rarifying Hercules's *eloquentia*, each successive woodcut individualizes its persuasive power as the rhetorical threads progressively acquire their own trajectories, dividing closer and closer to their source and stretching to the particular sensibilities of each ear that they strike. One unchanging feature in all of the woodcuts, however, is Hercules's bow and club, and while it is evidently the civilizing speech that persuades his followers to yield their literal and figurative arms to the rule of law, their leader in fact holds on to the power of violence to enforce that rule. Effective speech, the emblems imply, must always be guaranteed by the threat of effective action.

Emblems create for their audience a hermeneutic imperative through the interdependency of image and text, and "*Eloquentia fortitudine præstantior*" is no exception. But its various woodcuts also redouble that interdependency by showing through their subject matter that the effect of spoken words is intimately linked to what one sees in the process of hearing them. Although Hercules may well be skilled in the rhetorical arts, the visibility of his weapons—not to mention the skin of the Nemean lion, a testament to his fabled strength—offers his audience a daunting incentive to be led away by his words alone. Without threatening harm, the amphitheaters likewise provide incentives for playgoers to turn their eyes and ears toward the stage and to follow its lead and action. Spatially, the auditorium prepares theatergoers to concentrate their aural attention by first accommodating their physical and visual needs, which are met by distributing them radially around the stage on three to four vertical levels, giving each one a perspective incrementally different from her or his neighbor. In the final Alciati woodcut, Hercules works in a similar manner to individualize his followers by speaking to each one's particular ear, whereas in the first woodcut the same rhetorical line had succeeded in persuading all of his listeners—a kind of blunt style with little nuance and wide application, like violence.

The image of chains or lines that connect a speaker's words with the ears of listeners functions by turning an auditory sensation into a visual one through a kind of reverse ekphrasis. Further, in converting the heard into the seen, this image maps otherwise invisible sound waves into at least a curved or semicircular geometrical form so that it may illustrate how the speaker's words appeal to a wide audience, a form we see developing in the later Alciati woodcuts. Since the shape of the amphitheaters explicitly ties the practice of oratory to the configuration of their internal geometries, early modern writers pick up and elaborate this same image of lines or chains to describe the physical relationships between playgoers and the stage. In his *NEW AND CHOICE CHARACTERS*, for example, Thomas Overbury reveals the hypnotic effect that "*An excellent Actor*" can have on his audience: "[W]Hatsoeuer is commendable in the graue Orator, is most exquisitly perfect in him [i.e., the '*excellent Actor*']; for by a full and significant action of body, he charmes our attention : sit in a full Theater, and you will thinke you see so many lines drawne from the circumference of so many eares, whiles the *Actor* is the *Center*."[82] Grave orators as well as excellent actors make use of what Quintilian calls *pronuntiatio* or *actio*, which includes "voice and movement,"[83] and he joins Cicero in mentioning stage actors to illustrate the importance of this canon. Quintilian writes that *pronuntiatio* "itself has an extraordinary force and power in oratory," and that "Stage actors demonstrate this,"[84] whereas Cicero says that *actio* "has been abandoned by the orators, who are the players that act real life, and has been taken over by the actors, who only mimic reality."[85] Despite Cicero's censure, Overbury's actor presumably excels beyond the orator because he personifies a character with "a full and significant action of body," while the orator remains bound to whatever "graue" matter he argues.

If you "sit in a full Theater," Overbury suggests, "you will thinke you see so many lines drawne from the circumference of so many eares, whiles the *Actor* is the *Center*." First of all, the kind of space that he evokes here is amphitheatrical in shape, with the actor occupying a "*Center*" and the audience its "circumference." Second, the actor fastens his words to "so many eares" with "so many lines," which are initially the dramatic lines he so effectively speaks and only afterward become the many epiphenomenal lines we think we see.

Finally, he "charmes our attention" not just with his lines but with his "action of body," which appeals to our sense of sight as his voice does to our hearing. Although the oratorical power that Overbury puts on display belongs to the actor, Thomas Dekker had utilized the chain image in 1612 to differentiate between playwrights who compose bombastic plays and those who know and write "*Poesies* pure *Essence*."[86] In his *IF IT BE NOT GOOD*, *The Diuel is in it*, a Prologue asks for that poet who can fill the auditorium once again after another has "*Banishd*" theatergoers with his feeble plays:

> Giue me *That Man*,
> Who when the *Plague* of an Impostumd *Braynes*
> *(Breaking* out*)* infects a *Theater*, and hotly raignes,
> Killing the *Hearers* hearts, that the vast roomes
> Stand empty, like so many Dead=mens toombes,
> Can call the *Banishd* Auditor home, And tye
> His Eare (with golden chaines) to his Melody :
> Can draw with *Adamantine pen*, (euen creatures
> Forg'de out of th'*Hammer*, on tiptoe, to *Reach* vp,
> And (from *Rare silence*) clap their *Brawny hands*,
> T'*Applaud*, what their *charmd* soule scarce vnderstands.[87]

The dramatic invention of an unpoetic writer, the Prologue declares, is like a disease in the brain that contaminates the play—or "the *Plague*," to use Dekker's pun. And, when that play is staged, it disperses through the actors' words and "infects a *Theater*," "Killing the *Hearers* hearts, that the vast roomes | Stand empty, like so many Dead=mens toombes." Curiously, "Dead=mens toombes" are not empty of bodies but of life, so perhaps the "vast roomes | Stand empty" not because there is nobody there, but because such plays vacate and anesthetize the minds of their audiences. The Prologue describes an infectious chain reaction that moves from the playwright's sickened brain to his play, which is then transmitted through the actors to the theatergoers in the auditorium.

To turn this lazar house back into a playhouse, the Prologue summons the poet who "Can call the *Banishd* Auditor home, And tye | His Eare (with golden chaines) to his Melody." Such a poetic melody wins applause not only from the judicious but even from the "*Brawny hands*" of unrefined playgoers, whom the Prologue elsewhere calls a "Greasie-apron *Audience*" (A4r). The work of such dramatists, in other words, appeals to a broad spectrum of individuals, much like Hercules's rhetoric. His condescension notwithstanding, the Prologue focuses us here not on an audience or on Overbury's excellent actor but on a poet who wields the power of an "*Adamantine pen*," which is both unshakable in its integrity and magnetic in its effect: poetically, true north. Unlike Overbury, Dekker does not offer a glimpse of the architecture in which the audience's ears are tied "with golden chaines," but in his earlier

MAGNIFICENT *Entertainment* he had used the adamantine/magnetic metaphor to describe the English people's anticipation of James I's inaugural entry into London on March 15, 1603/4: "All mens eyes were presently turnd to the North, standing euen stone stil in their Circles, like the poynts of so many Geometricall needles, through a fixed & Adamantine desire" to see their new king.[88] The simultaneous orientation of so many eyes in the same direction, "like the poynts of so many Geometricall needles," is the visual equivalent of a theater audience's ears being tied by lines or chains to the stage. If eyes are magnetized and drawn toward a common desideratum, then playgoers are "*charmd*" by Dekker's true poet, while Overbury's excellent actor "charmes our attention."[89]

Alciati's Hercules equally charms his audience as he "cleaves the ears of men" (*fissa* [. . .] *aure uiros*),[90] which the Player in HAMLET might do "Had he the Motiue and the Cue for passion" that the Danish prince feels. "He would drowne the Stage with teares," Hamlet imagines,

> And cleaue the generall eare with horrid speech:
> Make mad the guilty, and apale the free,
> Confound the ignorant, and amaze indeed,
> The very faculty of Eyes and Eares.[91]

The way that Hercules "cleaves" is by pulling his audience to him as if in an embrace, and while we can certainly read Hamlet's "cleaue the generall eare with horrid speech" in light of his later criticism of excessively histrionic players who "split the eares of the | Groundlings,"[92] he in fact activates both senses of the word. Mark Robson writes that "Cleave can mean both to part or divide, to pierce or penetrate, and to adhere or cling to," but I would disagree with him that it is only "the first cluster of meanings that concerns Hamlet here" because it is the audience's "very faculty of Eyes and Eares" that the Player would "amaze" or transfix.[93] Paradoxically, one can cleave *to* something, but one can also cleave something *in two*. The circular geometry of the auditorium, I have argued, works to focus all of its playgoers' sensory energies on the stage, which optimizes their sight lines as well as their lines of hearing, imagined as chains that stretch from the actor's (or dramatic poet's) mouth to their ears. These sight and hearing lines are the channels through which the stage cleaves *to* the audience's attention. Yet, by distributing playgoers within a circular structure, an amphitheater at the same time casts a large proportion of the sights and sounds of its auditorium into the audience's perceptual field. The aural-visual lines through which the stage directs playgoers' attentions are therefore inevitably drawn into the offstage space of the auditorium, which cleaves their attention *in two* by diverting it away from the stage. These bifocal conditions create an atmosphere of distraction for playgoers, whose eyes and ears oscillate at unpredictable frequencies between the amphitheater's onstage and offstage spaces.

Distracted Globes

> That will aske some teares in the true perfor-
> ming of it : if I do it, let the audience looke to their eies:
> I will mooue stormes [. . .]
> I could
> play *Ercles* rarely, or a part to teare a Cat in, to make all
> split [. . .]
> . . . .
> This
> is *Ercles* vaine, a tyrants vaine
>
> —Bottom, in A MIDSOMMER *Nights Dreame*

I indicated earlier that "theater" stems from the Greek word for "sight" and originally meant "a place for viewing," but the same can be said for "amphitheater." The prefix *amphi-* ("two" or "both") alters the root word, however, by specifying how spectatorial space gets organized around performance space. Etymologically, "amphitheater" means "a place for viewing on both sides," the perceptual dynamics of which differ considerably from those of hall theaters, which by virtue of their shape situate their audiences at perpendicular angles toward the front of their stages. All buildings exercise control over their occupants through what modern architects call systems of "circulation," which both permit and restrict bodily movement as well as sensory access within their interior spaces.[94] On one hand, like James I's anticipated arrival in *THE MAGNIFICENT Entertainment*, rectilinear theaters tend to orient playgoers' bodies on the same bearing—partly through the auditorium's shape and partly by seating the entire audience—thereby compressing their sight lines into a narrow, largely unidirectional channel and limiting their literal perspectives onto the action. Amphitheaters, on the other hand, work to focus playgoers on the same onstage space with innumerable vectors instead of few. They do not therefore compress sight lines but rather circulate playgoers' senses on many levels around a thrust stage, which in fact multiplies their perspectives. John Orrell has cautioned that just because some hall theaters such as the Blackfriars were built in rectangular spaces does not mean that their auditoria followed the same shape, and he assembles substantial evidence to suggest that some of them might have been "segmental or U-shaped,"[95] like the new Sam Wanamaker Playhouse next to the Globe. If so, these hall auditoria would certainly broaden the radii of playgoers' sight lines, but their angles of incidence onto the stage would still be much more acute and thus restrictive than those in amphitheaters. Bruce Smith writes that "many-sided galleries, surrounding the thrust stage as a focal point, gave much better sight-lines than a square structure would for viewing not only the play but other members of the audience."[96]

To take in the whole scope of these places for viewing on both sides, let us investigate the various epiphenomenal sights and sounds that accompany the main event on the amphitheatrical stage. If early modern writers idealize the amphitheater's rhetorical and architectural design as a circular network of chains or lines that tie playgoers' senses directly to the stage's action, then they likewise reveal an array of ambient energies in these spaces against which this ideal must work and which could alienate them from the fiction onstage. As I have begun to suggest, such energies derive first from the interior geometry of the amphitheaters, which puts spectatorial space on view as much as it does the stage, but they are enhanced by microcultures of playgoing, which gave audience members certain customary freedoms within the auditorium's various spaces.

When Overbury urges us to "sit in a full Theater, and you will thinke you see so many lines drawne from the circumference of so many eares, whiles the *Actor* is the *Center*," he describes not just an ideal relationship between the audience and the stage but also real material conditions that allow playgoers to see much of the auditorium with no effort at all (figure 3.13). Regardless of where one sits or stands in an amphitheater, a large portion of the audience will always fall into view when looking at the stage; I would even surmise that the curve and rise of the inner galleries can create a sort of gravitational pull on playgoers' eyesight since it is always present in their periphery. The fact that early modern performances occurred in continuous light only helps to increase the range of playgoers' visibility, to say nothing of the visibility of other playgoers. Overbury and Dekker both imagine that sight and hearing lines converge on the central stage—that they are directed, become focused, and stop there—but geometrically speaking, these lines necessarily *intersect* the performance space, taking in offstage areas that these writers and their ideal spectatorial and auditorial conditions simply leave unacknowledged. Originating from as many as four vertical levels and from roughly 270 degrees around the stage, these sight lines are not purely convergent but more properly transversal because their radial directionality almost always allows them to cross over or through the performance space. From every standing that you might take up in an amphitheater, it's easy to get your sight lines tangled up in those of others (figure 3.14).

Yet, even though a large percentage of an audience remained in view when looking at the stage, this does not mean that playgoers necessarily concentrated their attentions there, and I am chary to suggest that whatever might have been visible in the auditorium drew people to the open-air playhouses more than the drama did. Nevertheless, the amount of physical activity that seems to have occurred amid playgoers during performances had a great potential to intensify the conditions of distraction that the circular auditorium already fostered through its transversal sight lines. Audience mobility, for instance, might easily give the otherwise fixed playgoing eye something else to fasten itself to. As we have already seen, Tiffany Stern argues that

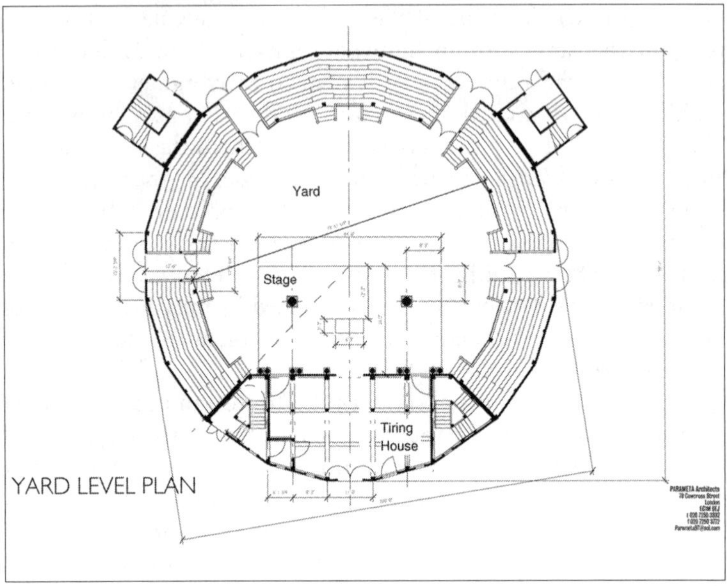

Figure 3.13. "Yard Level Plan" of the reconstructed Globe. Courtesy of Jon Greenfield, when at Pentagram Design Ltd.

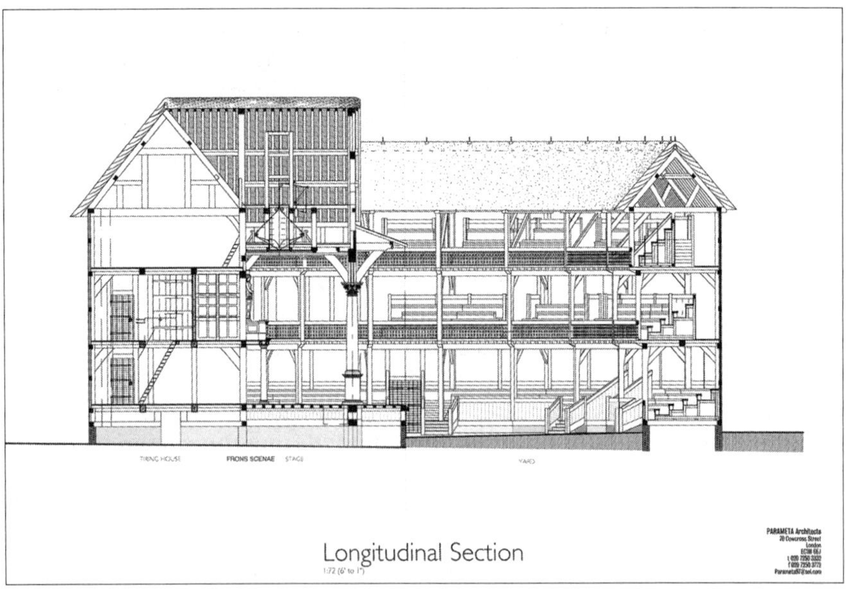

Figure 3.14. "Longitudinal Section" of the reconstructed Globe. Courtesy of Jon Greenfield, when at Pentagram Design Ltd.

among patrons in the gallery as well as in the yard, "all felt free to walk about during performances,"[97] and Andrew Gurr observes that early modern "audiences were active whereas we have been drilled for centuries into being passive. On stage the early players drew energy and inspiration from the audience's visible and audible participation in the experience. That, unstudied though it is, seems to be the essence of truly Shakespearean theatre."[98] Surely, we cannot judge the physical activity of earlier audiences according to modern conventions of docility in the theater, but Pauline Kiernan has documented the early seasons at the reconstructed Globe in London to suggest just how profitably research into contemporary performance in this space might benefit the study of early modern playgoing.

Kiernan writes, for example:

> Performances at the new Globe, where playgoers are free to move around the watching–listening space, to wander in and out of the theatre, to eat food and drink beer and wine sold by the hawkers during performances, have enabled us to gain a better understanding of how a highly visible, energized audience in close proximity to the actors on stage can have the potential to disrupt a performance.[99]

Disruption in such a venue can come in many forms, as we will momentarily see, but the consistent experience that actors and audiences reported during the early years at the new Globe was that the architectural space itself required a renegotiation of actor–audience roles and the "definitional constraint"[100] between the stage and the auditorium. Because the spectatorial area within the new Globe does not impose most of the behavioral restrictions of modern playgoing, audiences tended to feel freer to interact and interrupt, at least early on, which in turn gave actors new types of work to do in engaging with, disengaging from, and controlling the house. As Kiernan puts it, "Take away the controlling devices of lighting, set design and props, and the relationship between actor and audience changes. The physical conditions of an open playhouse offer a means of control to both actors and audience in a shared space. Control of the circumstances of performance then becomes, to some extent, up for grabs."[101] "Audience performance" is the collective term that she uses to describe the various freedoms Globe playgoers found themselves enjoying during those early years,[102] but if we turn to the early modern audience activities that are strewn throughout the documentary record, we find numerous sights, sounds, and movements offstage that would have potentially offered audiovisual competition with, and alienation from, the onstage scene.

Gurr states, "Once settled in place it was possible for playgoers at an amphitheatre to distract themselves with refreshments while the play was in progress,"[103] for which we have the testimony of the Swiss-born traveler Thomas Platter, who noted in his diary in 1599 that "during the performance food and drink are carried round the audience, so that for what one cares to pay one may also have refreshment."[104] Gurr conveniently catalogs the kind of gustatory distractions available to early modern theatergoers:

> The food seems principally to have been apples (there are several references to "pippins" being used as ammunition) and nuts. [. . .] Fletcher has a character in *Wit Without Money* (1614) describe youths who "break in at playes like prentices for three a groat, and crack Nuts with the Scholars in peny Rooms again, and fight for Apples" (2.111). John Tatham mentions pears used as ammunition in 1640 (2.212), and Overbury's Character "A Puny-Clarke" (a puisne or junior law clerk) "eates Ginger bread at a Play-house" (2.114). The drink offered was either water or bottle ale.[105]

In addition to food and beverages, smoking paraphernalia could also be purchased at plays—clay tobacco pipes have been found at the Globe, Theater, and Curtain sites. *THE ACTORS REMONSTRANCE*, a 1643 text that solicits Apollo and the nine Muses to reopen the London theaters, recalls "The Tobacco-men, that used to walk up and downe, selling for a penny pipe," and Henry Buttes complains about the disruption smoking could cause to other patrons:

> [I]*T chaunc'd me gazing at the Theater,*
> *To spie a Lock-Tabacco-Chevalier,*
> *Clowding the loathing ayr with foggie fume*
> *Of Dock-Tabacco, friendly foe to rume.*[106]

E. K. Chambers cites William Fennor's *Descriptions* for the practice of selling books at the theater, though this activity seems to have taken place before performances commenced: "[W]Orthy gentlemen, of what degree soeuer, I suppose this Pamphlet will hap into your hands, before a play begin, with the importunate clamour, of *Buy a new Booke*, by some needy companion, that will be glad to furnish you with worke for a turn'd Teaster."[107]

Aside from the distraction of refreshments—not to mention "The form of distraction that results from refreshments, the need for toilets"[108]—playgoers could sometimes influence the reactions of others through their unabashed or ostentatious behavior. Thomas Middleton mentions "a dull Audience of Stinkards sitting in the Penny-Galleries of a Theater, and yawning vpon the Players," and in John Day's *THE ILE OF GVLS* (which was incidentally produced by Paul's Boys and not at one of the amphitheaters), a Prologue contends with three gallants on the stage, saying, "Either see it all or none; for tis growne into a custome at playes, if any one rise (especially of any fashionable sort) about what serious busines soeuer, the rest thinking it in dislike of the play, tho he neuer thinks it, cry mew, by Iesus vilde; and leaue the poore hart-lesse children to speake their Epilogue to the emptie seates."[109]

Similarly, Fitz-dottrell in Ben Jonson's *THE DIUELL IS AN ASSE* imagines his own self-satisfaction were he to walk out on a performance: "Come but to one act, and I did not care—| But to be seene to rise, and goe away, | To vex the Players, and to punish their *Poet*."[110] Considering the range of other movements visible in the auditorium, those who came "*to detract, and ignorance their warrant*"[111] must have been placed in highly conspicuous locations such as on the stage itself, a practice that we see in *THE ILE OF GVLS*, which certainly occurred at the hall theaters and possibly even in the amphitheaters.[112]

The visual distractions of a restless or mobile audience; interruptions from the hawking, buying, and consuming of refreshments and tobacco (and possibly books); the clouding of others' eyes and nostrils with smoke; the exchange of topical news; and the behavior of surly gallants: each of these activities speaks to the bodily and sensory freedoms (and impositions) that amphitheaters afforded their patrons, generating microcultures of playgoing that, at times, diverted attention away from performances. Coupled with these mainly visual distractions are ambient noises emanating from within the auditorium. Writing of his days as a popular playwright, Michael Drayton recalls in "Sonnet. 47" the reverberating noise coming from the amphitheater's "circuite": "With showts and claps at euerie little pawse, | When the proud Round on euerie side hath rung."[113] If "euerie side" of the "proud Round" rings with applause, then most of the audience probably has its attentions trained on the stage rather than on the auditorium, but Drayton's anecdote reveals an environment in which acoustic intrusions from playgoers were routine, whether in the form of plaudite, hissing, or mewing. Staged at the square Fortune, Thomas Dekker's *THE VVHORE OF Babylon* presents a Prologue who tries to enchant the audience to quiet: "[T]He Charmes of silence through this Square be throwne, | That an vn-vsde Attention (like a Iewell) | May hang at euery eare," while the Prologue in his *IF IT BE NOT GOOD* hopes that the play will inspire "*Rare silence*" until it is time "T'*Applaud*."[114] The Chorus in Shakespeare's *The Life of Henry the Fift* beseeches theatergoers: "*your humble patience pray,* | *Gently to heare, kindly to iudge our Play*," asking again later to "Linger your patience on" and "Still be kind."[115] And Henry Chettle ventriloquizes the dead Richard Tarleton in *KIND-HARTS DREAME*, saying "lette *Tarleton* intreate the yoong people of the Cittie, either to abstaine altogether from playes, or at their comming thither to vse themselues after a more quiet order."[116]

"A large open auditorium with a good proportion of the audience on its feet would certainly generate a level of background noise much greater than the smaller gatherings, all seated, in the hall playhouses."[117] This background noise resulted not simply from the playgoing microcultures that produced these sounds and only occasionally found them to be intolerable. Such noise was also amplified by the material fabric out of which the open-air playhouses were built. Smith explains that the amphitheaters' "wooden beams, plaster over lath, and wooden boards over joists" would create an acoustically vibrant atmosphere for theatrical performances as they "return to the ambient air a high percentage of the sound waves that strike them."[118] In contrast to the rectilinear hall playhouses, the shapes of the polygonal amphitheaters also helped enhance the resonance of the buildings' materials: "The standing waves that create harmonically rich, in-filling sound are produced by reflections off many surfaces. In general, the more surfaces there are, the fuller the acoustic effect. As a twenty-sided polygon, the Globe provided plenty of reflective surfaces."[119] When Smith goes on to detail how actors' acoustical power differed significantly between the hall and open-air playhouses, he naturally focuses on the projection of voices from various areas on their stages, but he also considers the offstage space of the auditorium:

> Thanks to the absence of a roof over the yard, auditors in the yard and in the galleries would have found themselves in a perceptibly different relationship to the auditory events going on all around them. In a cylindrical space listeners can locate sounds horizontally far more accurately than they can in a space enclosed on six sides. Applause sounds on the left and the right, not all around; loud laughter comes from over *there*, a rude comment from over *there*. Performers in the reconstructed Globe in London have commented on the way audience response can start in one part of the theater and then spread laterally to the rest. The experience of broad sound comes not only from the actors onstage but from one's fellow auditors.[120]

For those audiences enchanted by the performance, the auditorium supplies exceptional sight lines and acoustics for concentrating on the stage. But for those theatergoers who happen to be uncharmed by the playing company's offerings for the day, the amphitheater's offstage areas provide sources of diversion and alienation that challenge the primacy of the onstage activity.

"Th'obseru'd of All Obseruers"

If the auditorium of an early modern amphitheater works to focus playgoers' bodies toward the lower center of the building, then it effectively generates centripetal pressures that draw their senses to the action on its thrust stage. As we have seen, writers including Thomas Overbury, Thomas Dekker, and even E. K. Chambers invoke this circular configuration because the shape maximizes the number of theatergoers whose sight and hearing lines can converge on either the work of an excellent actor or the words of a gifted poet. Since Overbury and Dekker are more intent on depicting actors and poets than an amphitheatrical space, however, their verbal images register as idealizations that are uninterested in the aural-visual intrusions of a playhouse crowd so visible and audible to itself. Gurr writes that "From whatever position in the auditorium you looked at the players the audience was visible behind them,"[121] which means that the centripetal pressures that turn playgoers' bodies toward the stage produce corresponding centrifugal forces that can redirect their attentions into the offstage circuit of the auditorium. That is to say, the amphitheatrical environment encourages playgoers to focus at once on the stage and off it, so alienating tendencies are built into the very structure of early modern theatergoing. One result of distributing playgoers radially below, above, and on level with the stage is that the amphitheaters make it impossible to locate an ideal position from which to observe a performance. Unlike the perspective staging techniques that were being imported to court theaters in the early seventeenth century from Continental thinkers such as Sebastiano Serlio, the phenomenology of playgoing in the amphitheaters is not explicitly theorized in the period. But the place to look for such a theory is in the same problematic: the organization of audience perspectives.

Virtually incomparable to theaters with perspective scenery and radically dissimilar from such other theatrical venues as hall playhouses, the amphitheaters that ringed the metropolis of early modern London offered their patrons an altogether different playgoing aesthetic. This aesthetic attempted neither to dictate the physical or intellectual perspectives that audiences took on the action, as began happening at court in the early seventeenth century, nor to gentrify the playgoing experience by subduing the audience's liveliness, which we see at the hall or "private" theaters—as they were sometimes called since they catered to a more privileged clientele. Instead, amphitheaters multiplied playgoers' sight lines within a vast and fluid spectatorial area, giving them heterogeneous and disunified perspectives on dramatic performances. As in any playhouse, the amphitheaters' material structures circumscribed audiences within spaces that restricted certain kinds of access while enabling others, with the prices of admission determining one's freedom of "circulation" inside the building, whether in the one-penny yard, the two-penny galleries, or the six-penny gentlemen's and lords' rooms. I have already argued how the banked degrees, the circling galleries, and the open yard surrounding a thrust stage compelled playgoers to turn themselves toward the performance. But, within these limitations of access and inducements of the body, audiences enjoyed significant autonomy to buy, sell, eat, crack nuts, open bottle ale, smoke, talk, report the news, applaud, mew, hiss, yawn, move about, distract others, walk out, and put themselves on display at will. Those who attended the amphitheaters paid for the option to participate, if they so desired, in any of these microcultures of playgoing.

To detail such microcultures is not to romanticize a theater atmosphere long since past but rather to estrange our contemporary sensibilities, first of all, as Gurr aims to do when he differentiates between "seeing" and "hearing" a play in the period. But, more important, I am arguing that the material conditions of playgoing in the amphitheaters encompassed appreciably more than simply going to see and hear a play onstage. It encompassed, in other words, a vigorous offstage space that frequently acquiesced neither to plays, players, nor playwrights. The collective motions, noises, and activities distributed throughout the auditorium produced a frenetic environment that was itself the phenomenal context for playgoing, and this context conditioned how audiences experienced the drama and the degree to which they disattended to the microcultures around them. Although early modern playgoers certainly tolerated such distractions more than our modern temperaments would bear, they were able to access performances only through the scrim of the auditorium's many sights and sounds. From ignorable white noise to deliberate interruptions, the ambient energies in the auditorium competed with the stage's dramatic action, requiring theatergoers to concentrate their minds actively on the performance. Further, by providing no ideal perspective from which to view the performance but rather a multiplicity of distinct standings, amphitheaters tended to *deanesthetize* their playgoers, making it difficult for them to be passive observers. We might say that perspective staging in the open-air playhouses is given in the kind of narrativized language that I discussed in chapter 2 rather than in stage effects or scenery. Much as the architecture works to achieve playgoers' bodily compliance, the performance onstage seeks to reward their concentration and mental labor with dramatic pleasures that exceed what they might otherwise find in the offstage area of the auditorium.

A theory of playgoing in the amphitheaters would have to begin with distraction—distraction in the sense of both the diversion of one's senses in space and a sort of divertissement of one's time. The geometrical relationship between the thrust stage and the offstage areas of the circular auditorium constitutes an architectural formation that activates a competitive dynamic between the two spaces. Even as it encourages playgoers to turn themselves toward the stage, neither does the auditorium constrain their bodies or their senses nor does it overdetermine their physical or intellectual perspectives onto the dramatic action. On the contrary, the auditorium bestows on playgoers tremendous freedoms regarding the spectatorial and related interpretive positions that a play might persuade them to adopt. Crucially, however, the theatrical performance is but one well-placed orator among many others. The performance must convince the audience to follow the stage's dramatic activity, making it more compelling than whatever microcultural activities might be taking place offstage in their midst. Thus the customary requests for quiet, attention, judgment, and applause are not empty rhetorical gestures that prologues, inductions, choruses, and epilogues make to theatergoers. They are, rather, genuine attempts to cleave playgoers from themselves while at once cleaving their attentions to the performance onstage, much as Hamlet's Player, with "Teares in his eyes, distraction in's Aspect," would "cleaue the generall eare with horrid speech," "amaze indeed, | The very faculty of Eyes and Eares."[122]

The power to cleave playgoers in such a way is emblematized no more evocatively than in the rituals that would herald afternoon performances in the amphitheaters. The presence of a flag over a playhouse announced that a play would be staged that afternoon, while a trumpeter would sound his instrument as a performance drew closer. Legend says that at least the first Globe playhouse flew a flag depicting either Atlas or Hercules bearing the terrestrial globe on his shoulders.[123] This flag—like those of the Rose, the Swan, and the other open-air playhouses—would beckon Londoners with a silent eloquence, drawing them as if so many lines snapped taut and drew their eyes and ears from their homes, their trades, and their daily routines to converge en masse within the diversionary atmosphere of an amphitheater, which fed "*Cauiarie* to the | Generall."[124]

Chapter 4

✦

Didascalic Space in Early Modern Printed Drama

John Marston's *THE MALCONTENT* opens with "*The vilest out of tune Musicke being heard*," which emanates, Bilioso tells Duke Pietro, "from the | Malecontent *Maleuoles* chamber," located somewhere offstage.[1] Ferrardo, "A Minion to Duke Pietro," calls to the disguised and "sometime | Duke of Genoa" ("*Dramatis personæ*," A2v): "*Maleuole*," as if to demand an explanation for the "discord rather then the Musique" that offends Pietro's ears (B1r). Malevole then responds:

> *Male*: *Yaugh,godaman what dost thou there : Dukes *Ganimed Iunoes* iealous of thy long stockings : shadowe of a woman, what wouldst Weesell ? thou lambe a Court : what doost thou bleat for? a you smooth chind *Catamite*! **Out of his chamber.*

to which the duke charges:

> *Pie:* Come downe thou ragged cur, and snarle heere , I giue thy dogged sullennes free libertie : trot about and be-spurtle whom thou pleasest. (B1r)

It takes half a page of solid prose as well as a song before Malevole finally comes out of his closet, prompting Pietro to ask: "And sir, | whence come you now?" (B1v). Himself dissimulating, the "Malecontent" Malevole speaks his first onstage lines in reply:

> *Mal*: From the publike place of much dissimulation, (the cowrt) (B1v)

This line originally read "(the | Church)," and G. K. Hunter states that it was probably the publishers who physically cut out the word from all but a few surviving copies of the first edition (QA), after which "(the | Church)" seems to have been removed altogether from the inner forme of sheet B.[2] Hunter goes on: "QB marks what is, I suppose, a partial restoration of the original;

it prints: 'the publick place of much dissimulation. ( )'; and QC completes the restoration: 'the publike place of much dissimulation, (the Church)'," observing that "In a number of the surviving copies of this edition [i.e., QC] 'the church' has again been cut out."[3]

In one copy of QC, British Library shelfmark C. 12. g. 8, "Church)" has not only been cut out but has also been overwritten. To be more precise, some early modern editor has glued or pasted a small piece of paper over the parallelogram-shaped hole left open after the excision of the single printed word "Church)" and then handwritten onto it the word "cowrt)"—mimicking quite dexterously the printed text's roman type. Also in the shape of a parallelogram, the inserted paper does not obscure the top half of the close parenthesis, so the writer has continued the bracket onto the paper and then back off of it, just nicking a "W" in the line below. With great skill but also with an artistry laid bare, the annotator simulates the typeface in the text, tidily furnishing new paper for a new word, all while revealing through the paper's raised plane that something in the text has been rendered inaccessible. I have elsewhere discussed the perceptual dynamics of overlaid paper and how such textual anomalies simultaneously elicit and frustrate a readerly desire to peer beneath the surface.[4] But here it is enough to note how fittingly the word "cowrt)" maps over the space left vacant by the word "Church)"—how the one materially, perceptually, and conceptually supplants the other. In what way the two words and their associations were related in this early editor's mind is impossible to know. Were church and court opposed to each other? Were they in theory parallel, like the physical shape of the hole and of the paper that was pasted in? Or did the editor perhaps care less about razing "(the | Church)" and more about foregrounding "(the | cowrt)" as the object of criticism? Was the alteration in fact a purely literary consideration, meant to relocate and sharpen the tooth of Malevole's "dogged sullennes"? Whatever the case may be, the two words occupy counterpoised places in the editor's mind, precisely because one *comes to mind* as a suitable substitute for the other: on the paper, "(the | cowrt)" displaces the textual and grammatical space of "(the | Church)."

Such a process of textual displacement, which includes the reader's eye movements around the surface of the page, is the subject of this last chapter devoted to the "didascalia" of Renaissance plays—that is, to the structure of stage directions and speech headings that is virtually unique to dramatic texts.[5] I will be suggesting that, through their perceived superfluity, stage directions and speech headings bestow on direct dramatic speech an impression of immediacy in exchange for didascalia's transparency, but upon closer examination both didascalia and dramatic lines rein in the other's proliferating meanings. Speech headings and stage directions represent a specifically textual formation of the offstage, giving the reader access to spaces and actions, at once dramatic and theatrical, that would otherwise be absent from the printed page. The temptation is to say that characters' speeches constitute the onstage space of dramatic texts, while didascalia comprise their offstage spaces. But, as previous chapters have argued, this binate model fails to account for the ways that onstage and offstage spaces interpenetrate and summon one another into existence. One of the first questions that will need to be addressed, then, is how we read didascalia and dialogue differentially. What are the representational registers within which we perceive these two sorts of dramatic textuality, and how do they each wrap the other in a veneer of either immediacy or transparency? To what do these separate dramatic utterances gesture? And, if didascalia and dialogue gesture or signify differently, then what gets lost or misrecognized through these transactions and the reading practices that they initiate? What textual effects do stage directions and speech headings obscure?

Much as the in-cut paper and the word "cowrt)" both conceptually and materially multiply the "publike place[s] of much dissimulation" in the text, the opening page of THE MALCONTENT (B1r) discloses a series of dramatic spaces just as it conceals them, which directs the reader to pursue actual and imaginative routes through several successive spaces and places as we take a second look at it:

> *Male*: * Yaugh,godaman what dost thou there : Dukes *Ganimed Iunoes* iealous of thy long stockings : shadowe of a woman, what wouldst Weesell ? thou lambe a Court : what doost thou bleat for? a you smooth chind *Catamite*! **Out of his chamber.*

The asterisk that comes after the speech heading stops the reader in his or her tracks, obstructing the smooth progression of Malevole's first words and sending the reader looking instead for an explanation to this interruption. This explanation, it turns out, is easy enough to locate in the page's right margin, yet it *displaces* the reader's attention from the immediate fiction of direct speech to the fictional context of that speech, which here resides spatially outside the central column of text where most of the play's dialogue and didascalia appear. Although the two asterisks literally frame Malevole's first line, creating a visual context within which he begins to speak, the direction "*Out of his* | *chamber*." transports the reader at least into an imaginary dramatic space within the play's fiction, and perhaps even into an imaginary theatrical space of a performance of that fiction. Comparable to *within* directions in other plays, this printed marginalium proceeds to displace the reader once again, expanding the fictional context for the speech into yet another offpage space, that of the interior chamber unseen even by those onstage.[6] Thus the first asterisk removes the reader from the ostensibly unmediated fiction of direct speech (about which I'll have more to say later) and into the page's margin; then "*Out of his* | *chamber*." guides the reader outside the text altogether to imagine what both Jean Alter and Margaret Jane Kidnie call a "virtual performance," which Alter describes as "an anticipation of, and substitution for, the elusive real performance" and Kidnie "a theater of the mind"[7]; and, finally, the sense of the direction points to the offstage "*chamber*" from which Malevole speaks his first lines.

I wish to address here neither the question of "virtual performance" nor the relation of didascalia to theater history or theater practice, and I am not inclined to engage in the long-standing text/performance debate that has absorbed dramatic critics for a couple of centuries now.[8] My focus in this chapter will instead be exclusively on the textual conventions that stage directions and speech headings enact and the reading practices that they elicit, using a couple of examples from early modern printed drama as illustrations. This chapter aims to grapple with aspects of the dramatic text that rarely receive attention in and of themselves, mainly because their very procedures of signification—specifically, their dislocative tendencies—impel the reader away from the text at hand, usually to answer questions about either the authorial provenance or the theatrical uses of didascalia. Printed drama, I will argue instead, conducts the reader on a disruptive itinerary around the surface of the pages of the dramatic text, an itinerary that is itself an active drama of shifting textual, cognitive, and eye movements. In this respect, didascalia continually dislocate the reader's eye from the presence of direct speech much as the auditorium and its various microcultures often dislodge the early modern playgoer's eye from the actors speaking onstage.

With its rather unusual graphic mark and locution, *THE MALCONTENT*'s cue "*" and stage direction "* *Out of his | chamber*." perform certain maneuvers on the reader that are in fact a pervasive practice of even the most routine didascalia. These maneuvers I would like to describe as dramatic "anacoluthon," which is a rhetorical figure that entails interruption and a confusion of sequence. Such dramatic anacoluthons are first of all spatial displacements of the reader's eye that transport him or her to other spaces on the paper's surface to stabilize and give meaning to dramatic lines. But these dislocations also involve temporal interruptions, which draw the reader *out* of characters' direct speech to localize and situate the reader *within* that direct speech. This dislocative and interruptive process has become so conventionalized a reading practice that it usually passes unobserved. When reading Malevole's first lines at the beginning of this chapter, for example, how easily were you able to decode the asterisk and marginal stage direction to know that the character or actor is speaking offstage, before moving on through the rest of the quotation? Was it really much of an effort at all? It is partly the effortlessness of this procedure that I would like to question, for the ease with which we read, or read through, speech headings and stage directions in printed drama bespeaks their conventional transparency, and often their near invisibility.[9] Because they guide the reader on an intratextual route, one which our reading practices have taught us to ignore, didascalia have not that *within*, but rather that *surface* which passeth show. And so to refrain from viewing their signifying procedure either as a "hermeneutic process of deepening" (whereby their meanings are thought to be buried somewhere within the text) or as an extratextual trip to the theater to discover their provenance, we shall have to attend to didascalia's inky cloak more as "a serial movement of dislocations, overlappings, and variations" that shuttle us, instead, around the configuration of the dramatic page.[10]

Narrative Registers; or, The "Invisible Life-Support System of Stage Directions"

Most of the limited theorization of didascalia assigns a specifically narrative voice to the discourse of speech headings and stage directions, which are often imagined to compensate for the page's disembodiment and decontextualization of dramatic characters' voices. The partition of dramatic documents into two kinds of textuality—that is to say, didascalia and direct speech—is above all a formal consideration, not only in the sense of the physical disposition of speech headings, stage directions, and dialogue across the surface of the page but also in the sense that the primary defining quality of drama's representational mode is that of unmediated speech, which is detached from and uncontrolled by the governing voice of a narrator. As I discussed in chapter 1, Aristotle makes a tripartite distinction between representational modes: "using the same means and imitating the same kinds of object, it is possible for the poet on different occasions to narrate the story ([1] either speaking in the person of one of his characters as Homer does or [2] in his own person without changing roles) or [3] to have the imitators performing and acting out the entire story."[11] Drama's unmediated dialogic form therefore necessitates the attribution of its speeches to individual characters, who have been freed from univocal narrative utterances that would deliver their words indirectly and who, as a result of this freedom, speak in their own personae. "The emergence of the visually distinct, freestanding speech attribution is significant in the evolution of English dramatic discourse," argues Linda McJannet: "Wherever a freestanding speech attribution is located (left, right or center), it signals the autonomy and integrity of the character. He or she has a vocal and therefore 'existential' independence, appearing in the dramatic text without introduction or qualification by any other discernible voice."[12]

Both on the page and within the logic of dramatic form, speech headings—which literally name speaking characters—are understood by critics to replace the solo narrating voice, which in epic, novelistic, and other literary forms assumes the responsibility of imparting characters' identities to the reader. Stage directions, too, supplant some of a conventional narrator's descriptive functions, such as indicating the presence or absence of characters, the actions and interactions between them, scene setting, and other nonverbal incidents that advance the fiction along its dramatic path. "From a literary point of view," Marvin Carlson remarks, "most stage directions seem at best rather stark and unadorned simplications [*sic*] of such matters as physical description, expression, and movement, all handled in far more elaborate and richly coded ways in other literary genres."[13] Because their deictic logic points beyond the printed page, stage directions and speech headings constantly invoke a fictional or theatrical elsewhere that nevertheless attempts to anchor the dialogue in place as well as within the dramatic present.

The apparent self-evidence of these statements about the basic functionality of speech headings and stage directions is doubtless one reason why they have garnered so little theoretical attention. Roman Ingarden, whom Pascale Aebischer calls "probably the most influential theorist of 'stage directions',"[14] makes key divisions between the didascalia and direct speech of printed drama. In his appendix on "The Functions of Language in the Theater," Ingarden explains:

> What is most conspicuous in a "written" drama is the existence, side by side, of two different texts: the "side text" or stage directions [*Nebentext*]—i.e., information with regard to where, at what time, etc., the given represented story takes place, who exactly is speaking, and perhaps also what he is doing at a given moment, etc.—and the main text itself [*Haupttext*]. The latter consists of sentences that are "really" *spoken* by the represented characters. Because we know which character is speaking, the sentences belonging to the main text acquire, so to speak, "quotation marks." These sentences themselves, as well as the characters that are indicated as speaking and, finally, the states of affairs of what is spoken itself, become what is *represented* by the elements of the stage directions: they belong to the "object stratum" of the "side text."[15]

Differentiating between the "main text" and the "side text," Ingarden considers the primary literary representation of "'written' drama" to be the lines that characters utter, which "acquire, so to speak, 'quotation marks.'" The implication of his figurative "so to speak" is that if we read the "main text" of dramatic discourse as quotation, then the textual agents who quote characters' lines become the stage directions and speech headings themselves. In other words, because drama's dialogic utterances "belong to the 'object stratum' of the 'side text,'" didascalia then occupy what must be the "subject stratum" of the main text, thus acquiring the status of a speaking subject, even if that which is spoken appears as quotation rather than as underived speech. While Ingarden does not say that didascalia *narrate* dramatic dialogue as such, his designation of "main" and "side" texts as well as the relation he establishes between the two produce, on the one side, a speaking subject and, on the other, a spoken object of literary representation.

Even as he assigns didascalia an implicit subject position, Ingarden resists privileging it or making it the more powerful of the two forms of textuality—perhaps the risk of associating subjecthood with stage directions and speech headings is what prevents him from completing the subject/object circuit in his discussion. Be that as it may, he goes on to insist that "the two texts work *together*," with the main text "supplementing the function of the stage directions," just as the side text "frequently completes the state of affairs projected by the main text."[16] "A drama that is read," states Ingarden, "would be totally impossible if this double projection [of side and main texts] were missing."[17] Before long, however, this mutual dependency begins to list to one side and the main text once again takes precedence:

> In other words, we should learn virtually everything that is essential for the given drama from the words that the characters speak. And, in a way, it is only a way of making things easier for the poet and the reader if one makes frequent use of the side text to obtain short-cut information about certain matters that in the main text are mentioned only in passing or not at all. This information, however, can almost be omitted if there is a suitable arrangement of the main text.[18]

The language of "virtually" and "almost" indicates didascalia's marginal status within Ingarden's schema, and he soon concludes his discussion of the two kinds of textuality by at once subordinating and essentializing speech headings and stage directions, which serve as a frame that renders intelligible the main text of direct speech. "[F]rom the start," he says, didascalia "cannot be absent. In this respect, the side text of a written drama can never be entirely removed. It is essential to this type of literary work. But it always remains only a *side* text, which in itself cannot constitute even the skeleton of a work. If we picture a work without a main text, we are left with an incomprehensible heap of rubble."[19]

Jacques Derrida's notion of the *parergon* is a critically useful figure for thinking through Ingarden's ranking of didascalia within the dramatic text. The *parergon*, for Derrida, takes many forms, such as a picture frame, a cartouche, and so on, but in all instances it is the constitutive work of a piece of art that nonetheless resides outside the work itself. When tendoned to a body of dialogue, didascalia contribute an internal structure to printed drama that is, Ingarden suggests, still outside of it, or just off to the side. His "side" text confers intelligibility on the "main" text, but by itself it is "an incomprehensible heap of rubble," like a disarticulated skeleton or a picture frame without a picture. Writes Derrida: "The frame labors [*travaille*] indeed. Place of labor, structurally bordered origin of surplus value, i.e., overflowed [*débordée*] on these two borders by what it overflows, it gives [*travaille*] indeed. Like wood. It creaks and cracks, breaks down and dislocates even as it cooperates in the production of the product, overflows it and is deduc(t)ed from it. It never lets itself be simply exposed."[20] This complicated exposure of the frame and its work corresponds to that of didascalia—simultaneously legible and transparent—which perform crucial labor and are almost expendable, both still "essential" and "only a *side* text." We thus learn from Ingarden's discussion that didascalia are not only narrative based but also readily narrativizable, becoming minor characters in a dramatic subplot that plays out on the margins of the main textual event.

Further, didascalia invite Ingarden to describe nonexistent textual states in order to give an account of their actual readerly functions: "This information [. . .] can almost be omitted," "the side text of a written drama can never be entirely removed," "[i]f we picture a work without a main text [. . .]," whereas they induce other critics to posit "virtual performances," to mine production histories, and/or to detail theater practices to offer critical explanations of stage directions and speech headings, all of which actually evade their status as material texts. For instance, Patricia A. Suchy asserts, "Stage directions must be considered in the totality of the theatre event, not as inscriptions on a page."[21] This critical tendency to move outside the dramatic text when addressing didascalia would seem entirely instinctive since stage directions, as Carlson puts it, "guid[e] the visual and aural imagination of the reader, by providing at least a partial substitute for the missing contributions of actor, director, and designers."[22] They are called *stage* directions, after all. Yet to eschew their materiality as *text* directions is to neglect a sizable component of the plays we read, and it is also to leave unexamined the *textual* dimensions of stage directions and speech headings, which perform their dislocative and interruptive maneuvers on readers without ever really being noticed. I don't dispute that didascalia actually tend to propel the reader outside the dramatic text and into "virtual performances" or theater practices (though this tendency reflects more than a disciplinary skirmish along the borders of literary and performance studies, as it's often characterized). But I do wish to investigate the unobserved effects that these endemic dislocations and interruptions have on the dramatic text and its reader.

Like Ingarden, I think that didascalia and direct speech do largely function according to two discursive orders, but the boundary and relation between those orders are immanently porous, making their absolute separation analytically problematic. In at least one respect, as we shall see, these two kinds of textuality operate according to the same signifying principle, which is that they refer only to each other. The challenge, then, is to account for these two orders within the same master discourse of "drama," all while resisting the prioritization of their functions precisely as textual, rather than theatrical, phenomena. Aebischer agrees, stating that "Ingarden's ranking of the 'main text' and 'side text' is not helpful in defining the status of the didascalia and the dramatic text as a whole," and she critiques "theoretical attempts at attributing dominance to certain components of the dramatic text."[23] Drawing on narratology, modern theater practices, and performance studies, she highlights various forms of authority within dramatic texts and argues that the particular uses to which plays are put, either in the theater or in reading, activate certain authoritative functions that are always site-specific and therefore shift from situation to situation.[24] In line with my aim to concentrate on textuality, moreover, Aebischer makes the important observation that the literally marginal placement of most didascalia in Western dramatic texts has encouraged especially literary critics to perceive their significance also as a marginal one compared to the direct speech of characters.[25] One way that Aebischer avoids prioritizing either direct speech or didascalia is by linking stage directions and speech headings to the storytelling agent of fiction, who narrates the kind of focalizing details that didascalia instead "display" to the reader.[26]

"Analogous to the narrator in a novel," Aebischer explains, "plays contain a narrative presence that, since dramatic action is not narrated but displayed, is more appropriately referred to as the playtext's *displaying agent*. This displaying agent displays the dialogue as its object."[27] Although her treatment of the dramatic text as a totality is far more nuanced than Ingarden's, she here reproduces his notion of the objecthood of direct speech as well as an imputed subjecthood of didascalia, whose power to "display" coincides with that of a storyteller who narrates. And because most dramatic texts qua texts are unimaginable and unintelligible without didascalia—excepting avant-garde plays such as Gertrude Stein's *Photograph*, which possesses no didascalia except act divisions; Samuel Beckett's *Act Without Words I* and *II*, which consist only of stage directions and no speech or speech headings; or Sarah Kane's *Crave*, which provides no stage directions and only single letters for speech headings—Aebischer embraces their essential status without trying to maintain the superior position of characters' direct speech: "Didascalia, even if reduced to mere speech prefixes, are thus revealed to be *an integral component of the dramatic text* because they are a part of the structuring instance responsible for the dialogue itself."[28] Suchy also considers "the stage direction as a kind of narration, belonging to both the realms of didascalia and dialogue," and under "Narrative referents" Alter groups together both didascalia and internal stage directions embedded in the dialogue: "This category includes all the referents which make up the 'story,' on the basis of either didascalia or discrete signs contained within the quoted text."[29] McJannet traces with great historical sensitivity the various narrative registers of stage directions and speech headings in both manuscript and print texts, stating that speech headings or "speech cues remain close to the conventions of narrative."[30] She adopts the figure of the "voice" to describe didascalic agency and writes that early modern dramatic texts "preserve a decorous separation of the voices of the dialogue and the voice of the stage directions."[31] Finally, Patrice Pavis writes that didascalia operate as "un observateur extérieur, un narrateur qui nous dit ce qui se passe" ("an outside observer, a narrator who tells us what is happening").[32]

Among those who have theorized the subject, then, the dominant conception of speech headings and stage directions involves a modal identification of their functions with narrativity. That modern explanations so consistently associate didascalia with the narrative mode is itself remarkable considering critics' efforts historically to dissociate it from the mode of drama. As chapter 1 demonstrated, Aristotle, Philip Sidney, and most other premodern critics do their best to segregate the two modes rather categorically, and whenever narrative discourse becomes unavoidable in the drama, they characterize it not as storytelling but as mere exposition or report delivered by *angeloi*, *nuntia*, and other minor characters. I began this chapter with the idea that didascalia mark out the play-text's offstage space in contradistinction to the onstage space of dramatic lines, and this book's frequent alignment of the onstage with drama and the offstage with narrative certainly makes this an appealing configuration. Even so, we have yet to examine the specifically textual relation between didascalia and direct speech, nor have we considered how their mutual mediation gives one a veneer of transparency and the other a veneer of immediacy. To begin this examination, I argue that a play-text's stage directions and speech headings, even when they are used dramaturgically in preparation of a production, *are never theatrical events*, though they may very well textualize details of past performances. Phenomenologically speaking, printed didascalia are *readerly* events that have specific consequences for how we navigate the terrain of the dramatic page. While they are not offpage or offstage in the strict sense, didascalia operate in the reader's imaginary as the offstage context for characters' unmediated speech.

The Supplemental Hypothesis

> [. . .] after all, these speech-prefixes are merely labels intended to show to whom the various speeches are to be attributed [. . .].
>
> —Ronald B. McKerrow, *Prolegomena for the Oxford Shakespeare*

> The first, broad and general assumption, is that we all know what a stage-direction is, or in other words that it presents no intellectual problem of interpretation.
>
> —Antony Hammond, "Encounters of the Third Kind in Stage-Directions in Elizabethan and Jacobean Drama"

For a long time, the story goes, didascalia simply supported drama's dialogic text, and we continue to be dominated by this critical view even today. Thus the image of the nearly superfluous didascalic structure in the dramatic text is emblazoned on our fixed, rote, and conventional practices of reading.

The critical treatment of stage directions and speech headings arises, as we have seen, from an assumption about their supplemental usage within the dramatic text—that is to say, the assumption that they provide an intelligibility which is otherwise absent from dialogic form—and it tends to associate that supplemental structure with narrative agents who, in other literary genres, manage and focalize their fictional representations. If modern critics associate didascalia with narrative agents, then the lines that characters speak become isomorphic with dramatic agents, who appear to possess autonomous voices that contribute to a play's literary core. The "characteristic for the dramatic mode of representation," says Ingarden, is "the *spoken* sentences, which are characteristically given in direct speech and never in indirect discourse, [and they] constitute the *main text* of the work."[33] The "quotation marks" that Ingarden employs Alter likewise encloses around direct speech, which he calls "*the quoted text*. Under normal circumstances, the quoted text, dialogue or monologue, emerges as the fundamental referential constant of the literary reading," and, he goes on to say, "The quoted text, as such, is thus almost 'complete': ideally, it needs a minimum of additional properties to become its own referent. It is the stablest of the signs—in literary readings" of dramatic texts.[34] And John Jowett speaks of "the usual [editorial] procedure that privileges the textual status of dialogue over that of stage directions, recognizing the greater instability that is inherent in the latter."[35] Questions will need to be raised about the stability and the literary/dramatic quality that Alter attributes more narrowly to the "quoted text"— Carlson states, in contrast, that it is the speech heading which "is so universal that normally within itself it serves as a distinguishing feature of the dramatic mode."[36] But the prevailing theoretical model frames the play-text with a narrative structure made out of stage directions and speech headings, while it portrays dialogic form as the very picture of dramatic literature itself.

Until now, I have discussed stage directions and speech headings almost indiscriminately, but they each perform their dramatic anacoluthon in distinct ways. The spatiotemporality of speech headings, first of all, is key. Aside from naming dramatic characters, which many plays throughout history accomplish within the dialogue as well, Renaissance speech headings precede characters' lines in a spatial sense. Because our English reading technology proceeds from left to right, the physical placement of speech headings on the left, "where the reader's eye enters the text,"[37] prepares the reader for the dramatic lines that follow. In addition, they give a microfictional heading or navigational bearing to the reader's movement through the dramatic lines, which conclude toward the right and then re/turn the reader's eye back to the left margin to pick up either with the continuation of the character's words or with the next speech heading. One effect of this spatial and, consequently, temporal configuration is that dramatic lines appear to *issue from* speech headings as if from the mouths or out of the heads of characters, who, like their agencies, also appear isomorphic with their names; in this respect, "speech prefix" might be the less subjectivizing of the two terms. In any case, the left-hand placement of speech headings—dictated by our "top to bottom, left to right" reading process[38]—creates an origin for characters' direct speech, ascribing to it an author by anchoring it to a name.

To counteract the borderline positivism in the previous paragraph, however, I think it important to note that the left-hand placement of speech headings also anticipates a legible deficit in characters' spoken lines. In other words, the spatial and temporal experience of reading speech headings prior to dramatic lines ends up forestalling the inherent unintelligibility that direct utterances *in print* exhibit, both individually and within the play's network of social dialogue. This "inherent unintelligibility" results not from dramatic lines having no meaning without speech attributions but instead from having an excess of meaning that immediately proliferates beyond the reader's control. In this respect, speech headings behave according to the third trait of Michel Foucault's "author-function": "The third characteristic of this author-function is that it does not develop spontaneously as the attribution of a discourse to an individual. It is, rather, the result of a complex operation which constructs a certain rational being that we call 'author.'"[39] The stakes of investment are certainly different between the author Foucault is contemplating and the dramatic character who seems to produce discourse spontaneously within a dramatic world, yet the attributive process as well as the mechanism of control are the same: "these aspects of an individual which we designate as making him [or her] an author are only a projection, in more or less psychologizing terms, of the operations that we force texts to undergo, the connections that we make, the traits that we establish as pertinent, the continuities that we recognize, or the exclusions that we practice."[40]

Speech headings therefore function as "the principle of thrift in the proliferation of meaning."[41] By locating the surplus of dialogic meaning within an origin and a name, speech headings forestall the unintelligibility of anonymous dramatic lines. They pre-fix proliferation. Further, their identificatory function, which McKerrow commonsensically cites in the epigraph opening this section, is then actually preceded by a compensatory need, which is created precisely through the ostensive directness or nonmediation of characters' speeches. Without speech headings, dramatic lines reach a level of nonmediation and signification that exceeds the reader's comprehension. Yet by suggesting here that speech headings are supplementary elements, I risk reinforcing the notion that characters' lines are the primary textual object of printed plays, that they are "the fundamental referential constant of the literary reading."[42] Hence I propose that characters' speeches are equally as compensatory to a text's didascalia. To follow conventional logic, if a speech heading were simply to identify and give an origin to the words that a character speaks, then those words must be understood to issue from a source that preexists the utterance itself. Dramatic lines would thus follow from and be subsequent to an autonomous, self-determining subject. But, at the same time, if our only way to identify such a subject is with a name or title, then the name that we read in the speech heading would ontologically precede his or her spoken words, making the lines themselves merely verbal appendages that augment this speaking subject. Instead of having a primary/secondary relationship, dialogue and didascalia are actually effects of one another and cannot exist intelligibly except within their shared textual dynamic. Through their spatial and temporal relations in the text, then, didascalia and direct speech enact the "complex operation which constructs a certain rational being that we call" "dramatic character."

In the wake of a poststructuralist critique of the autonomous humanist subject who has presided over character criticism since Alexander Pope, critics have argued that the unity of dramatic character, which even today we often take for granted in our interpretations of plays, is in fact performatively ascribed instead of existing prior to the act of reading. For instance, Harry Berger Jr. contends that dramatic "speakers are the effects rather than the causes both of the language assigned to their names and of the interpretations we give that language," partly because they are "the operators but not the owners of their discursive practices."[43] Initiating a reevaluation of editorial thinking about speech headings—which, alas, has led to limited effects in editorial practice—Random Cloud demonstrates that "[n]ot only is it not philosophically necessary to ascribe a primary or a transcendent unity to the notion of individual, isolated character that so obsesses modern history, but also the text and Shakespeare's nomenclutter resists [*sic*] such appropriation."[44] While Cloud illustrates that the lack of uniformity in the nomenclature of early texts often yields rich literary meaning, other critics have seized on the variability of those texts' speech headings both to demonstrate the instability of dramatic character and to censure the modern editorial project that has effaced that instability through the regularization of speech attributions, which creates fictions of self-identical characters.[45] Margreta de Grazia and Peter Stallybrass give the examples of Coriolanus's speech headings, which "include '*Mar.*,' '*Mart.*,' '*Martius.*,' and '*Cor.*,' '*Cori.*,' '*Corio.*,' '*Coriol.*,' as well as '*Com.*' and '*Mene.*'," adding that "within the single text of Q2 *Romeo and Juliet*, the 'Lady Capulet' of modern editions is fractured into '*Ca. W.*,' '*Capu. Wi.*,' '*La.*,' '*M.*,' '*Mo.*,' '*Old La.*,' '*Wi.*,' and '*Wife.*' "[46] We might also say that even regularized speech headings in modern editions necessarily introduce difference through their incessant repetitions within the dramatic text.

But early modern English drama reveals another axis of variability in the attribution of characters' speeches. Editors frequently refer to these textual differences as "classical" or "neoclassical" conventions, as opposed to "native" or vernacular ones, because they appear in the earliest imprints of Terence (1470), Plautus (1472), Seneca (1474), and Aristophanes (1498) as well as in medieval manuscripts of classical plays. These conventions involve what W. W. Greg terms "continuous printing" and what McJannet calls "embedded speech prefixes," each of which immediately follows the end of one character's speech and opens the next character's, all within the same line of type.[47] The speech headings, in other words, are not left-justified, while "The speeches in dialogue are printed continuously, running on in even lines."[48] Although the embedding of speech headings sometimes results from inaccurately casting off copy and typesetting within a compressed forme,[49] some play-texts adhere quite consciously to the neoclassical page layout, which curiously becomes more common in texts during the Caroline period, such as in *PERKIN VVARBECK*.[50] Considering his neoclassical propensities, it is perhaps unsurprising that some of Ben Jonson's early quarto, as well as the same folio, texts adopt this convention, such as *SEIANVS HIS FALL*, *VOLPONE or THE FOXE*, *CATILINE his CONSPIRACY*, and *THE ALCHEMIST*.[51] Relatively infrequent in early modern printed plays, however, embedded speech headings stand in contrast to the more familiar convention in which "speeches are introduced by a prefix or heading in which the speaker's name or title appears, usually in a brief or abbreviated form, in a contrasting, usually italic, typeface, indented slightly from the left margin of the text column."[52]

Whether embedded or left-justified, abbreviated or fully expanded, typographically distinct from or uniform with the rest of the text, the printed speech heading possesses one nearly universal attribute, which is its priority in space and time in relation to direct speech.[53] Upon reading, this spatiotemporal relationship creates a subjectivizing effect that might be described as grammatical insofar as drama's direct speech follows after and therefore seems to derive from the character whom the speech heading names. Like the subject in a sentence that acts upon an object, the speech heading's action is to speak, giving to the words on the page—which have a quality of plainness or objectivity about them since they appear to be unmediated—an individuated origin from which they spring. But even Aristotle had advised against confusing a temporal sequence with a cause-and-effect relationship. Discussing "the construction of the plot" and the emergence of reversal and recognition from within it, he says, "it makes quite a difference whether they occur *because* of those events or merely *after* them."[54]

Because speech headings seem to place dramatic lines within the mouths of named speakers, they function as locative devices that stabilize the proliferating meaning of direct speech. Yet because they also defer, however momentarily, characters' unmediated words through the simple but unrelenting process of assigning origins to those words, speech headings at the same time dislocate the reader from the dramatic dialogue, repeatedly shifting that reader's eye, as if a gear, out of and back into what is taken to be the main literary object. Jerome J. McGann observes, "The reading eye does not move only in a linear direction," but must "decipher the text in spatial as well as linear terms."[55] The spatiotemporal procedure of reading speech headings and characters' lines in quick and recurrent succession involves a cycle of conceptual relocations on the part of the reader, who navigates the dramatic fiction by shuttling between two kinds of textuality, each with its own interpretive demands and, as most theorists have it, its own modal register.

Like speech headings, stage directions are both locative and dislocative simultaneously. But while attributions serve chiefly to provide an origin for unmediated speech, both major and incidental directions aim to contextualize such speech, which differentiates the specific functions of these two kinds of didascalia within the printed play. Stage directions affect the temporality of reading by interrupting the flow of characters' lines, much as speech headings do, though their interruptions are far more intermittent since they are obviously not tied to each new speech. This temporal irregularity is furthermore linked to their spatial configuration in the text, which is more dispersed than speech headings even though their physical locations around the dialogue become for the most part regularized in print editions by the end of the sixteenth century.[56] In contrast to (nonembedded) speech headings, stage directions migrate about the surface of the page more freely, occupying positions on the left, center, and right. Although critics characterize both stage directions and speech headings as the principal structures of dramatic texts, the two kinds of didascalia in effect point in different directions. On the one hand, speech headings are introverted inasmuch as they name character-authors out of whom unmediated speech originates—or, put another way, they implant speeches within characters' mouths—whereas, on the other hand, stage directions are extroverted since they surround or provide a context for speech by highlighting the scene's actions, gestures, circumstances, and other conditioning details.

The sheer volume of contextual information that stage directions might convey—from: "*Enter Richard Duke of Gloster, solus.*" to: "*To get into the Charnell house, he takes holde of a Death's | head; it slips and staggers him.*"—is as wide and ranging as the offstage dramatic environments that previous chapters have elucidated.[57] Richard Hosley, for instance, divides stage directions into "two essential kinds":

> Some are "theatrical" in that they usually refer not to dramatic fiction but rather to theatrical structure or equipment: *upon the stage, at another door, within, a curtain being drawn, a scaffold thrust out, the throne descends, arising in the midst of the stage.* Others, conversely, are "fictional" in that they usually refer not to theatrical structure or equipment but rather to dramatic fiction: *upon the walls, before the gates, within the prison, on shipboard, from the bay, in the Tower, forth of the castle, enter the town.*"[58]

Michael Issacharoff names three functions for didascalia in addition to "nominative" speech headings, including the "addressee," which indicates to whom a speech is directed; the "melodic," which "describe[s] the manner of delivery envisaged, the intonation and attitude of the speaker"; and the "locative," which "stipulates the stage area where a speech act is to take place."[59] In a less systematizing way, Carlson differentiates "didascalia of attribution," "structural stage directions" and "performance didascalia."[60] Within the context of Renaissance drama, Hammond separates didascalia into six interrelated classes: "directions to get on and off stage"; "directions involving properties and effects"; "all other formal directions, which relate essentially to whatever the words leave out"; "directions implicit in the dialogue"; "speech-prefixes"; and "structural divisions within the play."[61] He even goes so far as to suggest "that the entire script of a play is a series of stage-directions, the great majority of which tell the actors what gestures to make with their vocal cords."[62]

Hammond's leveling of didascalia and dialogue, like Aebischer's, is refreshing since it discourages the prioritization of one over the other, though he also smartly insists on the physicality of spoken language. Rather than focusing either on the physicality of actors speaking in the theater or on the many types of stage directions, I want to return to the materiality of the text and address how printed didascalia and dialogue mutually compensate for each other, making neither as unmediated as it may seem. A notable example that Hammond actually discusses occurs at a pivotal moment in *THE DVTCHESSE Of Malfy*, where Antonio and Cariola trick the Duchess into carrying on her monologue in their absence, at which time her brother Ferdinand enters and eavesdrops on an undetermined stretch of her speech. The passage runs:

> *Ant.* 'Pray-thee *(Cariola)* let's steale forth the roome,
> And let her talke to her selfe : I haue diuers times
> Seru'd her the like, when she hath chafde extreamely :
> I loue to see her angry : softly *Cariola.* *Exeunt.*
> *Duch.* Doth not the colour of my haire 'gin to change?
> When I waxe gray, I shall haue all the Court
> Powder their haire, with Arras, to be like me :
> You haue cause to loue me, I entred you into my heart
> Before you would vouchsafe to call for the keyes.
> We shall one day haue my brothers take you napping :
> Me thinkes his Presence (being now in Court)
> Should make you keepe your owne Bed: but you'll say
> Loue mixt with feare, is sweetest : I'll assure you
> You shall get no more children till my brothers
> Consent to be your Ghossips : haue you lost your tongue? 'tis wel-
> For know whether I am doomb'd to liue, or die, *(*come :
> I Can Doe Both like a Prince. *Ferdinand Giues*
> *Ferd.* Die Then, Quickle : *Her a Ponyard.*
> Vertue, where art thou hid? what hideous thing
> Is it, that doth ecclipze thee?
> *Duch.* 'Pray sir heare me :[63]

Needless to say, the staging possibilities are virtually endless for these nineteen-odd lines and, in particular, for the timing and manner of Ferdinand's unmarked entry, but as Hammond says wryly, "one of the curses of editing is that you have to *choose*, when choice is impossible."[64] So when exactly does Ferdinand appear? Mercifully, I have little interest in exploring and exhausting an answer. But I would like to suggest that the numerous staging as well as editing possibilities for this passage demonstrate how the Duchess' so-called direct speech disseminates dramatic meaning beyond the reader's control, which asks for the mediating and stabilizing force of an editorial stage direction.

It would seem, but it is by no means absolutely necessary, that the conceit of the passage is Ferdinand's discovery of his sister's secret marriage and children, which the Duchess freely talks about in the presence, she thinks, of Antonio and Cariola. This common as well as commonsensical reading represents a kind of aural bed trick, which, if disastrous, is still apropos of Ferdinand's obsessions around his sister's sexuality. That he "*giues* | *her a ponyard*" and speaks onstage dictates that he must enter the scene, an entrance whose terminus a quo appears to be the silent exeunt of Antonio and Cariola—though, if he is unseen here by the Duchess, then why not by Antonio and Cariola even earlier in the scene? Furthermore, the terminus ad quem for his entry need only be the Duchess's "whether I am doomb'd to liue, or die, | I can doe both like a Prince," since his response, "Die then, quickle," might simply be a symptom of his lycanthropy and general psychological instability, and may actually have nothing to do with what she (thinks she) has disclosed to him. In other words, imagine the tragic irony if Ferdinand enters so late during her speech that he hears nothing at all incriminating—that is, until the Duchess directly reveals to him on the next page: "I pray sir, heare me: I am married" (F4v)—which would make his offer of the poniard merely a sign of his deteriorating mind. Regardless, the main question is: how much of the Duchess's speech does Ferdinand hear? Editorially placing his entrance at each line, even at each word, will subtly alter the significance not only of her incriminating revelations but also of the ratio between his own knowledge and ignorance. In the absence of a firm entry direction, the text engulfs the reader with potential meanings, making it at first difficult and then impossible to negotiate the multiplying consequences of a passage that will in fact support an entry direction *anywhere*. The editorial impulse to supply the text with a clear stage direction thus stems from a desire to rein in the unbounded meaning of direct speech.

Stanley Wells articulates the motivation for such emendation. In order "to make the staging intelligible," he recommends inserting stage directions because of "inconsistencies in early editions": "It seems to me *more* of an insult to a reader to suppose that he [or she] does not care about information essential to an intelligent reading of the play than to omit to provide such information just because it is not provided in an early edition."[65] But what, we might ask, is the experience of reading this passage from THE DVTCHESSE *Of Malfy* without knowing Ferdinand's point of entry—or even *that* he has entered, until we reach the poniard direction? Shock or confusion, to begin with. Yet such a sensation for readers, whether familiar or unfamiliar with the play, will likely stop them in their tracks, entice them to reread the passage to see what they have missed, and, upon discovering that there is no entry direction, maybe puzzle through some possible entry points and their rich implications for the scene. If a reader did so, then that would amount to quite an attentive and "intelligent reading of the play," to say nothing of performing an unexpected discovery that is not dissimilar to the Duchess's and Ferdinand's own. Too, this experience of reading entails a nonlinear shifting of the eye around the surface of the page, moving back and forth from direct speech to didascalia in an effort to locate a stage direction that confirms his entry, which is expected in turn to locate Ferdinand's stage presence. That Ferdinand speaks in the scene is therefore not in itself a sufficient cause for his presence. Characters must first be granted an entry direction before they may be allowed to speak.

My reading of THE DVTCHESSE *Of Malfy* illustrates how stage directions compensate for the unintelligibility of unmediated utterances, which derives, again, not from their meaninglessness but rather from their excesses of meaning. Demonstrating their compensatory nature, however, also helps fortify the supplemental hypothesis about didascalia that theorists tend to endorse. The text of *Much adoe about Nothing* reverses the direction of this hypothesis by showing how direct speech must likewise compensate for didascalia. The play's opening stage direction famously reads: "*Enter Leonato Gouernour of Messina, Innogen his wife, He- | ro his daughter, and Beatrice his Neece, with a messenger*," and several scenes later the text prints: "*Enter Leonato, his brother, his wife, Hero his daughter, and | Beatrice his neece, and a kinsman.*"[66] Yet, aside from facsimile editions of early imprints and Nicholas Rowe's inclusion of "Innogen, *Wife to* Leonato" in his 1709 dramatis personæ,[67] I know of no editor who has ever retained Innogen's presence in the play, despite two explicit entries in the two most authoritative Shakespearean texts of *Much adoe*. In 1733, Lewis Theobald sets the stage for all later editions:

> *Innogen*, (the Mother of *Hero*) in the oldest *Quarto* that I have seen of this Play, printed in 1600, is mention'd to enter in two several Scenes. The succeeding Editions [i.e., Rowe's, but not Pope's] have all continued her Name in the *Dramatis Personæ*. But I have ventur'd to expunge it; there being no mention of her thro' the Play, no one Speech address'd to her, nor one Syllable spoken by her. Neither is there any one Passage, from which we have any Reason to determine that *Hero*'s Mother was living. It seems, as if the Poet had in his first Plan design'd such a Character; which, on a Survey of it, he found would be superfluous; and therefore left it out.[68]

Refuting John Payne Collier's 1842 comment, "It is clear, therefore, that the mother of Hero made her appearance before the [early modern] audience, although she says nothing throughout the comedy, and is not entitled to have her name placed in the *Dramatis Personæ*," Alexander Dyce in 1853 contends, "The great probability is, that *she never appeared before any audience in any part of the play*," while Horace Howard Furness in 1899 rejoins, "[H]ow was the audience to know that she was 'the mother of Hero' or her aunt, or her grandmother, if she neither spoke one word herself nor a single remark was made to her by others?"[69]

The editorial tradition has thus made little ado about something in the early texts of the play, effectively writing out a named character who has two conspicuous entrances because there is "no one Speech address'd to her, nor one Syllable spoken by her." The editorial tradition, moreover, has framed Innogen either as a Shakespearean false start, whom he "found would be superfluous," or as an instance of Shakespearean nonediting: "Shakespeare, in remodelling an old play, perhaps even retaining the first manuscript page of it, carelessly suffered the old stage-direction to remain and merely omitted to erase the name of a character which did not enter his plan. A sin of omission is here more conceivable than a sin of commission."[70] Michael D. Friedman makes a compelling case for "the possibility that a modern director may utilize Innogen as a perpetually mute character," suggesting that "[i]f Innogen does hold her tongue and conspicuously supports Leonato when he turns against his daughter in the church scene, she will then have shown herself to possess all the characteristics of the virtuous Elizabethan wife: chastity, obedience, and silence."[71] As tantalizing as this possibility may be onstage, in reading it would still require additional entry directions for Innogen later in the play, which the early texts insistently withhold. In either case, editorial intervention serves to supplement a deficient text, stabilizing *Much adoe*'s didascalic structure either by enlarging her silent role throughout the play or by excising her stage presence altogether. The editorial treatment of this "ghost character" therefore stands in direct contrast to that of Ferdinand in THE DVTCHESSE *Of Malfy*.[72] That Innogen enters twice in *Much adoe* is not in itself a sufficient cause for her presence. Characters must first speak before they may be granted an entry direction.

Transparent Textuality; or, The Impulse to Fenestrate

> Editors traditionally treat the text of Shakespeare's dialogue as more or less sacrosanct, but feel no such compulsion about the original stage directions, which are often silently omitted, rewritten, rearranged, round-bracketed, square-bracketed, and even broken-bracketed. Compilers of concordances generally exclude stage directions. Literary critics, for their part, tend to accept—quite uncritically—the ideology that stage directions are subordinate and inferior textual features which neither require nor deserve interpretation.
>
> —Eric Rasmussen, afterword to *Stage Directions in* Hamlet

The supplemental hypothesis proposes that didascalia simply furnish the more literary portions of dramatic texts with a kind of scaffolding, or stage, on which the "main," "quoted," or "direct" speech does its unmediated performance. Because readers privilege characters' speeches as the prime repository of literary meaning, didascalia have acquired a reputation—they have in fact been calcified by a particular reading practice—as a surplus textual infrastructure to dramatic lines, which would nevertheless be deprived of intelligibility without the speech attributions that give them origins and without the stage directions that situate them into meaningful contexts. If structures consist in material patterns that create stability, then many critics conceive of didascalia as "the skeleton of a work,"[73] much like the load-bearing timbers that frame early modern amphitheaters, encircling and giving place to the main dramatic event onstage. Under the supplemental hypothesis, speech headings and stage directions would then function as a kind of textual theater—*θέᾱτρον*, *theātrum*, "a place for viewing"—for dramatic lines that appear to be unmediated. As Herbert Blau insists, however, "There is nothing more illusory in performance than the illusion of the unmediated," and Jonathan Goldberg says in a context about writing, "Immediacy is mediated."[74] The questions to which this discussion brings us, then, are: How does the dramatic text produce in its reader a perception of immediacy? And what textual operations occur on a material level to generate "the illusion of the unmediated" within the dramatic text?

The perception of immediacy in printed drama comes about, first of all, through the relative visibility of didascalia and direct speech, an issue which we have seen is linked to the critical and readerly prioritization of the two. Of course both kinds of text can readily be seen on the page and, while they are usually printed in dissimilar typefaces and in their own sectors on the paper, both are part of the same inking process and are thus equally visible to the reader's eye. Yet, as McJannet declares as she sets out her in-depth study, "What needs to be accounted for is why Elizabethan stage directions *seem* invisible."[75] Charting the complex historical development of didascalia in England, she argues that earlier drama in manuscript and print tends to employ "self-conscious" directions, whereas the popular drama that emerges in the second half of the sixteenth century evolves "self-effacing" directions. On the one hand, in a medieval play like *The Castle of Perseverance* the direction "*tunc* ascendet humanum ge[n]us ad mundum" ("*then* Mankind will go up to the World") is governed by a temporal marker that "self-consciously mediates the text to its various interpreters" so that "the stage directions collectively create a narrative that contains (or at least runs parallel to) the unmediated and developing present of the fictive world."[76] Eventually, on the other hand, temporal stage directions ("*Then*") are overtaken by spatial ones ("*Here*"), which has the effect of reorienting the reader from an outward-looking, performance-centered perspective to an inward-looking, text-centered one: "Whereas 'Then' locates readers or interpreters outside the text, 'Here' locates them inside it. And whereas the 'Then' formula seems to address itself to someone contemplating a production, looking ahead, with the whole of the narrative in mind, the 'Here' formula invokes a spatiotemporal present."[77]

The "spatiotemporal present" that McJannet speaks of here belongs to the dramatic fiction, but it is crucial to observe that it also coincides with that of the reading process, during which the moment-by-moment unfolding of the action through the progression of characters' lines is punctuated by the momentary anacoluthons of speech headings and stage directions. These temporal interruptions in and spatial dislocations from the central dramatic fiction become less visible—or, better, more transparent—as didascalia adopt particular print and grammatical conventions over the course of the sixteenth century, resulting in the "emergence of an efficient, unobtrusive, self-effacing dramatic code."[78] So as the reading eye proceeds through spoken lines on the page, gaps of unintelligibility arise as a direct result of the dramatic mode, which by definition withholds most of the fiction's unspoken particulars from its characters' words, requiring didascalia to supplement those words with origins and contexts. Pierre Corneille, for instance, clarifies their textual and epistemological relation:

> I should be of the opinion that the poet ought to take great care to indicate in the margin the less important actions which do not merit being included in the lines, and which might even mar the dignity of the verse if the author lowered himself to express them. The actor easily fills this need on the stage, but in a book one would often be reduced to guessing and sometimes one might even guess wrong, unless one were informed in this way of these little things.[79]

If such gaps in the reader's knowledge are at once supplemented by speech attributions or by details pertaining to "these little things," then didascalia tend to efface themselves just as those gaps close, allowing the reader to return almost immediately to the dialogue. We must bear in mind, however, that such dislocations from and compensations of the dialogue are not in truth immediate. They are in fact mediations of that dialogue, though our readerly tendency is to peer through speech headings and stage directions as if they were windows looking back onto dramatic action. One reason for this impulse to fenestrate didascalia is their perceived status as supplemental elements that take on the character of the *parergon*, performing indispensable work upon the work, but always from a place outside the work—a place to which the text repeatedly dislocates its reader.

Another reason for this impulse to treat didascalia as if they were transparent results from mistaking textual effects for textual features. When critics including Roman Ingarden, Jean Alter, Patricia Suchy, and others describe speech headings and stage directions as nearly superfluous features compared to the more literary portions of the dramatic text, they are not entirely incorrect. Their statements are accurate, I want to suggest, insofar as they describe the textual *effects* brought about by didascalia and direct speech, but they are off the mark insofar as they perceive these effects to be individual qualities inherent to the two kinds of text. For example, if speech headings and stage directions provide intelligibility to dramatic lines by anchoring them to specific origins and contexts—thereby arresting their proliferating meanings—then the stabilizing effects that they generate within the printed play appear to be qualities innate to themselves. But this appearance of innateness is actually *produced* as a result of the mutually compensatory relationship that the two kinds of text share. Like direct speech, didascalia possess no authority, stability, or structural integrity in and of themselves—their meanings, too, disseminate beyond the reader's control—and it is only by authorizing, stabilizing, and structuring dramatic lines that they seem to exhibit these qualities. As McJannet sees it, "the form and voice of Elizabethan stage directions result in their economy and 'invisibility,' and [. . .] these qualities, in turn, are the source of their relative authority."[80]

But, like most economies, that of the dramatic text is neither as smooth nor as economical as it purports to be. Despite the mode's ostensible immediacy and self-sufficiency, its textual economy is one of supplementation through displacement and distraction. Stage directions and speech headings compensate for the epistemological deficits that accompany direct speech, which is actually a rather conservative statement in light of the critical orthodoxy. A less orthodox view is that these epistemological deficits result from the superabundance rather than the deprivation of meaning, and an even more radical view is that direct speech compensates just as much for didascalia's exponential meanings. Thus, if characters' lines demand a context from stage directions to become situated and intelligible, then stage directions equally need those lines as textual objects onto which they bestow context and intelligibility. Similarly, if speech headings fasten direct speech to ontological origins by implanting them into the mouths of characters, then direct speech also turns out to be an indispensable adjunct to those attributions because it attests to the very existence and autonomy of the dramatic characters whom those speech headings name.[81] In short, didascalia and direct speech structure, supplement, and mediate each other, which means that direct speech is not so "direct" after all, but rather an effect of their textual dynamic. Because we read speech headings and stage directions as a kind of transparent textuality, their mediating function in the dramatic text vanishes, which has the effect of casting a veneer of immediacy or self-evidence onto characters' lines. The apparent "not-thereness" of didascalia works to produce the "right-thereness" of dramatic speeches.

What our reading practices habitually paper over, then, is that these perceptions of transparency and immediacy are but two sides of the same coin, which are rubbed smooth by the frequent handling of the dramatic text as if it were an unmediated surface for direct speech. What our reading practices obscure, in other words, are the processes by which didascalia and direct speech mediate each other by persistently interrupting and dislocating the reader's eye, shifting the reader's perceptual and cognitive energies in uneven ways around the surface of the text and, in the same moment, emulating the sudden movements of the dramatic fiction.

Sight Unseen

The correspondence between didascalic space in dramatic texts and the various kinds of offstage spaces that we have examined over the course of this book centers on their relative visibility, especially compared with that of other dramatic objects which have a propensity to upstage their less discernible counterparts. If the dramatic mode, unmediated action, the mise-en-scène itself, and direct speech all crowd quite effortlessly into our visual and aural fields, then the narrative mode, recounted dramatic action, the amphitheatrical auditorium, and didascalia all tend to fade rather unspectacularly into the background. Such quotients of visibility and nonvisibility are determined, as we have observed, not only by the limits of what the playgoing eye can actually see but also by critical conceptions about dramatic form, by the architectural construction of Renaissance amphitheaters, and by the textual layouts of early plays. While the limits of the visible in drama and theater have always predominated as a metaphor for the limits of knowability, those boundaries themselves have a history whose construction has alienated the offstage from onstage events, making its regions seem more unrepresentable and insignificant than they actually are in practice. As the textual analogues of offstage space, didascalia developed an unobtrusive quality in sixteenth- and seventeenth-century printed plays, a development which has in some ways contributed to their ongoing transparency in our contemporary reading practices.

But what precisely is gained when stage directions and speech headings efface themselves? What advantages ensue to the reader by looking through them like windows that frame dramatic action? Pascale Aebischer claims that didascalia have "a prescriptive, narrative, and, importantly, commentatorial presence in the playtext whose aim is to provide the reader with a reading strategy."[82] Although I wouldn't disagree with this, I think her statement is more productive if we reverse it, since this "reading strategy" is not the consequence of didascalia but rather their source. For speech headings and stage directions to give the reader a strategy as well as a structure for comprehending direct speech, that strategy would have to precede the dramatic text and therefore arrange its structure so as to yield a specific perceptual effect. So what strategy, exactly, do didascalia enact? And, to repeat my question from earlier in the chapter, what textual effects do stage directions and speech headings obscure?

I have argued that one such effect is the impression of the "right-thereness" of characters' spoken lines, and I would like to conclude by suggesting that the "reading strategy" which printed plays deploy is *the fiction of immediacy*. It is this readerly fiction of unmediated speech that didascalia obscure by turning themselves around as if to present the immediacy of dramatic action. ("Antimetabole" would be the rhetorical term for this dislocative and inversive maneuver.) While the unimpeded access to direct speech that dramatic texts offer up to readers is itself a fiction—perhaps the most foundational of dramatic illusions—it is one that readers accept, or more often never even recognize, because it comes with a substantial representational payoff. This payoff is, quite tautologically, the perception that dramatic speech is candid, self-evident, unadorned, and natural, a perception that is not unlike Lear's encounter with "vnaccommo- | dated man."[83]

The man Lear believes he sees standing before him "ow'st | the Worme no Silke ; the Beast, no Hide; the Sheepe, no | Wooll ; the Cat, no perfume": "Thou art," he says to the disguised Edgar, "the thing it selfe" (TLN 1883–86). In Lear's eyes, Edgar's "vncouer'd body" (TLN 1882) renders him natural, unadulterated, and readily comprehensible because he is stripped bare, a kind of pure and legible surface. He has not borrowed the (sartorial or olfactory) coverings of any other animal to compensate for the deficiencies of his own, which prompts the baffled king to speak to his own garments: "Off, off you Lendings : Come, vn- | button heere" (TLN 1888–89). The immense power of Lear's observation lies not in the fact that we realize he is mistaken about this naked fellow but that he speaks the truth about him even though that truth contradicts his intended meaning. Edgar is "vnaccommo- | dated man" inasmuch as his disguise is as bare as it can possibly be. But, even in his austerity, the unwitnessed stories that Edgar tells about Tom o' Bedlam serve to clothe him, arbitrating his interactions with others in this outcast world. Because we invest so heavily in and receive such pleasures from this fiction of immediacy, we tend to read dramatic texts as Lear does Edgar: as direct encounters with "the thing it selfe."

This book has sought not to bankrupt those investments and certainly not to anesthetize those pleasures, but rather to show how our investments and pleasures both thrive just as much on what we don't know and can't see as on the dramatic elements that we take to be self-evident. And if we read these structures of unknowing and unseeing as productive or weighted ignorances that impel us to carry on and to try to resolve our uncertainties, then we come to understand how vital such structures are to the drama's representational work. We have been concerned with a routinely unapproachable dramatic space, which has consisted of theoretically dubious fictional locales, imaginary scenes somewhere beyond the stage's boundaries, disregarded theatrical areas occupied by playgoers, as well as transparent textual sites within printed drama. In its array of dramatic formations, the offstage gives audiences the perspective of juxtaposed distances, which creates the sensation that the play's action is *right there*, up close and immediate. Because the offstage has so often seemed unthinkable, obscured, extraneous, and transparent, it's become a representational vanishing point. Yet even Lear believes that we "may see how this world | goes, with no eyes." "Looke with thine eares," he intones (TLN 2594–95).

NOTES

Preface

1. Robert Weimann, *Shakespeare and the Popular Tradition in the Theater: Studies in the Social Dimension of Dramatic Form and Function*, ed. Robert Schwartz (Baltimore: Johns Hopkins University Press, 1978), 78, 79.

2. Ibid., 80–81, his emphases.

3. Ibid., 224.

4. Ibid., 230.

5. Ibid.

Introduction

1. William Shakespeare, *THE TRAGEDIE OF Othello, the Moore of Venice*, in *MR. WILLIAM SHAKESPEARES COMEDIES, HISTORIES, & TRAGEDIES* (London: by Isaac Iaggard and Ed. Blount, 1623), TLN 420–21, 429. I have omitted a stray 'u' in the line, which reads in some Folios: "I will a round vn-varnish'd uTale deliuer." Subsequent citations appear in the text.

2. "As it hath beene diuerse times acted at the Globe, and at the Black-Friers, by his Maiesties Seruants," VVilliam Shakespeare, *THE Tragœdy of Othello, The Moore of Venice* (London: by N.O. for Thomas Walkley, 1622), A1r.

3. William Shakespeare, *THE TRAGEDIE OF HAMLET, Prince of Denmarke*, in *MR. WILLIAM SHAKESPEARES COMEDIES, HISTORIES, & TRAGEDIES* (London: by Isaac Iaggard and Ed. Blount, 1623), TLN 3175.

4. William Shakespeare, *The Winters Tale*, in *MR. WILLIAM SHAKESPEARES COMEDIES, HISTORIES, & TRAGEDIES* (London: by Isaac Iaggard and Ed. Blount, 1623), TLN 3066–67.

5. Thomas Middleton, *WOMEN BEWARE WOMEN*, in *TWO NEW PLAYES* (London: for Humphrey Moseley, 1657), K2r.

6. William N. West, "The Idea of a Theater: Humanist Ideology and the Imaginary Stage in Early Modern Europe," *Renaissance Drama*, n.s., 28 (1997 [1999]): 247, 248.

7. Patricia Parker, "Dilation and Delay: Renaissance Matrices," *Poetics Today* 5 (1984): 520.

8. Lorna Hutson, *The Invention of Suspicion: Law and Mimesis in Shakespeare and Renaissance Drama* (Oxford: Oxford University Press, 2007), 7. See also the thematic contributions to the special issue *Shakespeare and Narrative*, ed. Peter Holland, *Shakespeare Survey* 53 (2000): 1–357.

9. William Shakespeare, *The life and death of King Richard the Second*, in *MR. WILLIAM SHAKESPEARES COMEDIES, HISTORIES, & TRAGEDIES* (London: by Isaac Iaggard and Ed. Blount, 1623), TLN 969–72.

10. See especially James Barrett, *Staged Narrative: Poetics and the Messenger in Greek Tragedy* (Berkeley: University of California Press, 2002).

11. See Bruce R. Smith, *The Acoustic World of Early Modern England: Attending to the O-Factor* (Chicago: University of Chicago Press, 1999); and Pauline Kiernan, *Staging Shakespeare at the New Globe* (Basingstoke, UK: Macmillan Press, 1999).

12. See Roman Ingarden, *The Literary Work of Art: An Investigation on the Borderlines of Ontology, Logic, and Theory of Literature: With an Appendix on the Functions of Language in the Theater*, trans. George G. Grabowicz (Evanston, Ill.: Northwestern University Press, 1973); and Pascale Aebischer, "Didascalia and Speech in the Dramatic Text," *Journal of Dramatic Theory and Criticism* 17, no. 2 (2003): 25–44.

13. M. C. Bradbrook, *Elizabethan Stage Conditions: A Study of Their Place in the Interpretation of Shakespeare's Plays* (London: Cambridge University Press, 1968), 118.

14. Georg von Greyerz, *The Reported Scenes in Shakespeare's Plays* (Bern: Fritz Pochon-Jent, 1965), 73.

15. Francis Berry, *The Shakespeare Inset: Word and Picture* (Carbondale: Southern Illinois University Press, 1965), 56.

16. B. G. Tandon, "Off-Stage Action in *Macbeth*," in *Some Early Greek Scholars in England*, ed. James Hogg (Salzburg: Salzburg Studies in English Literature, Universität Salzburg, 1981), 68.

17. Peter Holland, "'Travelling Hopefully': The Dramatic Form of Journeys in English Renaissance Drama," in *Travel and Drama in Shakespeare's Time*, ed. Jean-Pierre Maquerlot and Michèle Willems (Cambridge: Cambridge University Press, 1996), 160–61. Other discussions of offstage action include Ethel Arnold, "An Explanation of the Use of Off-Stage Scenes in Shakespearean Drama" (M.A. thesis, Colorado State Teachers College, 1933); John H. Astington, "Malvolio and the Dark House," *Shakespeare Survey* 41 (1989): 55–62; William Bache, "Hamlet, Macbeth, and Lear Offstage: The Significance of Absence," *Dalhousie Review* 59 (1979): 308–20; Anthony Brennan, *Onstage and Offstage Worlds in Shakespeare's Plays* (London: Routledge, 1989); Michael D. Bristol, "Vernacular Criticism and the Scenes Shakespeare Never Wrote," special issue *Shakespeare and Narrative*, ed. Peter Holland, *Shakespeare Survey* 53 (2000): 89–102; John Russell Brown, *Shakespeare and the Theatrical Event* (Basingstoke, UK: Palgrave Macmillan, 2002), 180–96; Maurice Charney, "Asides, Soliloquies, and Offstage Speech in *Hamlet:* Implications for Staging," in *Shakespeare and the Sense of Performance: Essays in the Tradition of Performance Criticism in Honor of Bernard Beckerman*, ed. Marvin Thompson and Ruth Thompson (Newark: University of Delaware Press, 1989), 116–31; Maurice Charney, "The Stage Situation of Asides, Soliloquies, and Offstage Speech in *Hamlet*," *Shakespeare Bulletin* 4, no. 3 (1986): 5–8; Aurélie Coulon, "Le sujet hors-scène," *Agôn: Revue des arts de la scène*, no. 0 (2007): 59 pars., August 19, 2015, http://agon.ens-lyon.fr/index.php?id=305; Germaine Greer, "The Offstage Mob: Shakespeare's Proletariat," in *Shakespeare and Cultural Traditions*, ed. Tetsuo Kishi, Roger Pringle, and Stanley W. Wells (Newark: University of Delaware Press, 1994), 54–75; Beliz Güçbilmez, "An Uncanny Theatricality: The Representation of the Offstage," *New Theatre Quarterly* 23 (2007): 152–60; Margaret Hicks, "*Dentro:* The Imaginary World

Offstage in Lope de Vega's Early Plays," in *Looking at the* Comedia *in the Year of the Quincentennial*, ed. Barbara Mujica, Sharon D. Voros, and Matthew D. Stroud (Lanham, Md.: University Press of America, 1993), 69–74; Martha Barbour Hobson, "Action Behind the Scenes in Shakespeare and in Ibsen" (M.A. thesis, University of Chicago, 1918); Martha Barbour Hobson, "The Development of Off-Stage Action in the English Drama" (Ph.D. thesis, Northwestern University, 1932); John D. Lyons, "Unseen Space and Theatrical Narrative: The 'Récit de Cinna,'" *Yale French Studies* 80 (1991): 70–89; Lois Potter, "*The Two Noble Kinsmen*: Spectacle and Narrative," in *The Show Within: Dramatic and Other Insets; English Renaissance Drama (1550–1642)*, 2 vols., ed. François Laroque (Montpellier, Fr.: Publications de Université Paul-Valery, 1992), 2.235–51; Stephen Ratcliffe, *Reading the Unseen: (Offstage)* Hamlet (Denver: Counterpath Press, 2010); June Schlueter and James P. Lusardi, "Offstage Noise and Onstage Action: Entrances in the Ophelia Sequence of *Hamlet*," in *Stage Directions in Hamlet: New Essays and New Directions*, ed. Hardin L. Aasand (Madison, N.J.: Fairleigh Dickinson University Press, 2003), 33–41; Frances Ann Shirley, *Shakespeare's Use of Off-Stage Sounds* (Lincoln: University of Nebraska Press, 1963); Arthur Colby Sprague, "Off-Stage Sounds," *University of Toronto Quarterly* 15 (1945): 70–75; Arthur Colby Sprague, "'True, Gallant Raleigh': Some Off-Stage Conversations in Shakespeare's Plays," in *Shakespeare's Styles: Essays in Honour of Kenneth Muir*, ed. Philip Edwards, Inga-Stina Ewbank, and G. K. Hunter (Cambridge: Cambridge University Press, 1980), 183–90; B. G. Tandon, "Offstage Action in the Plays of Shakespeare," in *Indian Response to Shakespeare*, ed. Basavaraj S. Naikar (New Delhi: Atlantic Publishers and Distributors, 2002), 132–38; B. G. Tandon, "Why Does Ophelia Die Offstage?", *Aligarh Journal of English Studies* 15, nos. 1–2 (1993): 1–5; Charles Whitworth, "Reporting Offstage Events in Early Tudor Drama," in *Tudor Theatre: "Let There Be Covenants . . .": Convention et Theatre*, ed. André Lascombes (Bern: Peter Lang, 1998), 45–66; John Wilders, *The Off-Stage Life of Shakespeare's Characters* (Middlebury, Vt.: Middlebury College Press, 1984); and Peter Womack, "Noises Off," *Textual Practice* 1 (1987): 309–28.

18. Richard Meek, *Narrating the Visual in Shakespeare* (Farnham, UK: Ashgate, 2009), 142.

19. William Gruber, *Offstage Space, Narrative, and the Theatre of the Imagination* (New York: Palgrave Macmillan, 2010), 6. See also Barrett, *Staged Narrative*; Barbara Hardy, *Shakespeare's Storytellers: Dramatic Narration* (London: Peter Owen, 1997); and Rawdon Wilson, *Shakespearean Narrative* (Newark: University of Delaware Press, 1995).

20. Gruber, *Offstage Space*, 178.

21. Andrew Sofer, *Dark Matter: Invisibility in Drama, Theater, and Performance* (Ann Arbor: University of Michigan Press, 2013), 4, his emphasis.

22. Michael Issacharoff, "Space and Reference in Drama," *Poetics Today* 2, no. 3 (1981): 211–24; Hanna Scolnicov, "Theatre Space, Theatrical Space, and the Theatrical Space Without," in *The Theatrical Space*, ed. James Redmond (Cambridge: Cambridge University Press, 1987), 11. See also Michael Issacharoff, *Discourse as Performance* (Stanford, Calif.: Stanford University Press, 1989), particularly chapter 5, "Space in Drama."

23. Marvin Carlson, "Indexical Space in the Theatre," *Assaph* 10 (1994): 4. This notion of an "indexical" sign, which forms "a direct physical connection"

with its referent, Carlson adapts from C. S. Peirce, *Peirce on Signs: Writings on Semiotic by Charles Sanders Peirce*, ed. James Hoopes (Chapel Hill: University of North Carolina Press, 1991), 183.

24. Peter Womack, "Off-Stage," in *Early Modern Theatricality*, ed. Henry S. Turner (Oxford: Oxford University Press, 2013), 73, his emphasis; Tim Fitzpatrick, *Playwright, Space and Place in Early Modern Performance* (Farnham, UK: Ashgate, 2011), 5. Other terms that have been proposed to name these spaces include "within" in W. W. Greg, *Dramatic Documents from the Elizabethan Playhouses: Stage Plots, Actors' Parts, Prompt Books*, 2 vols. (Oxford: Clarendon, 1931), 1.208; "espace environnant" and "espace référé" in Steen Jansen, "Le Rôle de l'espace scénique dans la lecture du texte dramatique," in *Semiotics of Drama and Theatre*, ed. Herta Schmid and Aloysius van Kesteren (Amsterdam: John Benjamins, 1984), 254–89, esp. 265; "unlocalized off" and "localized off" in Gay McAuley, *Space in Performance: Making Meaning in the Theatre* (Ann Arbor: University of Michigan Press, 1999), 25 and 29–32; "espace dramatique" in Patrice Pavis, *Dictionnaire du théâtre* (Paris: Messidor/Éditions Sociales, 1980), 146–47; "macrocosme théâtral" in Étienne Souriau, *Les Deux cent mille situations dramatiques* (Paris: Flammarion, 1950), 22; "without" in Henry S. Turner, "*King Lear* Without: The Heath," *Renaissance Drama*, n.s., 28 (1997 [1999]): 177; and "espaces dramatiques" in Anne Ubersfeld, *Lire le théâtre I*, rev. ed. (Paris: Belin, 1996), 137–41. See also "obscæne" in Jonathan Walker, "Rhetorics of the Obscæne," *Theatre Survey* 48 (2007): 77–97.

25. Henry S. Turner, *The English Renaissance Stage: Geometry, Poetics, and the Practical Spatial Arts 1580–1630* (Oxford: Oxford University Press, 2006), 37.

26. Ibid., 24, his emphasis.

27. Mariko Ichikawa, *The Shakespearean Stage Space* (Cambridge: Cambridge University Press, 2013), 1.

28. Turner, *English Renaissance Stage*, 29.

29. Shakespeare, TRAGEDIE OF HAMLET, TLN 3158–75. THE *Tragicall Historie of* HAMLET, *Prince of Denmarke* (London: by I.R. for N.L., 1604/5), M1v, prints the penultimate line as: "Puld the poore wretch from her melodious lay."

30. The phrase "evidential uncertainty" belongs to Hutson, *Invention of Suspicion*, 105.

31. Bertolt Brecht, "A Short Organum for the Theatre," in *Brecht on Theatre: The Development of an Aesthetic*, ed. and trans. John Willett (New York: Hill and Wang, 1992), 181. Brecht writes specifically about "an aesthetics of the exact sciences" in a discussion of the A-effect and how he wants not only to embrace "the realm of the merely enjoyable" but also "to take up lodging there" (180).

32. Bertolt Brecht, *The Messingkauf Dialogues*, trans. John Willett (London: Methuen, 1965), 102, his emphases.

33. Ibid., 103, his emphasis.

34. Jonathan Dollimore, *Radical Tragedy: Religion, Ideology, and Power in the Drama of Shakespeare and His Contemporaries*, 2nd ed. (Durham, N.C.: Duke University Press, 1993), 3, 6.

35. S. L. Bethell, *Shakespeare and the Popular Dramatic Tradition* (London: Staples Press, 1944), 33.

36. Samuel Johnson, *Mr. Johnson's* PREFACE *To his* EDITION *of Shakespear's Plays* (London: for J. and R. Tonson, H. Woodfall, J. Rivington, R. Baldwin, L.

Hawes, Clark and Collins, T. Longman, W. Johnston, T. Caslon, C. Corbet, T. Lownds, and the Executors of B. Dodd, 1765), xxii.

37. Philip Sidney, *THE DEFENCE OF Poesie* (London: for VVilliam Ponsonby, 1595), H4r.

38. Thomas Dekker, *IF IT BE NOT GOOD, The Diuel is in it* (London: for I.T., by Edward Marchant, 1612), A4v.

39. Turner, *English Renaissance Stage*, 30.

40. See Smith, *Acoustic World*, esp. chap. 8.

41. See Stephen Orgel, *The Illusion of Power: Political Theater in the English Renaissance* (Berkeley: University of California Press, 1975).

42. Linda McJannet, *The Voice of Elizabethan Stage Directions: The Evolution of a Theatrical Code* (Newark: University of Delaware Press, 1999), 133.

43. Shakespeare, *TRAGEDIE OF HAMLET*, TLN 1229–30.

44. Ibid., TLN 1203, 1230.

45. Jacques Derrida, *The Truth in Painting*, trans. Geoff Bennington and Ian McLeod (Chicago: University of Chicago Press, 1987), 61.

46. Ingarden, *Literary Work of Art*, 209.

47. Henri Lefebvre, *The Production of Space*, trans. Donald Nicholson-Smith (Malden, Mass.: Blackwell, 1991), 96.

Chapter 1. Scene Individable, or Poem Unlimited

1. Froma I. Zeitlin, *Playing the Other: Gender and Society in Classical Greek Literature* (Chicago: University of Chicago Press, 1996), 385n17.

2. Aristotle, *Aristotle's Poetics: A Translation and Commentary for Students of Literature*, trans. Leon Golden, comm. O. B. Hardison Jr. (Englewood Cliffs, N.J.: Prentice Hall, 1968), 5.1449a31–32, with reference to Aristotle, *Poetics*, ed. and trans. Stephen Halliwell (Cambridge, Mass.: Harvard University Press, 1995). Unless otherwise noted, subsequent citations to Golden's translation appear in the text by chapter and Bekker numbers.

3. William Shakespeare, *A MIDSOMMER Nights Dreame*, in *MR. WILLIAM SHAKESPEARES COMEDIES, HISTORIES, & TRAGEDIES* (London: by Isaac Iaggard and Ed. Blount, 1623), TLN 1869, 1853–54. Subsequent citations appear in the text.

4. Varro, the only classical writer to link the word with the theater, explains that "*Obscaenum* 'foul' is said from *scaena* 'stage'," concluding that "anything shameful is called *obscaenum*, because it ought not to be said openly except on the *scaena* 'stage' " (Varro, *On the Latin Language*, 2 vols., trans. Roland G. Kent [Cambridge, Mass.: Harvard University Press, 1993], book 7, sec. 96, 1.349–51). The *Oxford Latin Dictionary* offers the following: *ob*, prep. 1: "in the direction of, towards"; 2a: "In front of or in the way of (so as to block)" (1210). See *obscenus* 1 (*~a, ~um*), adj. 2: "Exciting disgust by its unwholesomeness, filthy, polluted, loathsome" (1219); and *scaena* (*~ae*), n. 1a: "The background (representing a building, etc.) against which a play, etc., is performed" (1697). In the entry for *obscenus*, *Harper's Latin Dictionary* offers the etymological suggestion: "[perh. ob and caenum, filth]" (1240). E. A. Andrews, Charleton T. Lewis, and Charles Short, eds., *Harper's Latin Dictionary* (New York: American Book, 1907).

5. Marvin Carlson, *Places of Performance: The Semiotics of Theatre Architecture* (Ithaca, N.Y.: Cornell University Press, 1989), 131; see also his figs. 63 and 64 (132–33).

6. Keir Elam, *The Semiotics of Theatre and Drama*, 2nd ed. (London: Routledge, 2001), 25.

7. Carlson, "Indexical Space" (see intro., n. 23).

8. Gruber, *Offstage Space*, 144 (see intro., n. 19).

9. There are of course ways other than storytelling for audiences to perceive offstage action. For example, the classical Greek theater employed the *ekkyklema* or "rolled-out thing," which would wheel tableaux, usually of carnage, out onto the stage. Likewise "teichoscopy," technically a form of narration (originating in the third book of the *Iliad*), is used by characters in elevated positions above the stage to relay events taking place simultaneously in the distance. In recent years video has become a powerful means of mediating offstage action, as in a London warehouse production of *Pericles* by Cardboard Citizens: the attempted rape of Marina was staged in an enclosed structure representing the brothel, during which stage personnel led several men from the audience up to the structure's windows to peer in while a video of the interior scene was projected onto a large wall next to the brothel for the rest of the audience to see, creating a layered and troubling experience of voyeurism. And, because sound carries, audiences can usually acquire access to offstage noises and sound effects much more directly than offstage spectacles; see Shirley, *Shakespeare's Use of Off-Stage Sounds* (see intro., n. 17).

10. Horace, *Ars Poetica*, in *Horace for Students of Literature: The* "Ars Poetica" *and Its Tradition*, trans. Leon Golden, ed. Leon Golden and O. B. Hardison Jr. (Gainesville: University Press of Florida, 1995), 12–13, with references in the Latin to Horace, *Satires, Epistles, Ars Poetica*, trans. H. Rushton Fairclough (Cambridge, Mass.: Harvard University Press, 1999). Subsequent text citations refer to Golden's translation.

11. The idea that seeing something produces belief more readily than hearing about it certainly does not originate with Horace. See Herodotus, *The Persian Wars*, 4 vols., trans. A. D. Godley (Cambridge, Mass.: Harvard University Press, 1920), 1.1.§8: "men trust their ears less than their eyes." My thanks to Jody Enders for alerting me to this reference. Curiously, research in the field of cognitive psychology has recently suggested that the opposite is sometimes true. When test subjects were told a distorted verbal account of an event that they had visually witnessed for themselves, the narrative tended to overwrite their firsthand memory of the event; see Jonathan W. Schooler and Tonya Y. Engstler-Schooler, "Verbal Overshadowing of Visual Memories: Some Things Are Better Left Unsaid," *Cognitive Psychology* 22 (1990): 36–71, a study Gruber discusses in *Offstage Space*.

12. Gruber, *Offstage Space*, 12.

13. O. B. Hardison Jr., "A Commentary on Aristotle's *Poetics*," in Aristotle, *Aristotle's Poetics*, 114. In *Plato and Aristotle on Poetry*, ed. Peter Burian (Chapel Hill: University of North Carolina Press, 1986), 80–81, Gerald F. Else explains that "*Πρᾶξις* ['Things to be done'] here has not the connotation of mere activeness, stirring about, nor does it refer to physical action. From its parent word, the verb *πράττειν*, it has in it the notion of a moral or intellectual *program* aimed at a goal [. . .]. Action in this sense is what the plot, *ὁ μῦθος*, imitates" (his emphasis). For Aristotle's distinction between "story" and "episodes," see chapter 17 of the *Poetics*.

14. Julie Stone Peters, *Theatre of the Book 1480–1880: Print, Text, and Performance in Europe* (Oxford: Oxford University Press, 2000), 170–73.

15. Halliwell's translation of this passage reads: "the deus ex machina should be employed for events outside the drama—preceding events beyond human knowledge, or subsequent events requiring prediction and announcement; for we ascribe to the gods the capacity to see all things. There should be nothing irrational in the events; if there is, it should lie outside the play, as with Sophocles' Oedipus" (Aristotle, *Poetics*, 15.1454b2–8).

16. Hardison, "Commentary," 209, his emphasis.

17. Ibid., 209.

18. Halliwell's translation: "Stories should not comprise irrational components; ideally there should be no irrationality, or, failing that, it should lie outside the plot (as with Oedipus' ignorance of how Laius died), not inside the drama (as with those who report events at Delphi in *Electra*, or the silent figure who comes from Tegea to Mysia in the *Mysians*). The excuse that the plot would have been ruined is ridiculous; one should not construct plots like this in the first place" (Aristotle, *Poetics*, 24.1460a26–34).

19. Scolnicov, "Theatre Space," 17 (see intro., n. 22).

20. In an instructive essay, Andrew Ford proposes a similar constitutive function for *katharsis* in the *Poetics*. See his "*Katharsis*: The Ancient Problem," in *Performativity and Performance*, ed. Andrew Parker and Eve Kosofsky Sedgwick (New York: Routledge, 1995), 109–32. Also highly relevant here is Steven Mullaney, *The Place of the Stage: License, Play, and Power in Renaissance England* (Chicago: University of Chicago Press, 1988), in which he argues that the political and cultural legitimacy that the city of London garnered to itself in the early modern period was locked in a definitional relationship with the margins or Liberties encircling the city, where such illegitimate political and cultural forms as the Renaissance theater found a place and voice beyond the city's limits—limits that also declared the symbolic limitations of the governing order's ability to accommodate such forms.

21. See 24.1460a11–18: "Now then, it is necessary in tragedy to create the marvelous, but the epic admits, even more, of the irrational, on which the marvelous especially depends, because the audience does not see the person acting. The whole business of the pursuit of Hector would appear ridiculous on the stage with some men standing about and not pursuing and Achilles nodding at them to keep them back; but in the narrative description of epic, this absurdity escapes notice. The marvelous is pleasant, and the proof of this is that everyone embellishes the stories he tells as if he were adding something pleasant to his narration."

22. Halliwell's translation differentiates the three forms of representation more clearly than Golden's: "in the same media one can represent the same objects by combining narrative with direct personation, as Homer does; *or* in an invariable narrative voice; *or* by direct enactment of all roles" (3.1448a20–24, emphasis in original).

23. Irene J. F. de Jong, *Narrative in Drama: The Art of the Euripidean Messenger-Speech* (Leiden: Brill, 1991), 117, her emphasis, my brackets.

24. Gerald Else gives an invaluable account of how Aristotle conceives of narrative and spectacle, discussing his conflicted evaluation in the *Poetics* of Homer's use

of both modes; see his *Plato and Aristotle on Poetry*, esp. 170–73. In his fragmentary *On Poets*, Aristotle curiously makes two statements that associate narrative with drama in a way that the *Poetics* seems at pains to avoid. Richard Janko explains in *Aristotle: Poetics* (Indianapolis: Hackett, 1987) that the context for both fragments is a discussion of tragedy in relation to epic, and Aristotle would again appear to be positioning tragedy as a superior poetic form. The fragments read: "In tragedy the narrative is [done] only with messengers, and what is enacted is in the other [parts], but in epics there is narrative only"; and "Narrative must be added as a part of the dramatic" (Janko, *Aristotle: Poetics*, 57, frags. 3.8a and 3.8b).

25. In *Staged Narrative*, 81 (see intro., n. 10), James Barrett explains that in the ancient Greek theater messengers who traveled from afar were called *angeloi*, and those appearing from within the *skēnē* were called *exangeloi*. For a discussion of how Plato and Aristotle use the same term, *apangelia*, to designate both the genre of narrative and the speeches delivered by messengers in drama, see Barrett, *Staged Narrative*, 69–73.

26. Plato, *The Republic*, 2 vols., trans. Paul Shorey (Cambridge, Mass.: Harvard University Press, 1969), 3.394b–c. Subsequent citations appear in the text by chapter and Stephanus pagination.

27. On this passage, Halliwell notes that "imitates," "*Mimeisthai* here implies full enactment; cf. Pl. *Rep*. 3.397a" (Aristotle, *Poetics*, 137nb).

28. One classical critic, Philodemus, anticipates my argument that Aristotle tries both to include and to exclude onstage narration within his theory. Unfortunately, his *On Poems* is understudied and highly fragmented. See Richard Janko, "Philodemus' *On Poems* and Aristotle's *On Poets*," *Cronache Ercolanesi* 21 (1991): 5–64, esp. 14; and Nathan A. Greenberg, *The Poetic Theory of Philodemus* (New York: Garland, 1990), 129.

29. Edited and translated by S. Georgia Nugent, "Ancient Theories of Comedy: The Treatises of Evanthius and Donatus," in *Shakespearean Comedy*, ed. Maurice Charney (New York: New York Literary Forum, 1980), 271, emphases in original; subsequent citations appear in the text. Nugent provides a discussion of the two treatises (259–67), English translations (267–77), and transcriptions of the fourth-century CE Latin texts (277–80). Evanthius positions both *peripeteia* and *anagnorisis* together in the catastrophe, a conjunction that Aristotle in *Poetics* commends as part of a successful complex plot: "The most effective recognition is one that occurs together with reversal" (11.1452a32–33).

30. This view would likewise bring Evanthius's divisions between the protasis, epitasis, and catastrophe into line with Aristotle's assertion that "To be a whole is to have a beginning and a middle and an end" (7.1450b27–28).

31. My gratitude goes to Paul D. Streufert for helping me unpack the phrase *protatika prosopa*.

32. Turner, *English Renaissance Stage*, 3 (see intro., n. 25). My epigraph is from Julius Caesar Scaliger, *Poetices libri septem*, in *Select Translations from Scaliger's* Poetics, trans. Frederick Morgan Padelford (New York: Henry Holt, 1905), 3.

33. Turner, *English Renaissance Stage*, 35.

34. Ibid., 84.

35. Ibid., 83, his emphases.

36. Sidney, *DEFENCE OF Poesie*, H4r (see intro., n. 37). Subsequent citations appear in the text.

37. The phrases "conceived space" and "perceived space" belong to Scolnicov, "Theatre Space," 11.

38. Nearly a century after Sidney's *DEFENCE*, Richard Flecknoe, *A Short DISCOURSE of the English Stage* (London: by R. Wood for the Author, 1664), G5v, makes a similar assessment by comparing English drama to that of other nations: "The chief faults of ours, are our huddling too much matter together, and making them too long and intricate; we imagining we never have intrigue enough, till we lose our selves and Auditors, who shu'd be led in a Maze, but not a Mist; and through turning and winding wayes, but sô still, as they may finde their way at last."

39. I have supplied the "[by]" from Philip Sidney, *AN APOLOGIE for Poetrie* (London: for Henry Olney, 1595), K2r, which reads: "the body of the child is taken vp by *Hecuba*."

40. Parker, "Dilation and Delay," 52 (see intro., n. 7), my emphases.

41. Peters, *Theatre of the Book*, 174–75.

42. Turner, *English Renaissance Stage*, 35.

43. Lodovico Castelvetro, *Castelvetro on the Art of Poetry*, trans. Andrew Bongiorno (Binghamton: State University of New York Press, 1984), 33. My epigraph is from William Shakespeare, *Pericles, Prince of Tyre* (London: for Henry Gosson, 1609), G2v.

44. In "Unseen Space," 80n18 (see intro., n. 17), John D. Lyons notes, "It is an odd aspect of the history of poetics that the concept of mixture should apply only to mixing in one direction but not to the other. If the narrator speaks as a character, the mode is mixed. But if the character speaks as narrator, we are still in a purely mimetic (dramatic) mode."

45. Else, *Plato and Aristotle on Poetry*, 25, his emphasis.

46. Gruber, *Offstage Space*, 83.

47. Castelvetro, *Castelvetro on the Art of Poetry*, 34. Page numbers in the subsequent paragraph of text refer to this source.

48. Castelvetro explains the distinction: "The dramatic mode differs from the similitudinary as the metaphor from the simile. In the metaphor the proper word for a thing is replaced by a word of different meaning; in a drama one person is made to represent another and is accepted by the audience as a person whom he or she represents. The simile, on the other hand, uses the word of different meaning not in place of the proper word but only in so far as it is similar to it and yet recognizably different" (ibid., 34).

49. Gruber, *Offstage Space*, 129.

50. Celia R. Daileader, *Eroticism on the Renaissance Stage: Transcendence, Desire, and the Limits of the Visible* (Cambridge: Cambridge University Press, 1998).

51. Turner, "*King Lear* Without," 185 (see intro., n. 24).

52. Raphael Holinshed [et al.], *THE Third volume of Chronicles* (London, 1587), 840.

53. "The Booke of Sir Thomas Moore," fol. 3a, Harley MS. 7368, British Library, London, my transcription. Modernized, the note reads: "Leave out [. . .] the insurrection wholly with the cause thereof and begin with Sir Thomas More at the Mayor's sessions with a report afterwards of his good service done being Sheriff of London upon a mutiny against the Lombards only by a short report and not otherwise at your own perils."

54. Jody Enders, "Performing Miracles: The Mysterious Mimesis of Valenciennes (1547)," in *Theatricality*, ed. Tracy C. Davis and Thomas Postlewait (Cambridge: Cambridge University Press, 2003), 46.

55. For this insight, I am indebted to Andrew Sofer, *The Stage Life of Props* (Ann Arbor: University of Michigan Press, 2003), which has helped me understand the importance of diachrony in relation to offstage action.

Chapter 2. The Narrative Economy of Social Commerce

1. Hayden White, "The Value of Narrativity in the Representation of Reality," *Critical Inquiry* 7 (1980): 8. My epigraphs are from Roland Barthes, *S/Z: An Essay*, trans. Richard Miller (New York: Hill and Wang, 1974), 213; and White, "Value of Narrativity," 8–9.

2. White, "Value of Narrativity," 6. White's uncited quotation of Roland Barthes is from *Image, Music, Text*, trans. Stephen Heath (New York: Hill and Wang, 1977), 119.

3. Barthes, *S/Z*, 213, his emphases.

4. The line belongs to Helena in Shakespeare, *A MIDSOMMER Nights Dreame*, TLN 609 (see chap. 1, n. 3). Subsequent citations appear in the text.

5. White, "Value of Narrativity," 8.

6. Barthes, *S/Z*, 213.

7. Hutson, *Invention of Suspicion* (see intro., n. 8).

8. Meek, *Narrating the Visual*, 116 (see intro., n. 18), his emphasis.

9. Parker, "Dilation and Delay," 530 (see intro., n. 7).

10. Joel B. Altman, *The Tudor Play of Mind: Rhetorical Inquiry and the Development of Elizabethan Drama* (Berkeley: University of California Press, 1978), 34.

11. See Frank Whigham, *Ambition and Privilege: The Social Tropes of Elizabethan Courtesy Theory* (Berkeley: University of California Press, 1984).

12. The five canons are discussed in Cicero, *De Oratore*, 2 vols., trans. E. W. Sutton and H. Rackham (Cambridge, Mass.: Harvard University Press, 1959), 1.31.142; and in Quintilian, *The Orator's Education* [*Institutio Oratoria*], 5 vols., trans. Donald A. Russell (Cambridge, Mass.: Harvard University Press, 2001), 3.3.1. Citations are to book, chapter, and section numbers.

13. Quintilian, *Orator's Education*, 4.2.31. See also Cicero, *De Inventione*, trans. H. M. Hubbell (Cambridge, Mass.: Harvard University Press, 1949), 1.28; and *Rhetorica ad Herennium*, trans. Harry Caplan (Cambridge, Mass.: Harvard University Press, 1954), 1.9.

14. Quintilian, *Orator's Education*, 4.2.34–35.

15. Ibid., 4.2.61.

16. Lorna Hutson, "Law, Probability and Character in Shakespeare," in *Fictions of Knowledge: Fact, Evidence, Doubt*, ed. Yota Batsaki, Subha Mukherji, and Jan-Melissa Schramm (New York: Palgrave Macmillan, 2012), 65.

17. Hutson, *Invention of Suspicion*, 121.

18. Hutson, "Law, Probability and Character," 79.

19. Hutson, *Invention of Suspicion*, 7.

20. Horace, *Ars Poetica*, 12–13 (see chap. 1, n. 10).

21. Lyons, "Unseen Space," 76–77 (see intro., n. 17).

22. Keith M. Botelho, *Renaissance Earwitnesses: Rumor and Early Modern Masculinity* (New York: Palgrave Macmillan, 2009), 7.

23. Hutson, *Invention of Suspicion*, 7.

24. [Thomas Kyd,] *THE SPANISH TRAGEdie* (London: by Edward Allde, for Edward White, n.d.), D2v. Subsequent citations appear in the text.

25. For Keir Elam's discussion of "iconic *identity*" and "indexical signs," see *Semiotics of Theatre*, 18–27, esp. 20 and 19; the emphasis is his (see chap. 1, n. 6). As I detail in chapter 2, Marvin Carlson develops the notion of "indexical signs" in "Indexical Space," 1–10 (see intro., n. 23). In *The Shakespearean Stage 1574–1642*, 4th ed. (Cambridge: Cambridge University Press, 2009), 244, Andrew Gurr observes how apparel could function as a kind of "indexical sign" on the early modern stage: "Some costumes gave information about locality or setting. Nightcaps and candles signified night scenes and bedrooms, riding boots signified travel."

26. See James Calderwood, *Metadrama in Shakespeare's Henriad: Richard II to Henry V* (Berkeley: University of California Press, 1979), especially the chapter "*Henry V:* English, Rhetoric, Theater," 162–81; and also Tiffany Stern, "'The Curtain is Yours,'" in *Locating the Queen's Men, 1583–1603: Material Practices and Conditions of Playing*, ed. Helen Ostovich, Holger Schott Syme, and Andrew Griffin (Farnham, UK: Ashgate, 2009), 77–96. While the 1600 quarto of *THE CRONICLE History of Henry the fift* (London: by Thomas Creede, for Tho. Millington, and Iohn Busby, 1600), prints no choruses at all, the 1623 *The Life of Henry the Fift*, in *MR. WILLIAM SHAKESPEARES COMEDIES, HISTORIES, & TRAGEDIES* (London: by Isaac Iaggard and Ed. Blount, 1623), h1r, calls the opening speaker a "Prologue," who nonetheless asks the audience to "*Admit me* Chorus *to this Historie*" (TLN 33). Subsequent in-text citations are to the Folio printing.

27. Ch. Marl., *THE TRAGICALL History of D. Faustus* (London: by V.S. for Thomas Bushell, 1604), A2r–v. *Faustus* is set in black letter with roman type for proper names, so I have converted the text to roman and used italic for proper names.

28. [Thomas Norton and Thomas Sackville,] *The Tragidie of Ferrex and Porrex* (London: by Iohn Daye, n.d.), A3r. Although it is the first to be "Seen and allowed," as the title page states, this is the second printing of *THE TRAGEDIE OF GORBODVC* (London: by William Griffith, 1561) and should not be confused with the lost play *Ferrex and Porrex*, for which Philip Henslowe paid William Haughton 20*s* in March 1599/1600. In *The Elizabethan Dumb Show: The History of a Dramatic Convention* (London: Methuen, 1965), Dieter Mehl provides an invaluable discussion of this dramatic device; see Mehl's two appendices, 173–99, for partial lists of early modern plays that contain dumb shows. See also Norman Jones and Paul Whitfield White, "*Gorboduc* and Royal Marriage Politics: An Elizabethan Playgoer's Report of the Premiere Performance," *English Literary Renaissance* 26 (1996): 3–17.

29. Shakespeare, *TRAGEDIE OF HAMLET*, TLN 2006–7 (see intro., n. 3).

30. Ben Jonson, *SEIANVS HIS FALL* (London: by G. Elld, for Thomas Thorpe, 1605), A4r.

31. [Norton and Sackville,] *Ferrex and Porrex*, A1v.

32. Turner, *English Renaissance Stage*, 225 (see intro., n. 25).

33. T. Middleton and T. Dekkar, *The Roaring Girle* (London: for Thomas Archer, 1611), A4r.

34. Ben Jonson, BARTHOLMEW FAYRE, in THE VVORKES OF BENIAMIN IONSON. *The second Volume* (London: for Richard Meighen, 1640), A5r. For a discussion of inductions, see Thelma N. Greenfield, *The Induction in Elizabethan Drama* (Eugene: University of Oregon Books, 1969), which gives a list of plays containing inductions in appendix 2, 161–66.

35. In "Dramatic Presence and Absence: A Structural Phenomenology of Revenge Tragedy in the Tradition of Kyd" (Ph.D. thesis, Boston University, 1992), 56, Bin Zhu lists nine accounts of the play's prehistory, each told by a different character (except Balthazar, who gives two), but four of these are only brief allusions. See Brennan, *Onstage and Offstage Worlds* (see intro., n. 17), for a discussion of how reports about offstage action shape the audience's understanding of dramatic characters.

36. George Puttenham, THE ARTE OF ENGLISH POESIE (London: by Richard Field, 1589), Dd2r; "*Hypotiposis*, or the counterfait representation" is printed in the outer margin of Dd2r. See especially chapter 3 of Hutson's *Invention of Suspicion* and Meek's *Narrating the Visual.*

37. Puttenham, ARTE OF ENGLISH POESIE, Dd2v, brackets in original.

38. Katharine Eisaman Maus, *Four Revenge Tragedies* (Oxford: Oxford University Press, 1995), 332n.

39. Hutson, *Invention of Suspicion*, 125–26.

40. Shakespeare, *Henry the Fift*, TLN 84–85.

41. Berry, *Shakespeare Inset*, 14 (see intro., n. 15).

42. Ibid., 20, his emphasis.

43. Ibid., 6.

44. Frank R. Ardolino, *Thomas Kyd's Mystery Play: Myth and Ritual in "The Spanish Tragedy"* (New York: Peter Lang, 1985), 50–51.

45. The EPILOGVE to *The Second Part of Henry the Fourth*, in MR. WILLIAM SHAKESPEARES COMEDIES, HISTORIES, & TRAGEDIES (London: by Isaac Iaggard and Ed. Blount, 1623), TLN 3344–47, had promised theatergoers:

> *if you be not too much cloid with Fat Meate, our humble Author will continue the Story (with* Sir Iohn *in it) and make you merry, with faire* Katherine *of* France: *where (for any thing I know)* Falstaffe *shall dye of a sweat, vnlesse already he be kill'd with your hard Opinions*[.]

46. George W. Bush, "President Welcomes President Chirac to White House," news release, November 6, 2001, http://www.whitehouse.gov/news/releases/2001/11/20011106–4.html [content no longer available].

47. Barthes, *S/Z*, 213.

48. Turner, *English Renaissance Stage*, 24.

49. In *The Norton Shakespeare*, ed. Stephen Greenblatt et al. (New York: W. W. Norton, 1997), 2471n3, the editors note: "In no version of the story previous to Shakespeare's does Cordelia die at this point." For a compelling discussion of *Lear* and offstage action, see chapter 4 of Meek's *Narrating the Visual.*

50. Turner, *English Renaissance Stage*, 24.

51. Ann Rosalind Jones and Peter Stallybrass, *Renaissance Clothing and the Materials of Memory* (Cambridge: Cambridge University Press, 2000), 5.

52. Wilfrid Hooper, "The Tudor Sumptuary Laws," *English Historical Review* 30 (1915): 437. For Mary and Philip's 1554 law on dress, see *The Statutes of the Realm* [1101–1713], 12 vols., ed. A. Luders, Sir T. Edlyn Tomlins, J. France, W. E. Taunton, and J. Raithby (London: Record Commission, 1810–1828), 4.239. See also Joan Kent, "Attitudes of Members of the House of Commons to the Regulation of 'Personal Conduct' in Late Elizabethan and Early Stuart England," *Bulletin of the Institute of Historical Research* 46 (1973): 41–71.

53. Jones and Stallybrass, *Renaissance Clothing*, 5.

54. Ibid., 2.

55. Ibid., 5.

56. William Shakespeare, *Much adoe about Nothing*, in *MR. WILLIAM SHAKESPEARES COMEDIES, HISTORIES, & TRAGEDIES* (London: by Isaac Iaggard and Ed. Blount, 1623), TLN 1354–55. Subsequent citations appear in the text. Before play's end, Borachio's story will be repeated in various forms by Claudio and Don Pedro at the interrupted wedding (TLN 1743–54), by the two watchmen who have eavesdropped on Borachio (TLN 2039–51), and again by Borachio himself (TLN 2312–25).

57. John A. Allen, "Dogberry," *Shakespeare Quarterly* 24 (1973): 41.

58. *A second and third blast of retrait from plaies and Theaters* (London: by Henrie Denham, 1580), E7v. The anonymous writer, who calls himself "Anglophile Eutheo" on the title page, is conventionally identified with Anthony Munday during his priest-catching days. Offering no evidence, Frederick Gard Fleay makes the attribution to Munday in *A Chronicle History of the London Stage 1559–1642* (London: Reeves and Turner, 1890), 51, but in "Anthony Munday, Pamphleteer and Pursuivant," *Modern Language Review* 4 (1908–9): 484–90, John Dover Wilson explains in considerable detail why Munday could reasonably be the author of the antitheatrical tract. In *The Antitheatrical Prejudice* (Berkeley: University of California Press, 1981), Jonas A. Barish takes Munday to be the author of *A second and third blast*.

59. There is a turned letter in the final word "husbaud." In the 1600 quarto, *Much adoe about Nothing* (London: by V.S. for Andrew Wise, and William Aspley, 1600), F1r, Conrad's line reads "they" instead of "thy": "And thought they Margaret was Hero?"

60. Jean E. Howard, *The Stage and Social Struggle in Early Modern England* (London: Routledge, 1994), 67. For a compelling discussion of the play's management of theatricality and antitheatricality, see particularly 57–72.

61. Ibid., 62, 63.

62. Harry Berger Jr., "Against the Sink-a-Pace: Sexual and Family Politics in *Much Ado About Nothing*," *Shakespeare Quarterly* 33 (1982): 307.

63. Howard, *Stage and Social Struggle*, 63.

64. [John Ford,] *THE CHRONICLE HISTORIE OF PERKIN VVARBECK. A Strange Truth* (London: by T.P. for Hugh Beeston, 1634), E1r. Subsequent citations appear in the text. Although it might also have been performed in an amphitheater under continuous lighting, *PERKIN VVARBECK* seems to have been written for the indoor venue of the Phoenix playhouse, according to its title page.

65. "*Edwards Sister*" is Margaret, Duchess of Burgundy, younger sister to Edward IV, a supporter of Yorkist exiles, and aunt to Richard, Duke of York, whom Warbeck claims to be.

66. William Shakespeare, *The Tragedy of Richard the Third*, in *MR. WILLIAM SHAKESPEARES COMEDIES, HISTORIES, & TRAGEDIES* (London: by Isaac Iaggard and Ed. Blount, 1623), TLN 2712. In the first quarto of Shakespeare's play, *THE TRAGEDY OF King Richard the third* (London: by Valentine Sims, for Andrew Wise, 1597), I2r, Tyrrell's line reads: "Wept like *two* children in their deaths sad stories" (my emphasis).

67. In "John Ford's Substantive Accidentals in *Perkin Warbeck*," *The Library* 16 (2015): 446–57, Gilles Monsarrat argues that the fifty-one instances of capitalized words in the play's 1634 printing (such as in "E V R O P E" in the passage just quoted) constitute Ford's deliberate but subtle stance on Warbeck as a legitimate claimant to Henry VII's throne.

68. For a compelling discussion of the surprisingly topical relevance of writing a chronicle history play as late as the 1630s, see Lisa Hopkins, *John Ford's Political Theatre* (Manchester, UK: Manchester University Press, 1994), especially her chapter "*Perkin Warbeck*: a Stuart succession play?"

69. Ibid., 59.

70. Shakespeare, *Henry the Fift*, TLN 2299. My epigraph is from Shakespeare, *TRAGEDIE OF HAMLET*, TLN 1682–83 (see intro., n. 3).

71. Shakespeare, *TRAGEDIE OF Othello*, TLN 96 (see intro., n. 1).

72. Pierre Corneille, "Of the Three Unities of Action, Time, and Place," trans. Donald Schier, in *Critical Theory since Plato*, ed. Hazard Adams (New York: Harcourt Brace Jovanovich, 1971), 219–20; Pierre Corneille, "Discours des trois unités d'action, de jour et de lieu," in *Trois discours sur le Poème dramatique (Texte de 1660)*, 2nd ed., ed. Louis Forestier (Paris: Société d'Édition d'Enseignement Supérieur, 1982), 125–26:

> Quand je dis qu'il n'est pas besoin de rendre compte de ce que font les acteurs cependant qu'ils n'occupent point la scène, je n'entends pas dire qu'il ne soit quelquefois fort à propos de le rendre, mais seulement qu'on n'y est pas obligé, et qu'il n'en faut prendre le soin que quand ce qui s'est fait derrière le théâtre sert à l'intelligence de ce qui se doit faire devant les spectateurs.

73. Shakespeare, *Richard the Second*, TLN 1354–56, 1361 (see intro., n. 9).

74. Sidney, *DEFENCE OF Poesie*, H4r (see intro., n. 37).

75. Ibid.

76. Ibid., I1r, H4v.

77. In-text citations will be to the first octavo, [Christopher Marlowe,] *Tamburlaine the Great* (London: by Richard Ihones, 1590). The text is printed in black letter, which I have converted to roman, while the roman type used for proper nouns I have converted to italic.

78. Sidney, *DEFENCE OF Poesie*, H4r.

79. Aristotle, *Aristotle's Poetics*, 24.1459b22–28 (see chap. 1, n. 2).

80. Middleton, *WOMEN BEWARE WOMEN*, in *TWO NEW PLAYES*, G7r (see intro., n. 5). Subsequent citations appear in the text. There is no record of the kind of theatrical venue in which *WOMEN BEWARE WOMEN* was performed. Modern editions of the play invariably adopt the name "Bianca" since Middleton's character seems to be based on the historical Bianca Capello (1548–1587), a mistress of Francesco de' Medici. In their edition of the play, Bryan Loughrey and Neil Taylor explain

that "in O the name is 'Brancha' throughout, but this is probably a misreading of 'Beancha'" (Thomas Middleton, *Women Beware Women*, in *Five Plays*, ed. Loughrey and Taylor [London: Penguin Books, 1988], 241n. I have retained the spelling "Brancha" in my discussion.

81. Daileader, *Eroticism on the Renaissance Stage*, 26 (see chap. 1, n. 50). Daileader offers a sensitive treatment of Middleton's scene. See also William Gruber's discussion of this scene in *Offstage Space*, 67–70 (see intro., n. 19), which wrongly identifies Mother as Brancha's, not Leantio's, parent.

82. Daileader, *Eroticism on the Renaissance Stage*, 25.

83. *Oxford English Dictionary*, s.v. "duke," *n.*, 4.: "The castle or rook at chess. *Obs.*" In "Middleton's Chess Strategies in *Women Beware Women*," *Studies in English Literature* 24 (1984): 349, Neil Taylor and Bryan Loughrey puzzle over the identity of Livia's king and rook, writing: "The duke–rook must surely be Guardiano, and the king the Duke of Florence. But at lines 300–301 she had seemed to identify the 'duke' (who would 'strike a sure stroke for the game anon') with the Duke." In my reading I assume that because Livia and Guardiano are the two closest players conspiring to curry favor with the Duke of Florence, they are to be identified as the queen and king on the chessboard.

84. *Oxford English Dictionary*, s.v. "thing," *n.*1, 11c.: "*euphem.* The genitals."

85. Daileader, *Eroticism on the Renaissance Stage*, 4.

86. The earliest example that the *Oxford English Dictionary* gives for "come," *v.*, 17: "To experience sexual orgasm" is 1650, but see Eric Partridge, *Shakespeare's Bawdy* (London: Routledge, 1990), 81: "**come.** To experience a sexual emission" (bold in original); and Gordon Williams, *A Dictionary of Sexual Language and Imagery in Shakespearean and Stuart Literature* (London: The Athlone Press, 1994), 277: "**come** experience orgasm" (bold in original).

87. Ania Loomba, *Gender, Race, Renaissance Drama* (Manchester, UK: Manchester University Press, 1989), 123.

88. For an intriguing discussion that emphasizes how temporality is bound up with epistemology, see Subha Mukherji, "Trying, Knowing and Believing: Epistemic Plots and the Poetics of Doubt," in *Fictions of Knowledge: Fact, Evidence, Doubt*, ed. Yota Batski, Subha Mukherji, and Jan-Melissa Schramm (New York: Palgrave Macmillan, 2012), 84–109.

89. Barthes, *S/Z*, 213, his emphases.

90. Ibid., 10.

Chapter 3. Cleaving the General Ear

1. See Cicero, *De Oratore*, 1.99 (see chap. 2, n. 12); and Quintilian, *Orator's Education* [*Institutio Oratoria*], 2.23 (see chap. 2, n. 12). My epigraphs are from E. K. Chambers, *The Elizabethan Stage*, 4 vols. (Oxford: Clarendon Press, 1923), 2.525; Andrew Gurr, "The Shakespearean Stage," in Greenblatt et al., *Norton Shakespeare*, 3294 (see chap. 2, n. 49); and Shakespeare, *A MIDSOMMER Nights Dreame*, TLN 1995–96 (see chap. 1, n. 3).

2. Bruce R. Smith, *Ancient Scripts and Modern Experience on the English Stage 1500–1700* (Princeton, N.J.: Princeton University Press, 1988), 29.

3. Irby B. Cauthen Jr., introduction to *Gorboduc or Ferrex and Porrex*, by Thomas Sackville and Thomas Norton, ed. Cauthen (Lincoln: University of Nebraska Press, 1970), xii–xiii: "Not just for the hearing of the grave subject

matter discussed by young law students but, one suspects, for the satisfaction of her own curiosity, Elizabeth commanded that second performance at Whitehall."

4. Glynne Wickham, *Early English Stages 1300 to 1660*, 4 vols. in 5 (London: Routledge and Kegan Paul, 1959–2001), 1.xl.

5. Elam, *Semiotics of Theatre and Drama*, 79 (see chap. 1, n. 6).

6. Ibid., 81.

7. Bethell, *Popular Dramatic Tradition*, 33 (see intro., n. 35).

8. Tho. Nash, *Pierce Penilesse* HIS SVPPLICATION *to the Diuell* (London: by Abell Ieffes, 1592), f3r.

9. Weimann, *Shakespeare and Popular Tradition*, 73 (see pref., n. 1).

10. Erving Goffman, *Frame Analysis* (Harmondsworth: Penguin, 1974), 201.

11. Brecht's many ideas on alienation effects are distributed throughout his writings, but the most sustained treatments are in *The Messingkauf Dialogues* (see intro., n. 32), and in his essays "Alienation Effects in Chinese Acting," "Short Description of a New Technique of Acting which Produces an Alienation Effect," and "A Short Organum for the Theatre," in *Brecht on Theatre: The Development of an Aesthetic*, ed. and trans. John Willett (New York: Hill and Wang, 1992), 91–99, 136–47, 179–205.

12. Colin Counsell, *Signs of Performance: An Introduction to Twentieth-Century Theatre* (London: Routledge, 1996), 17, his emphasis.

13. Andrew Gurr, *Playgoing in Shakespeare's London*, 3rd ed. (Cambridge: Cambridge University Press, 2004), 1.

14. Gabriel Egan, "Hearing or Seeing a Play? Evidence of Early Modern Theatrical Terminology," *Ben Jonson Journal* 8 (2001): 332.

15. Tho. Middleton, *NO WIT [NO] HELP LIKE A VVOMANS* (London: for Humphrey Moseley, 1657), A2r. In "Hearing or Seeing a Play?," 332, Egan writes: "Nearly half (three-eighths) of the rare aural examples are by Shakespeare, and we may guess that his pre-eminence in the field is the reason that Shakespeare's unusual way of putting it has, wrongly, been taken for the period's norm."

16. William Webbe, *A Discourse of English Poetrie* (London: by Iohn Charlewood for Robert Walley, 1586), L1r.

17. Puttenham, *ARTE OF ENGLISH POESIE*, L4v (see chap. 2, n. 36).

18. Sidney, DEFENCE OF *Poesie*, C4v, D1v (see intro., n. 37).

19. Thomas Heywood, *AN APOLOGY For Actors* (London: by Nicholas Okes, 1612), B3v. In *Elizabethan Drama and the Viewer's Eye* (Chapel Hill: University of North Carolina Press, 1977), 9, Alan C. Dessen makes this connection between Sidney's triad of philosophy, history, and poetry and Heywood's triad of oratory, painting, and theater. For more on the *Ut pictura poesis* tradition, see Horace, *Ars Poetica*, e.g., line 361 (see chap. 1, n. 10); D. J. Gordon, "Poet and Architect: The Intellectual Setting of the Quarrel between Ben Jonson and Inigo Jones," *Journal of the Warburg and Courtauld Institutes* 12 (1949): 152–78; and Henryk Markiewicz, "Ut Pictura Poesis . . . A History of the Topos and the Problem," trans. Uliana Gabara, *New Literary History* 18 (1987): 535–58.

20. Smith, *Acoustic World*, 31, his emphasis (see intro., n. 11). See Lefebvre, *Production of Space*, 199–200 (see intro., n. 47): "the hearing plays a decisive role in the lateralization of space. Space is listened for, in fact, as much as seen, and heard before it comes into view."

21. Russ McDonald, *The Bedford Companion to Shakespeare: An Introduction with Documents* (Boston: Bedford Books, 1996), 45. For exhaustive detail on the Rose site, see Julian Bowsher and Pat Miller, *The Rose and the Globe—Playhouses of Shakespeare's Bankside, Southwark: Excavations 1988–91* (London: Museum of London Archaeology, 2009), esp. 32–64.

22. Bowsher and Miller, *Rose and Globe*, 93. See also Simon Blatherwick, "The Archeological Evaluation of the Globe Playhouse," in *Shakespeare's Globe Rebuilt*, ed. J. R. Mulryne and Margaret Shewring (Cambridge: Cambridge University Press, 1997), 78, who explains that in England, thanks to "the introduction of Policy Planning Guidance 16, large scale archeological excavation is not as commonplace as it was. Its place has been taken by a process known as archeological evaluation which involves an assessment of the surviving archeological remains" (68), a less-invasive procedure undertaken at the Globe site. A detailed interpretive diagram of the site can be found in Andrew Gurr, "A First Doorway into the Globe," *Shakespeare Quarterly* 41 (1990): 98.

23. Bowsher and Miller, *Rose and Globe*, 94.

24. See Anthony Mackinder with Lyn Blackmore, Julian Bowsher, and Christopher Phillpotts, *The Hope Playhouse, Animal Baiting and Later Industrial Activity at Bear Gardens on Bankside: Excavations at Riverside House and New Globe Walk, Southwark, 1999–2000* (London: Museum of London Archaeology, 2013).

25. Julian Bowsher, *Shakespeare's London Theatreland: Archaeology, History and Drama* (London: Museum of London Archaeology, 2012), 58.

26. Julian M. C. Bowsher and Simon Blatherwick, "The Structure of the Rose," in *New Issues in the Reconstruction of Shakespeare's Theater: Proceedings of the Conference Held at the University of Georgia, February 16–18, 1990*, edited by Franklin J. Hildy (New York: Peter Lang, 1990), 63.

27. Bowsher and Miller, *Rose and Globe*, 94.

28. Christine Eccles, *The Rose Playhouse* (London: Nick Hern, 1990), 86.

29. Julian M. C. Bowsher, "The Rose and Its Stages," *Shakespeare Survey* 60 (2007): 36. For more on the archeology of the Rose, see Julian M. C. Bowsher, *The Rose Theatre: An Archaeological Discovery* (London: Museum of London, 1998); and on the Rose and the Globe, see Bowsher and Miller, *Rose and Globe*.

30. Carly Hilts, "Raising the Curtain: Excavating Shakespeare's Lost Playhouse," *Current Archaeology* 269 (2012): 11. Some ten meters from the principal remains at the Globe site, "The top of a *possible* pier base was revealed within site D (south-west of site C) at approximately 1.09m OD. The pier base [. . .] consisted of a 'plinth' of grey mortar, with fragments of brick" (Bowsher and Miller, *Rose and Globe*, 98, my emphasis).

31. Hilts, "Raising the Curtain," 12.

32. Scott Simon and Heather Knight, "Archaeologists Find Early Shakespeare Theater Was Rectangular," *Weekend Edition*, aired May 21, 2016, transcript accessed November 18, 2016, http://www.npr.org/2016/05/21/478962867/archaeologists-find-early-shakespeare-theater-was-rectangular.

33. Maev Kennedy, "Excavation Finds Early Shakespeare Theatre Was Rectangular," *Guardian*, May 17, 2016, accessed November 19, 2016, https://www.theguardian.com/culture/2016/may/17/curtain-excavation-early-shakespeare-theatre-rectangular-shoreditch.

34. Maev Kennedy, "Did Shakespeare Write *Henry V* to Suit London Theatre's Odd Shape?" *Guardian*, November 10, 2016, accessed November 19, 2016, https://www.theguardian.com/culture/2016/nov/10/shakespeare-write-henry-v-suit-london-theatre-the-curtain-odd-shape.

35. Ibid. Might this have been used as an understage effect or place for sound effects in *Henry the Fift*, first performed at the Curtain? Fluellen argues that

> the Mynes
> is not according to the disciplines of the Warre;the con-
> cauities of it is not sufficient : for looke you, the'athuer-
> sarie, you may discusse vnto the Duke, looke you, is digt
> himselfe foure yard vnder the Countermines"?
> (TLN 1176–1180)

36. Bowsher, "Rose and Its Stages," 36.

37. Wickham, *Early English Stages*, 2.2.110, his emphases. See also Andrew Gurr, "The Shakespearian Stages, Forty Years On," *Shakespeare Survey* 41 (1989): 1–12.

38. Chambers, *Elizabethan Stage*, 2.466. The quote is from the Hope Theater's building contract, Dulwich College, Muniment 49. Based on measurements at the Theater site, Julian Bowsher argues that "In the 20th century a myth grew up that the Globe was the old Theatre 're-erected,' that the dimensions and layout of the Globe were exactly the same as the Theatre," but "we now know the relative sizes of the Theatre and the Globe, which shows that the former was considerably smaller than the latter" (*Shakespeare's London Theatreland*, 62).

39. For a discussion of Hollar's accuracy in the engraving, see especially John Orrell, *The Quest for Shakespeare's Globe* (Cambridge: Cambridge University Press, 1983). Tim Fitzpatrick disputes Orrell's claims that Hollar used a topographical glass to achieve his accuracy in "From Archaeological Remains to Onion Dome: At the Upper Limits of Speculation," *Shakespeare* 7 (2011): 434. In *The Site of the Globe Playhouse, Southwark*, 2nd ed. (London: Hodder and Stoughton, 1924), 57–60, W. W. Braines was the first to argue that the names had been reversed, but see also I. A. Shapiro, "The Bankside Theatres: Early Engravings," *Shakespeare Survey* 1 (1948): 25–37.

40. Bowsher and Blatherwick "Structure of the Rose," 58.

41. Bowsher, "Rose and Its Stages," 37.

42. John Orrell, "Beyond the Rose: Design Problems for the Globe Reconstruction," in *New Issues in the Reconstruction of Shakespeare's Theater: Proceedings of the Conference Held at the University of Georgia, February 16–18, 1990*, ed. Franklin J. Hildy (New York: Peter Lang, 1990), 95. But see Bowsher and Miller, *Rose and Globe*, 126–30, who argue that the original Globes were (if identical in size) sixteen- or eighteen-sided polygons.

43. Jon Greenfield, "Design as Reconstruction: Reconstruction as Design," in Mulryne and Shewring, *Shakespeare's Globe Rebuilt*, 93.

44. John Orrell, "Peter Street at the Fortune and the Globe," *Shakespeare Survey* 33 (1980): 140. See also S. P. Cerasano, "Raising a Playhouse from the Dust," *Shakespeare Quarterly* 40 (1989): 483–90; and John Summerson, *Architecture in Britain 1530 to 1830* (New Haven, Conn.: Yale University Press, 1993), 50–57. For the Vitruvian arguments, see Frances A. Yates, *Theatre of the World*

(London: Routledge and Kegan Paul, 1969); Richard C. Kohler, "The Fortune Contract and Vitruvian Symmetry," *Shakespeare Studies* 6 (1970): 311–26; and Kohler, "Excavating Henslowe's Rose," *Shakespeare Quarterly* 40 (1989): 475–82.

45. Orrell, "Peter Street," 144. Orrell discusses the *ad triangulum* and *ad quadratum* methods in relation to the amphitheaters (142–46), but see also Paul Frankl, "The Secret of the Mediaeval Masons," *Art Bulletin* 27 (1945): esp. 57–59. For a biography of Peter Street, builder of at least the first Globe and first Fortune, see Mary Edmond, "Peter Street, 1553–1609: Builder of Playhouses," *Shakespeare Survey* 45 (1992): 101–14. See also Mary Edmond, "The Builder of the Rose Theatre," *Theatre Notebook* 44 (1990): 50–54.

46. Valentine Leigh, *THE MOST PROFITABLE AND Commendable Science of Surueying of Lands, Tenements, and Hereditaments* (London: by Robert Robinson, for Robert Dexter, 1596), O2v.

47. Orrell, "Peter Street," 144.

48. Jon Greenfield, "Reconstructing the Rose: Development of the Playhouse Building between 1587 and 1592," *Shakespeare Survey* 60 (2007): 32–34.

49. Richard Harris, *Discovering Timber-framed Buildings*, 2nd ed. (Aylesbury, UK: Shire Publications, 1979), 5. Indispensable information about period building practices and the process of timber framing the new Globe can be found in Jon Greenfield, "Timber Framing, The Two Bays and After," in Mulryne and Shewring, *Shakespeare's Globe Rebuilt*, 97–120.

50. At least for the first Fortune, the two upper galleries were also jettied, as the playhouse's contract states: "All which Stories shall conteine Twelue foote and a half of lawfull assize in breadth througheoute besides a Juttey forward[es] in eyther of the saide Two vpper Stories of Tenne ynches of lawfull assize" (R. A. Foakes and R. T. Rickert, eds., *Henslowe's Diary* [Cambridge: Cambridge University Press, 1961], 307, Dulwich College, Muniment 22). These jetties or overhanging ledges were adopted in the building of the reconstructed Globe, but instead of "Tenne ynches" they extend 11.75 inches over the yard at both the second and third levels (Greenfield, "Timber Framing," 106). Orrell contends that the second Globe could not "have had the juttying galleries of the Fortune; such overhangings were specifically forbidden by two proclamations issued in 1611 and in any case cannot have improved the sightlines from the upper galleries. Therefore the upper parts of the walls of the yard directly reflected the proportions of the lowermost parts" (Orrell, "Peter Street," 147).

51. Orrell, *Quest for Shakespeare's Globe*, 127.

52. Hilts, "Raising the Curtain," 11.

53. William Lambarde, *A Perambulation of Kent* (London: by Edm. Bollifant, 1596), Q2r; this page is either missigned as O2 or the tail of the Q has fouled. I have converted the text's black letter to roman and its roman to italic.

54. Gurr, *Shakespearean Stage 1574–1642*, 150 (see chap. 2, n. 25).

55. Tiffany Stern, "'You that walk i'th Galleries': Standing and Walking in the Galleries of the Globe Theatre," *Shakespeare Quarterly* 51 (2000): 211.

56. Ibid., 213; Orrell, *Quest for Shakespeare's Globe*, 137.

57. Foakes and Rickert, *Henslowe's Diary*, 307, 308; W. W. Greg, ed., *Henslowe Papers: Being Documents Supplementary to Henslowe's Diary* (London: A. H. Bullen, 1907), 20.

58. *Oxford English Dictionary*, s.v. "ceil, ciel," *v*. 2. "To cover with a lining of woodwork, sometimes of plaster, etc. (the interior roof or walls of a house or apartment)." In "The Situation of the 'Lords Room': A Revaluation," *Review of English Studies* 48 (1997): 302, Gabriel Egan argues against reading "to be seeled" and "seelinge" in the Fortune contract as referring to walls.

59. Ben Jonson, *EVERY MAN OVT OF HIS HVMOR* (London: for Nicholas Linge, 1600), F1r. *Oxford English Dictionary*, s.v. "over," *prep*. "I. In sense 'above'. 1a Above, higher up than. Used of position or motion within the space above."

60. T. Deckar, *THE GVLS Horne-booke* (London: for R.S., 1609), E2v.

61. Stern, "'You that walk i'th Galleries,'" 215.

62. Gurr, *Playgoing in Shakespeare's London*, 42.

63. During a tour of the new Globe in 2000, a guide offered the specious suggestion that playgoers standing under the eaves and listening to the conversations of gallery patrons was the etymology of "eavesdropping." He also claimed, rather cleverly, that the modern "green room," as a place for actors to wait before going onstage, derived from a grassed area behind the tiring house.

64. Bowsher and Blatherwick "Structure of the Rose," 66–67.

65. Chambers, *Elizabethan Stage*, 2.466.

66. Foakes and Rickert, *Henslowe's Diary*, 307.

67. Ibid., 308.

68. Bowsher and Blatherwick "Structure of the Rose," 67, 71.

69. For the Latin transcript and English translation of the Red Lion dispute, see Janet S. Loengard, "An Elizabethan Lawsuit: John Brayne, his Carpenter, and the Building of the Red Lion Theatre," *Shakespeare Quarterly* 34 (1983): 306–10. The account is in the plea roll, National Archives, KB 27/1229, m. 30.

70. R. A. Foakes, "The Discovery of the Rose Theatre: Some Implications," *Shakespeare Survey* 43 (1991): 146.

71. Ibid., 147.

72. West, "Idea of a Theater," 247 (see intro., n. 6). My epigraphs are from Gaston Bachelard, *The Poetics of Space*, trans. Maria Jolas (Boston: Beacon Press, 1964), 232; and Smith, *Acoustic World*, 207.

73. Chambers, *Elizabethan Stage*, 2.525.

74. Early modern theater companies favored a vocabulary of traditional social categories while capitalizing on the emergent ability of moneyed classes to transgress those categories. See, for instance, Howard, *Stage and Social Struggle*, 75 (see chap. 2, n. 60): "While the public theaters were hierarchically designed to reflect older status categories (common men in the pit; gentlemen in the galleries; lords on the very top), in actuality one's place at the public theater was determined less by one's rank than by one's ability or willingness to pay for choice or less choice places. Money thus stratified the audience in ways at least potentially at odds with older modes of stratification."

75. In *The English Renaissance Stage*, 258 (see intro., n. 25), Henry S. Turner argues that, theoretically at least, the practices of rhetoric and of architecture shared a technical relationship and even a vocabulary in the period: "both Jonson and Vitruvius tended to think of built structure and *geometrical* systems of ordering in terms that were also used to describe syntactical and *verbal* structure in classical rhetoric" (his emphases). For the evidence that Vitruvius's *De Architectura* drew on a rhetorical vocabulary to conceptualize the processes of

designing and constructing buildings as one would an argument, see Louis Callebat, "Rhétorique et Architecture dans le 'De Architectvra' de Vitruve," in *Le Projet de Vitruve: Objet, Destinataires et Réception du* De Architectura, Actes du colloque international (Rome, 26–27 March 1993) (Rome: École Française de Rome, 1994), 31–46.

76. Andree Alciati, *Emblematum liber* (Augsburg: by Heinrich Steyner, 1531), E6r, from which I take the Latin quotations. All English translations are from *Alciato's* Book of Emblems: *The Memorial Web Edition in Latin and English*, ed. William Barker, Mark Feltham, and Jean Guthrie (Department of English, Memorial University of Newfoundland), last modified April 26, 2005, http://www.mun.ca/alciato/, with reference to Peter M. Daly with Virginia W. Callahan, eds., *Index emblematicus: Andreas Alciatus*, 2 vols. (Toronto: University of Toronto Press, 1985).

77. Alciati, *Emblematum liber*, E6r.

78. For this phrase, the website *Alciato at Glasgow*, Glasgow University Library, accessed July 12, 2016, http://www.emblems.arts.gla.ac.uk/alciato/emblem.php?id=A31a092, observes in note 2: "Cf. Cicero's notorious line, *Cedant arma togae, concedat laurea linguae*, 'Let weapons yield to the arts of peace, let laurels yield to eloquence' (quoted in Quintilian, *Institutio Oratoria*, 11.1.24)."

79. Alciati, *Emblematum liber*, E6r.

80. Andre Alciat, *LES EMBLEMES* (Paris: by Christian Wechel, 1540), N4v. Lucian of Samosata offers what seems to be the earliest description of Hercules's tongue leading others' ears with chains; see Lucian, "Heracles," in *Lucian*, vol. 1, trans. A. M. Harmon (Cambridge, Mass.: Harvard University Press, 1961), 63–71.

81. Alciato, *DIVERSE IMPRESE* (Lyons: by Gvlielmo Rovillio, 1564), L4v.

82. Thomas Ouerburie, *NEW AND CHOICE CHARACTERS* (London: by Thomas Creede for Laurence Lisle, 1615), M5v. In *The Elizabethan Stage*, 4.257–58, Chambers attributes the authorship of "*An excellent Actor*" to John Webster.

83. Quintilian, *Institutio Oratoria*, 5.87.

84. Ibid.

85. Cicero, *De Oratore*, 2.171.

86. Dekker, *IF IT BE NOT GOOD*, A4r (see intro., n. 38).

87. Ibid., A4v.

88. Tho. Dekker, *THE MAGNIFICENT Entertainment* (London: by T.C. for Tho. Man the yonger, 1604), A3r.

89. See Sidney in *DEFENCE of Poesie*: "For *Poesie* must not be drawne by the eares, it must be gently led, or rather it must lead" (H3r). See also Ralph Bathurst, "On the Death of Mr. WILLIAM CARTVVRIGHT, and the now publishing of his POEMS," in William Cartwright, *COMEDIES, TRAGI-COMEDIES, With other POEMS* (London: for Humphrey Moseley, 1651), sigs. **2r–v:

> *But who could hear without an Extasie,*
> *When with a gracefull conquering presence He*
> *Stood forth, and, like Almighty Thunder, flung*
> *His numerous strains amongst th' amazed throng?*
> *A pleasing horror strook through every limb,*
> *And every Ear was close chain'd up to Him:*
> *Such Masculine vigour ravish'd our ascent;*

> *What He Perswaded, was Commandement:*
> *A sweeter plenty Rhetorick ne'r knew*
> *In* Chysostome's *Pulpit, nor in* Tully's *Pew.*

For a discussion of the etymological relationship between "sweet" and "persuade" in this and other texts, see Jeffrey Masten, "Toward a Queer Address: The Taste of Letters and Early Modern Male Friendship," *GLQ* 10 (2004): 367–84.

90. Alciati, *Emblematum liber*, E6r.

91. Shakespeare, *TRAGEDIE OF HAMLET*, TLN 1603–6 (see intro., n. 3).

92. Ibid., TLN 1858–59.

93. Mark Robson, "Looking with Ears, Seeing with Eyes: Shakespeare and the Ear of the Early Modern," *Early Modern Literary Studies* 7.1 (2001): paragraph 17. See also *Oxford English Dictionary*, s.v. "cleave," *v.*[2] B3 and "cleave," *v.*[1] B1.

94. See, for example, Le Corbusier, *Precisions on the Present State of Architecture and City Planning*, trans. Edith Schreiber Aujame (Cambridge, Mass.: MIT Press, 1991), 47: "*architecture is circulation*" (his emphasis); and Adrian Forty, *Words and Buildings: A Vocabulary of Modern Architecture* (London: Thames and Hudson, 2000), 87–94. My epigraph is taken from Shakespeare, *A MIDSOMMER Nights Dreame*, TLN 293–302.

95. John Orrell, "The Private Theatre Auditorium," *Theatre Research International* 9 (1984): 79.

96. Smith, *Acoustic World*, 206.

97. Stern, "'You that walk i'th Galleries,'" 211.

98. Gurr, *Shakespearean Stage*, 259.

99. Kiernan, *Staging Shakespeare*, 16 (see intro., n. 11). If there were "hawkers during performances" in the early seasons, they have since been ushered out.

100. Elam, *Semiotics of Theatre and Drama*, 79.

101. Kiernan, *Staging Shakespeare*, 6.

102. Ibid., 28.

103. Gurr, *Playgoing in Shakespeare's London*, 43.

104. Clare Williams, *Thomas Platter's Travels in England, 1599* (London: J. Cape, 1937), 167.

105. Gurr, *Playgoing in Shakespeare's London*, 43.

106. *THE ACTORS REMONSTRANCE* (London: for Edw. Nickson, 1643), A4r; and Henry Buttes, *DYETS DRY DINNER* (London: by Tho. Creede, for William Wood, 1599), P3v.

107. Chambers, *Elizabethan Stage*, 2.549; William Fennor, *FENNORS Descriptions* (London: by Edvvard Griffin, for George Gibbs, 1616), A3v, his emphasis. A "Teaster" is idiomatic for a teston, originally a shilling coin from the reign of Henry VIII that depreciated to 6*d.* before being recalled in 1548. Colloquially, a tester is an almost worthless coin.

108. Gurr, *Playgoing in Shakespeare's London*, 44.

109. [Thomas Middleton,] *FATHER Hubbards Tales* (London: by T.C. for William Cotton, 1604), B4r; Iohn Day, *THE ILE OF GVLS* (London: by Iohn Hodgets, 1606), A3r.

110. Ben Ionson, *THE DIUELL IS AN ASSE*, in *THE VVORKES OF BENIAMIN IONSON. The second Volume.* (London: for Richard Meighen, 1640), T1r.

111. Middleton, *NO WIT [NO] HELP*, A2r.

112. See Leslie Thomson, "Playgoers on the Outdoor Stages of Early Modern London," *Theatre Notebook* 64 (2010): 3–11.

113. Michaell Draiton, *POEMS* (London: for N. Ling, 1605), Cc4v.

114. Thomas Dekker, *THE VVHORE OF Babylon* (London: for Nathaniel Butter, 1607), A3r; Dekker, *IF IT BE NOT GOOD*, A4v.

115. Shakespeare, *Henry the Fift*, TLN 34–35, 493, 1079 (see chap. 2, n. 26).

116. H.C. [Henry Chettle], *KIND-HARTS DREAME* (London: for William Wright, [?1593]), E4r.

117. Gurr, *Playgoing in Shakespeare's London*, 43.

118. Smith, *Acoustic World*, 209.

119. Ibid., 211.

120. Ibid., 214, his emphases.

121. Andrew Gurr, "The 'State' of Shakespeare's Audiences," *Shakespeare and the Sense of Performance: Essays in the Tradition of Performance Criticism in Honor of Bernard Beckerman*, ed. Marvin Thompson and Ruth Thompson (Newark: University of Delaware Press, 1989), 177.

122. Shakespeare, *TRAGEDIE OF HAMLET*, TLN 1595, 1603, 1605–6.

123. See Ernest Schanzer, "Hercules and His Load," *Review of English Studies*, n.s. , 19 (1968): 51–53; Kent van den Berg, *Playhouse and Cosmos: Shakespearean Theater as Metaphor* (Newark: University of Delaware Press, 1985), esp. 36–38; and Richard Dutton, "*Hamlet, An Apology for Actors*, and the Sign of the Globe," *Shakespeare Survey* 41 (1988): 35–43.

124. Shakespeare, *TRAGEDIE OF HAMLET*, TLN 1481–82.

Chapter 4. Didascalic Space in Early Modern Printed Drama

1. [John] Marston, *THE MALCONTENT* (London: by V.S. for William Aspley, 1604), B1r, British Library, shelfmark C. 12. g. 8. Subsequent citations to this copy appear in the text.

2. G. K. Hunter, introduction to *The Malcontent*, by John Marston, ed. G. K. Hunter (Manchester: Manchester University Press, 1999), xxviii–xxix. *THE MALCONTENT* appeared in three separate editions in 1604, all printed by Valentine Sims for William Aspley, and given the designations QA, QB, and QC by W. W. Greg, "Notes on Old Books," *Library*, 4th ser., 2 (1922): 49. In the British Library holdings are two other copies of QC, shelfmarks Ashley 3625 and C. 34. e. 17.

3. Hunter, introduction to *The Malcontent*, xxix.

4. See Jonathan Walker, "Reading Materiality: The Literary Critical Treatment of Physical Texts," *Renaissance Drama*, n.s., 41 (2013): 199–232.

5. Technically, didascalia include features such as dramatis personae, act and scene divisions, and even production notes, but I limit my discussion here to speech headings and stage directions. See "didascaliae" and "Didaskalia" in *The Oxford Classical Dictionary*, 3rd ed., ed. Simon Hornblower and Antony Spawforth (Oxford: Oxford University Press, 1999), 466. For a related discussion of act and scene divisions, see Turner, "*King Lear* Without," 178–83 (see intro., n. 24), in which he writes: "*On the page*, act and scene divisions do not simply reproduce a break in performance: they contribute a conceptual unity to the play by subdividing its action into discrete parts, and these parts are then presumed by the reader to fit together into a coherent structural whole" (180, his emphasis). See also Peters, *Theatre of the Book* (see chap. 1, n. 14).

6. *THE MALCONTENT* uses similar cueing techniques again on C1v, G3v, I2v, and I4r. In *A Dictionary of Stage Directions in English Drama, 1580–1642* (Cambridge: Cambridge University Press, 1999), 253, Alan C. Dessen and Leslie Thomson note that there are "roughly 800 examples" of the *within* stage direction in the five hundred or so plays they examined for their study. See also Ichikawa, *Shakespearean Stage Space* (see intro., n. 27), esp. chap. 3, "'*Music within*' and '*Music above*.'"

7. Jean Alter, "Waiting for the Referent: Waiting for Godot? On Referring in Theatre," in *On Referring in Literature*, ed. Anna Whiteside and Michael Issacharoff (Bloomington: Indiana University Press, 1987), 49; and Margaret Jane Kidnie, "Text, Performance, and the Editors: Staging Shakespeare's Drama," *Shakespeare Quarterly* 51 (2000): 465. Alter had used the notion of "virtual performance" in "From Text to Performance: Semiotics of Theatrality [*sic*]," *Poetics Today* 2 (1981): 113–39, but Michael Issacharoff also employs it in his "Inscribed Performance," *Rivista di Letterature moderne e comparate* 39 (1986): 94.

8. For a brief account of and persuasive intervention into this debate, see Marvin Carlson, "Theatrical Performance: Illustration, Translation, Fulfillment, or Supplement?" *Theatre Journal* 37 (1985): 5–11. In "The Book of the Play," in *From Performance to Print in Shakespeare's England*, ed. Peter Holland and Stephen Orgel (Basingstoke: Palgrave Macmillan, 2006), 13–54, Stephen Orgel offers an even earlier account, showing "how Renaissance readers read" plays as either performance or textual events (45). Other criticism is legion. But for some of the parameters of the debate, see Richard Levin, "Performance-Critics *vs* Close Readers in the Study of English Renaissance Drama," *Modern Language Review* 81 (1986): 545–59; Harry Berger Jr., *Imaginary Audition: Shakespeare on Stage and Page* (Berkeley: University of California Press, 1989); Anthony B. Dawson, "The Impasse over the Stage," *English Literary Renaissance* 21 (1991): 309–27; W. B. Worthen, *Shakespeare and the Authority of Performance* (Cambridge: Cambridge University Press, 1997); Genevieve Love, "'As from the waste of Sophonisba'; or, What's Sexy about Stage Directions," *Renaissance Drama*, n.s., 32 (2003): 3–31; and Margaret Jane Kidnie, *Shakespeare and the Problem of Adaptation* (London: Routledge, 2009).

9. Such textual "transparency" stands in contrast to theatrical manuscripts in the period, which I will not be addressing. In "'A bed / for woodstock': A Warning for the Unwary," *Medieval and Renaissance Drama in England* 2 (1985): 107, William B. Long explains that in manuscript plays "the motivating factor [for directions and notations] is noticeability," usually being written conspicuously for theatrical personnel.

10. Roland Barthes, "From Work to Text," in *Textual Strategies: Perspectives in Post-Structuralist Criticism*, ed. and trans. Josué V. Harari (Ithaca, N.Y.: Cornell University Press, 1979), 76. Although I do not address the authorial, theatrical, and/or printing house provenances of didascalia, the bibliographical criticism on the subject is substantial. See, for instance, Alan C. Dessen's chapter "Interpreting Stage Directions," in his *Elizabethan Stage Conventions and Modern Interpreters* (Cambridge: Cambridge University Press, 1984), 19–52; Antony Hammond, "Encounters of the Third Kind in Stage-Directions in Elizabethan and Jacobean Drama," *Studies in Philology* 89 (1992): 71–99, an astute and balanced discussion; E. A. J. Honigmann, "Re-Enter the Stage Direction: Shakespeare and Some Contemporaries," *Shakespeare Survey* 29 (1976): 117–25; T. H. Howard-Hill,

"The Evolution of the Form of Plays in English during the Renaissance," *Renaissance Quarterly* 43 (1990): 112–45; MacD. P. Jackson, "Stage Directions and Speech Headings in Act 1 of *Titus Andronicus* Q (1594): Shakespeare or Peele?" *Studies in Bibliography* 49 (1996): 134–48; Long, "'A bed / for Woodstock,'" 91–118; and William B. Long, "Stage-Directions: A Misinterpreted Factor in Determining Textual Provenance," *TEXT* 2 (1985): 121–37.

11. Aristotle, *Aristotle's Poetics*, 3.1448a20–24 (see chap. 1, n. 2). The quotation in my section title comes from Gary Taylor, general introduction to *William Shakespeare: A Textual Companion*, by Stanley Wells and Gary Taylor with John Jowett and William Montgomery (Oxford: Clarendon, 1987), 2. With the phrase "an invisible life-support system of stage directions," Taylor does not mean written or printed stage directions, but rather "an unwritten para-text [. . .] which Shakespeare could either expect his first readers [i.e., playhouse personnel] to supply, or which those first readers would expect Shakespeare himself to supply orally" (2).

12. McJannet, *Voice of Elizabethan Stage Directions*, 61 (see intro., n. 42).

13. Marvin Carlson, "The Status of Stage Directions," *Studies in the Literary Imagination* 24 (1991): 37.

14. Aebischer, "Didascalia and Speech," 26 (see intro., n. 12).

15. Ingarden, *Literary Work of Art*, 208 (see intro., n. 12), his emphases, my brackets.

16. Ibid., 208, his emphasis, 209.

17. Ibid., 209.

18. Ibid.

19. Ibid., his emphasis.

20. Derrida, *Truth in Painting*, 75 (see intro., n. 45), translators' brackets.

21. Patricia A. Suchy, "When Words Collide: The Stage Direction as Utterance," *Journal of Dramatic Theory and Criticism* 6 (1991): 77.

22. Carlson, "Status of Stage Directions," 39.

23. Aebischer, "Didascalia and Speech," 29, 28.

24. Suchy makes this point in her earlier article "When Words Collide," 77: "Linguistic function shifts with context," but she does not develop it as fully as Aebischer does.

25. Aebischer, "Didascalia and Speech," 28. McJannet would qualify this, however, since she shows how didascalia and their relation to marginality vary within a wide range of play-texts. She writes: "As it happens, what is 'marginal' or 'central' in the theoretical or figurative sense is not altogether decided by literal marginality or centrality on the page" (*Voice of Elizabethan Stage Directions*, 107). See also Evelyn B. Tribble, *Margins and Marginality: The Printed Page in Early Modern England* (Charlottesville: University Press of Virginia, 1993), 103.

26. Aebischer, "Didascalia and Speech," 32.

27. Ibid., her emphasis.

28. Ibid., 33, her emphasis. See also Kidnie, "Text, Performance, and the Editors," 462: "stage directions remain an element of the literary dramatic text as integral as dialogue." In "Evolution of the Form of Plays," 133, T. H. Howard-Hill notes that the first edition of Seneca in 1474 prints centered character lists that open each scene, but thereafter the text "does not indicate to whom subsequent speeches belong."

29. Suchy, "When Words Collide," 77; Alter, "Waiting for the Referent," 46.

30. McJannet, *Voice of Elizabethan Stage Directions*, 58.

31. Ibid., 106. Issacharoff, in "Inscribed Performance," 95–96, had earlier used the figure of the "voice," specifically that of the author, to characterize the authority of didascalia.

32. Pavis, "Remarques sur le discours théâtral," *Degrés* 6 (1978): 2, my translation.

33. Ingarden, *Literary Work of Art*, 209, his emphases. My epigraphs are from Ronald B. McKerrow, *Prolegomena for the Oxford Shakespeare: A Study in Editorial Method* (Oxford: Oxford University Press, 1939), 57; and Hammond, "Encounters of the Third Kind," 71.

34. Ibid., 208; Alter, "Waiting for the Referent," 46, his emphasis.

35. John Jowett, "From Print to Performance: Looking at the Masque in *Timon of Athens*," in Holland and Orgel, *From Performance to Print in Shakespeare's England*, 79.

36. Carlson, "Status of Stage Directions," 37.

37. McJannet, *Voice of Elizabethan Stage Directions*, 69.

38. Ibid.

39. Michel Foucault, "What Is an Author?" in *Textual Strategies: Perspectives in Post-Structuralist Criticism*, ed. and trans. Josué V. Harari (Ithaca, N.Y.: Cornell University Press, 1979), 150.

40. Ibid.

41. Ibid., 44.

42. Alter, "Waiting for the Referent," 46.

43. Harry Berger Jr., "What Did the King Know and When Did He Know It? Shakespearean Discourses and Psychoanalysis," *South Atlantic Quarterly* 88 (1989): 812. Other important studies of the coherency of the subject are Catherine Belsey, *The Subject of Tragedy: Identity and Difference in Renaissance Drama* (London: Routledge, 1985); and Alan Sinfield, *Faultlines: Cultural Materialism and the Politics of Dissident Reading* (Berkeley: University of California Press, 1992), esp. chap. 3.

44. Random Cloud, "'The very names of the Persons': Editing and the Invention of Dramatick Character," in *Staging the Renaissance: Reinterpretations of Elizabethan and Jacobean Drama*, ed. David Scott Kastan and Peter Stallybrass (New York: Routledge, 1991), 93. See also the extended version of this essay, titled "What's the Bastard's Name? Random Cloud," in *Shakespeare's Speech Headings: Speaking the Speech in Shakespeare's Plays*, ed. George Walton Williams (Newark: University of Delaware Press, 1997), 133–209.

45. In *The Struggle for Shakespeare's Text: Twentieth-Century Editorial Theory and Practice* (Cambridge: Cambridge University Press, 2010), 212–13, Gabriel Egan outlines a series of arguments and editorial experiments that have accentuated such variability.

46. Margreta de Grazia and Peter Stallybrass, "The Materiality of the Shakespearean Text," *Shakespeare Quarterly* 44 (1993): 268.

47. W. W. Greg, *A Bibliography of the English Printed Drama to the Restoration*, 4 vols. (London: Oxford University Press, 1939–59), 4.clx; McJannet, *Voice of Elizabethan Stage Directions*, 69.

48. C. H. Herford, Percy Simpson, and Evelyn Simpson, eds., *Ben Jonson*, 11 vols. (Oxford: Clarendon, 1925–52), 9.46.

49. McJannet, *Voice of Elizabethan Stage Directions*, 66–67.

50. Ibid., 68.

51. Jonson, SEIANVS HIS FALL (see chap. 2, n. 30); Ben Jonson, VOLPONE Or THE FOXE ([London:] for Thomas Thorppe, 1607); Ben Jonson, CATILINE *his* CONSPIRACY (London: for Walter Burre, 1611); Ben Jonson, THE ALCHEMIST (London: by Thomas Snodham, for Walter Burre, 1612). For more on Jonson's use of neoclassical textual conventions, see Herford, Simpson, and Simpson, *Ben Jonson*, 9.46–47. See also Peter M. Wright, "Jonson's Revision of the Stage Directions for the 1616 Folio *Works*," *Medieval and Renaissance Drama in England* 5 (1991): 257–85.

52. McJannet, *Voice of Elizabethan Stage Directions*, 57. McJannet describes here early texts printed in roman, but those printed in black letter tend to use roman and occasionally italic as contrasting typefaces, a point she makes in "Elizabethan Speech Prefixes: Page Design, Typography, and Mimesis," in *Reading and Writing in Shakespeare*, ed. David M. Bergeron (Newark: University of Delaware Press, 1996), 61n2. See, for instance, Ch. Marl., THE TRAGICALL *History of D. Faustus* (see chap. 2, n. 27), which for the most part uses black letter for dialogue, roman for speech headings, and italic for stage directions and Latin.

53. A number of medieval English dramatic manuscripts position speech headings in the right margin with horizontal rules that connect them to the speeches, including the earliest *Interludium de Clerico et Puella* as well as *The Castle of Perseverance* and the Northampton *Abraham and Isaac*, among others. See Howard-Hill, "Evolution of the Form of Plays," esp. 114–29; and McJannet, *Voice of Elizabethan Stage Directions*, 57–62.

54. Aristotle, *Aristotle's Poetics*, 10.1452a20–21, translator's emphases.

55. Jerome J. McGann, *The Textual Condition* (Princeton, N.J.: Princeton University Press, 1991), 113.

56. Throughout *The Voice of Elizabethan Stage Directions*, McJannet discusses at length this process of standardization in early modern printed drama. For an extensive look at the theatricality of entrances and exits in Renaissance plays, see Mariko Ichikawa, *Shakespearean Entrances* (Basingstoke: Palgrave Macmillan, 2002); and Fitzpatrick, *Playwright, Space and Place* (see intro, n. 24).

57. Shakespeare, *Tragedy of Richard the Third*, TLN 2 (see chap. 2, n. 66); Cyril Tourneur, THE ATHEIST'S TRAGEDIE: OR *The honest Man's Reuenge* (London: for Iohn Stepneth, and Richard Redmer, 1611), H4v. For an analysis of stage direction grammar throughout the period, see McJannet, *Voice of Elizabethan Stage Directions*, esp. "Part Two: The Grammar and Rhetoric of Elizabethan Stage Directions."

58. Richard Hosley, "The Gallery over the Stage in the Public Playhouse of Shakespeare's Time," *Shakespeare Quarterly* 8 (1957): 16–17.

59. Issacharoff, *Discourse as Performance*, 23, 24, 25 (see intro., n. 22).

60. Carlson, "Status of Stage Directions," 37, 39.

61. Hammond, "Encounters of the Third Kind," 73–77.

62. Ibid., 73. Bruce R. Smith makes a similar argument regarding "physiological" v. "syntactical" punctuation marks in "Prickly Characters," in Bergeron, *Reading and Writing in Shakespeare*, 25–44.

63. John Webster, THE TRAGEDY OF THE DVTCHESSE *Of Malfy* (London: by Nicholas Okes, for Iohn Waterson, 1623), F4r. Subsequent citations appear in the text. In "The Printing of John Webster's Plays (II)," *Studies in Bibliography* 8 (1956):

118–19, John Russell Brown shows through his collation that the stage direction about Ferdinand's poniard is a stop-press correction that is missing in three extant copies, and Hammond, "Encounters of the Third Kind," 95, notes that it is not until the 1708 Q4 that an entry direction for Ferdinand is added.

64. Hammond, "Encounters of the Third Kind," 95, his emphasis.

65. Stanley Wells, *Re-Editing Shakespeare for the Modern Reader* (Oxford: Clarendon, 1984), 68, 75, 76, his emphasis. It is worth noting that, in "The Printing of John Webster's Plays (I)," *Studies in Bibliography* 6 (1954): 133, John Russell Brown writes of "the care taken with the nomenclature in speech directions and stage directions" in *THE DVTCHESSE Of Malfy*.

66. Shakespeare, *Much adoe about Nothing* (1623), TLN 2–3, 415–16 (see chap. 2, n. 56). Except for lineation and two majuscules, the first direction in the 1600 quarto is identical: "*Enter Leonato gouernour of Messina, Innogen his wife, Hero | his daughter, and Beatrice his neece, with a | messenger*," while the second direction only alters spacing: "*Enter Leonato,his brother,his wife,Hero his daughter,and | Beatrice his neece,and a kinsman*" (Shakespeare, *Much adoe about Nothing* [1600], A2r, B3r [see chap. 2, n. 59]).

67. N. Rowe, ed., *THE WORKS OF Mr. William Shakespear*, 6 vols. (London: for Jacob Tonson, 1709), 1.Y1v.

68. Lewis Theobald, ed., *THE WORKS OF SHAKESPEARE*, 7 vols. (London: for A. Bettesworth and C. Hitch, J. Tonson, F. Clay, W. Feales, and R. Wellington, 1733), 1.Dd2r n. 1.

69. John Payne Collier, ed., *THE WORKS OF WILLIAM SHAKESPEARE*, 8 vols. (London: Whittaker & Co., 1842), 2.187 n. 1; Alexander Dyce, *A FEW NOTES ON SHAKESPEARE* (London: John Russell Smith, 1853), 37, his emphasis; and Horace Howard Furness, ed., *A NEW VARIORUM EDITION OF SHAKESPEARE* (Philadelphia: J. B. Lippincott Company, 1899), 7.

70. Furness, *A NEW VARIORUM*, 7. In "'Surpris'd with all': Rereading Character in *Much Ado about Nothing*," in *Second Thoughts: A Focus on Rereading*, ed. David Galef (Detroit: Wayne State University Press, 1998), 242–243n6, David Weil Baker suggests, "The source for Innogen may be Messer Lionato's unnamed wife in 'La Prima Parte de le Nouvelle del Bandello,'" and he directs the reader to this text in Geoffrey Bullough, *Narrative and Dramatic Sources of Shakespeare*, 8 vols. (London: Routledge and Kegan Paul, 1957–1975), 2.112–134.

71. Michael D. Friedman, "'Hush'd on Purpose to Grace Harmony': Wives and Silence in *Much Ado About Nothing*," *Theatre Journal* 42 (1990): 360, 360–61. In note 41, Friedman also lists three productions in 1896, 1903, and 1971 that retained Innogen as a character. In his "Shakespeare in Production" edition (William Shakespeare, *Much Ado About Nothing*, ed. John F. Cox [Cambridge: Cambridge University Press, 1998], 87), Cox mentions only that "[Augustin] Daly's initial stage direction (1896) included Leonato's wife Innogen, as in Q"; and in William Shakespeare, *Much Ado About Nothing*, ed. Barbara Mowat and Paul Werstine (New York: Washington Square Press, 2005), 199, the editors suggest that Innogen's "presence in this opening scene when Benedick jokes about her possible adultery, and her silence in the wedding scene as Hero is being attacked, would certainly alter the tone of the play." See also Alison Findlay, *The Shakespeare Handbooks: Much Ado About Nothing* (Basingstoke: Palgrave Macmillan, 2011), esp. 3, 9–10.

72. See Kristian Smidt, "Shakespeare's Absent Characters," *English Studies* 61 (1980): 397–407, esp. 399, in which Smidt discusses numerous "ghost characters," including three others besides Innogen in *Much adoe about Nothing*.

73. Ingarden, *Literary Work of Art*, 209. My epigraph is from Eric Rasmussen, afterword to *Stage Directions in* Hamlet: *New Essays and New Directions*, ed. Hardin L. Aasand (Madison, N.J.: Fairleigh Dickinson University Press, 2003), 226.

74. Herbert Blau, "Universals of Performance; or, Amortizing Play," *SubStance* 11–12, nos. 37–38 (1982–1983): 143; Jonathan Goldberg, *Writing Matter: From the Hands of the English Renaissance* (Stanford, Calif.: Stanford University Press, 1990), 251.

75. McJannet, *Voice of Elizabethan Stage Directions*, 17, her emphasis.

76. Ibid., 118. *The Castle of Perseverance*, in *The Macro Plays:* The Castle of Perseverance, Wisdom, Mankind*; A Facsimile Edition with Facing Transcriptions*, ed. David Bevington (New York: Johnson Reprint Corp., 1972), 29, line 614 s.d., my emphasis, which McJannet cites in *Voice of Elizabethan Stage Directions*, 119; the line in ms. reads: "tūc ascend[et] hūanū gē[us] ad mūdū" (Bevington 28), with brevigraphs in the bracketed portions.

77. McJannet, *Voice of Elizabethan Stage Directions*, 120.

78. Ibid., 137.

79. Pierre Corneille, "Of the Three Unities of Action, Time, and Place," trans. Donald Schier, in *Critical Theory Since Plato*, ed. Hazard Adams (New York: Harcourt Brace Jovanovich, 1971), 222–23. Pierre Corneille, "Discours des trois unités d'action, de jour et de lieu," in *Trois discours sur le Poème dramatique (Texte de 1660)*, 2nd ed., ed. Louis Forestier (Paris: Société d'Édition d'Enseignement Supérieur, 1982), 135–36:

> Je serais d'avis que le poëte prît grand soin de marquer à la marge les menues actions qui ne méritent pas qu'il en charge ses vers, et qui leur ôteraient même quelque chose de leur dignité, s'il se ravalait à les exprimer. Le comédien y supplée aisément sur le théâtre; mais sur le livre on serait assez souvent réduit à deviner, et quelquefois même on pourrait deviner mal, à moins que d'être instruit par là de ces petites choses.

80. McJannet, *Voice of Elizabethan Stage Directions*, 17.

81. It should be noted that plenty of unnamed mutes populate the early modern stage and are still taken to be dramatically "real," though I might argue that their unspoken presence is but another form of supplementation since they ratify the social privilege of the named and titled characters on whom they attend simply by being superfluously at the ready. See Arthur Colby Sprague, "Shakespeare's Unnecessary Characters," *Shakespeare Survey* 20 (1967): 75–82.

82. Aebischer, "Didascalia and Speech," 32.

83. William Shakespeare, *THE TRAGEDIE OF KING LEAR*, in *MR. WILLIAM SHAKESPEARES COMEDIES, HISTORIES, & TRAGEDIES* (London: by Isaac Iaggard and Ed. Blount, 1623), TLN 1886–87. Subsequent citations appear in the text.

BIBLIOGRAPHY

The Actors Remonstrance. London: for Edw. Nickson, 1643.

Aebischer, Pascale. "Didascalia and Speech in the Dramatic Text." *Journal of Dramatic Theory and Criticism* 17, no. 2 (2003): 25–44.

Alciat, Andre. *Les Emblemes*. Paris: by Christian Wechel, 1540.

Alciati, Andree. *Emblematum liber*. Augsburg: by Heinrich Steyner, 1531.

Alciato. *Diverse Imprese*. Lyon: by Gvlielmo Rovillio, 1564.

Alciato at Glasgow. Glasgow University Library. Accessed July 12, 2016. http://www.emblems.arts.gla.ac.uk/alciato/emblem.php?id=A31a092.

Alciato's Book of Emblems: *Memorial Web Edition in Latin and English*. Edited by William Barker, Mark Feltham, and Jean Guthrie. Department of English, Memorial University of Newfoundland. Last modified April 26, 2005. http://www.mun.ca/alciato/.

Allen, John A. "Dogberry." *Shakespeare Quarterly* 24 (1973): 35–53.

Alter, Jean. "From Text to Performance: Semiotics of Theatrality [*sic*]." *Poetics Today* 2 (1981): 113–39.

———. "Waiting for the Referent: Waiting for Godot? On Referring in Theatre." In *On Referring in Literature*, edited by Anna Whiteside and Michael Issacharoff, 42–56. Bloomington: Indiana University Press, 1987.

Altman, Joel B. *The Tudor Play of Mind: Rhetorical Inquiry and the Development of Elizabethan Drama*. Berkeley: University of California Press, 1978.

Andrews, E. A., Charleton T. Lewis, and Charles Short, eds. *Harper's Latin Dictionary*. New York: American Book Company, 1907.

Ardolino, Frank R. *Thomas Kyd's Mystery Play: Myth and Ritual in "The Spanish Tragedy."* New York: Peter Lang, 1985.

Aristotle. *Aristotle's Poetics: A Translation and Commentary for Students of Literature*. Translated by Leon Golden. Commentary by O. B. Hardison Jr. Englewood Cliffs, N.J.: Prentice-Hall, 1968.

———. *Poetics*. Edited and translated by Stephen Halliwell. Cambridge: Harvard University Press, 1995.

Arnold, Ethel M. "An Explanation of the Use of Off-Stage Scenes in Shakespearean Drama." M.A. thesis, Colorado State Teachers College, 1933.

Astington, John H. "Malvolio and the Dark House." *Shakespeare Survey* 41 (1989): 55–62.

Bache, William B. "Hamlet, Macbeth, and Lear Offstage: The Significance of Absence." *Dalhousie Review* 59 (1979): 308–20.

Bachelard, Gaston. *The Poetics of Space*. Translated by Maria Jolas. Boston: Beacon Press, 1964.

Baker, David Weil. "'Surpris'd with all': Rereading Character in *Much Ado about Nothing*." In *Second Thoughts: A Focus on Rereading*, edited by David Galef, 228–45. Detroit: Wayne State University Press, 1998.

Barish, Jonas A. *The Antitheatrical Prejudice*. Berkeley: University of California Press, 1981.

Barrett, James. *Staged Narrative: Poetics and the Messenger in Greek Tragedy*. Berkeley: University of California Press, 2002.

Barthes, Roland. "From Work to Text." In *Textual Strategies: Perspectives in Post-Structuralist Criticism*, edited and translated by Josué V. Harari, 73–81. Ithaca, N.Y.: Cornell University Press, 1979.

———. *Image, Music, Text*. Translated by Stephen Heath. New York: Hill and Wang, 1977.

———. *S/Z: An Essay*. Translated by Richard Miller. New York: Hill and Wang, 1974.

Bathurst, Ralph. "On the Death of Mr. WILLIAM CARTVVRIGHT, and the now publishing of his POEMS." In William Cartwright, *COMEDIES, TRAGI-COMEDIES, With other POEMS*. London: for Humphrey Moseley, 1651. Sigs. **1v–**2v.

Belsey, Catherine. *The Subject of Tragedy: Identity and Difference in Renaissance Drama*. London: Routledge, 1985.

Berger, Harry Jr. "Against the Sink-a-Pace: Sexual and Family Politics in *Much Ado About Nothing*." *Shakespeare Quarterly* 33 (1982): 302–13.

———. *Imaginary Audition: Shakespeare on Stage and Page*. Berkeley: University of California Press, 1989.

———. "What Did the King Know and When Did He Know It? Shakespearean Discourses and Psychoanalysis." *South Atlantic Quarterly* 88 (1989): 811–62.

Bergeron, David M., ed. *Reading and Writing in Shakespeare*. Newark: University of Delaware Press, 1996.

Berry, Francis. *The Shakespeare Inset: Word and Picture*. Carbondale: Southern Illinois University Press, 1965.

Bethell, S. L. *Shakespeare and the Popular Dramatic Tradition*. London: Staples Press, 1944.

Bevington, David, ed. *The Macro Plays:* The Castle of Perseverance, Wisdom, Mankind; *A Facsimile Edition with Facing Transcriptions*. New York: Johnson Reprint, 1972.

Blatherwick, Simon. "The Archeological Evaluation of the Globe Playhouse." In Mulryne and Shewring, *Shakespeare's Globe Rebuilt*, 67–80.

Blau, Herbert. "Universals of Performance; or, Amortizing Play." *SubStance* 11–12, nos. 37–38 (1982–1983): 140–61.

"The Booke of Sir Thomas Moore." Harley MS. 7368. British Library, London.

Botelho, Keith M. *Renaissance Earwitnesses: Rumor and Early Modern Masculinity*. New York: Palgrave Macmillan, 2009.

Bowsher, Julian M. C. "The Rose and Its Stages." *Shakespeare Survey* 60 (2007): 36–48.

———. *The Rose Theatre: An Archaeological Discovery*. London: Museum of London Archaeology, 1998.

———. *Shakespeare's London Theatreland: Archaeology, History and Drama*. London: Museum of London Archaeology, 2012.

Bowsher, Julian M. C., and Simon Blatherwick. "The Structure of the Rose." In *New Issues in the Reconstruction of Shakespeare's Theater: Proceedings of the Conference Held at the University of Georgia, February 16–18, 1990*, edited by Franklin J. Hildy, 55–78. New York: Peter Lang, 1990.

Bowsher, Julian M. C., and Pat Miller. *The Rose and the Globe—Playhouses of Shakespeare's Bankside, Southwark: Excavations 1988–91*. London: Museum of London Archaeology, 2009.

Bradbrook, M. C. *Elizabethan Stage Conditions: A Study of Their Place in the Interpretation of Shakespeare's Plays*. London: Cambridge University Press, 1968.

Braines, W. W. *The Site of the Globe Playhouse, Southwark*. 2nd ed. London: Hodder and Stoughton, 1924.

Brecht, Bertolt. "Alienation Effects in Chinese Acting." In Brecht, *Brecht on Theatre*, 91–99.

———. *Brecht on Theatre: The Development of an Aesthetic*, edited and translated by John Willett. New York: Hill and Wang, 1992.

———. *The Messingkauf Dialogues*. Translated by John Willett. London: Methuen, 1965.

———. "Short Description of a New Technique of Acting which Produces an Alienation Effect." In Brecht, *Brecht on Theatre*, 136–47.

———. "A Short Organum for the Theatre." In Brecht, *Brecht on Theatre*, 179–205.

Brennan, Anthony. *Onstage and Offstage Worlds in Shakespeare's Plays*. London: Routledge, 1989.

Bristol, Michael D. "Vernacular Criticism and the Scenes Shakespeare Never Wrote." Special issue, *Shakespeare and Narrative*, edited by Peter Holland, *Shakespeare Survey* 53 (2000): 89–102.

Brown, John Russell. "The Printing of John Webster's Plays (I)," *Studies in Bibliography* 6 (1954): 117–40.

———. "The Printing of John Webster's Plays (II)," *Studies in Bibliography* 8 (1956): 113–27.

———. *Shakespeare and the Theatrical Event*. Basingstoke, UK: Palgrave Macmillan, 2002.

Bullough, Geoffrey. *Narrative and Dramatic Sources of Shakespeare*. 8 vols. London: Routledge and Kegan Paul, 1957–1975.

Bush, George W. "President Welcomes President Chirac to White House." News release. November 6, 2001. The White House: President George W. Bush. http://www.whitehouse.gov/news/releases/2001/11/20011106-4.html [content no longer available].

Buttes, Henry. *DYETS DRY DINNER*. London: by Tho. Creede, for William Wood, 1599.

Calderwood, James. *Metadrama in Shakespeare's Henriad: Richard II to Henry V*. Berkeley: University of California Press, 1979.

Callebat, Louis. "Rhétorique et Architecture dans le 'De Architectvra' de Vitruve." In *Le Projet de Vitruve: Objet, Destinataires et Réception du* De Architectura. Actes du colloque international (Rome, 26–27 March 1993). Rome: École Française de Rome, 1994. 31–46.

Carlson, Marvin. "Indexical Space in the Theatre." *Assaph* 10 (1994): 1–10.

———. *Places of Performance: The Semiotics of Theatre Architecture*. Ithaca, N.Y.: Cornell University Press, 1989.

———. "The Status of Stage Directions," *Studies in the Literary Imagination* 24 (1991): 37–48.

———. "Theatrical Performance: Illustration, Translation, Fulfillment, or Supplement?" *Theatre Journal* 37 (1985): 5–11.

Castelvetro, Lodovico. *Castelvetro on the Art of Poetry*. Translated by Andrew Bongiorno. Binghamton: State University of New York Press, 1984.

Cauthen, Irby B. Jr. Introduction to *Gorboduc or Ferrex and Porrex*, by Thomas Sackville and Thomas Norton, edited by Irby B. Cauthen Jr., xi–xxx. Lincoln: University of Nebraska Press, 1970.

Cerasano, S. P. "Raising a Playhouse from the Dust." *Shakespeare Quarterly* 40 (1989): 483–90.

Chambers, E. K. *The Elizabethan Stage*. 4 vols. Oxford: Clarendon Press, 1923.

Charney, Maurice. "Asides, Soliloquies, and Offstage Speech in *Hamlet:* Implications for Staging." In *Shakespeare and the Sense of Performance: Essays in the Tradition of Performance Criticism in Honor of Bernard Beckerman*, edited by Marvin Thompson and Ruth Thompson, 116–131. Newark: University of Delaware Press, 1989.

———. "The Stage Situation of Asides, Soliloquies, and Offstage Speech in *Hamlet.*" *Shakespeare Bulletin* 4, no. 3 (1986): 5–8.

[Chettle, Henry] H. C. *KIND-HARTS DREAME*. London: for William Wright, [?1593].

Cicero. *De Inventione*. Translated by H. M. Hubbell. Cambridge, Mass.: Harvard University Press, 1949.

———. *De Oratore*. 2 vols. Translated by E. W. Sutton and H. Rackham. Cambridge, Mass.: Harvard University Press, 1959.

Cloud, Random. "'The very names of the Persons': Editing and the Invention of Dramatick Character." In *Staging the Renaissance: Reinterpretations of Elizabethan and Jacobean Drama*, edited by David Scott Kastan and Peter Stallybrass, 88–96. New York: Routledge, 1991.

———. "What's the Bastard's Name? Random Cloud." In *Shakespeare's Speech Headings: Speaking the Speech in Shakespeare's Plays*, edited by George Walton Williams, 133–209. Newark: University of Delaware Press, 1997.

Collier, John Payne, ed. *THE WORKS OF WILLIAM SHAKESPEARE*. 8 vols. London: Whittaker & Co., 1842.

Corneille, Pierre. "Discours des trois unités d'action, de jour et de lieu." In *Trois discours sur le Poème dramatique (Texte de 1660)*, 2nd ed. Edited by Louis Forestier. Paris: Société d'Édition d'Enseignement Supérieur, 1982.

———. "Of the Three Unities of Action, Time, and Place." Translated by Donald Schier. In *Critical Theory Since Plato*, edited by Hazard Adams, 219–226. New York: Harcourt Brace Jovanovich, 1971.

Coulon, Aurélie. "Le sujet hors-scène." *Agôn: Revue des arts de la scène*. No. 0 (2007): 59 pars. August 19, 2015. http://agon.ens-lyon.fr/index.php?id=305.

Counsell, Colin. *Signs of Performance: An Introduction to Twentieth-Century Theatre*. London: Routledge, 1996.

Daileader, Celia R. *Eroticism on the Renaissance Stage: Transcendence, Desire, and the Limits of the Visible*. Cambridge: Cambridge University Press, 1998.

Daly, Peter M., with Virginia W. Callahan, eds. *Index emblematicus: Andreas Alciatus*. 2 vols. Toronto: University of Toronto Press, 1985.

Dawson, Anthony B. "The Impasse over the Stage." *English Literary Renaissance* 21 (1991): 309–27.

Day, Iohn. *THE ILE OF GVLS*. London: by Iohn Hodgets, 1606.

Deckar, T. *THE GVLS Horne-booke*. London: for R.S., 1609.

de Grazia, Margreta, and Peter Stallybrass. "The Materiality of the Shakespearean Text." *Shakespeare Quarterly* 44 (1993): 255–83.

de Jong, Irene J. F. *Narrative in Drama: The Art of the Euripidean Messenger-Speech*. Leiden: Brill, 1991.

Dekker, Tho. *THE MAGNIFICENT Entertainment*. London: by T.C. for Tho. Man the yonger, 1604.

Dekker, Thomas. *IF IT BE NOT GOOD, The Diuel is in it*. London: for I.T., by Edward Marchant, 1612.

———. *THE VVHORE OF Babylon*. London: for Nathaniel Butter, 1607.

Derrida, Jacques. *The Truth in Painting*. Translated by Geoff Bennington and Ian McLeod. Chicago: University of Chicago Press, 1987.

Dessen, Alan C. *Elizabethan Drama and the Viewer's Eye*. Chapel Hill: University of North Carolina Press, 1977.

———. *Elizabethan Stage Conventions and Modern Interpreters*. Cambridge: Cambridge University Press, 1984.

Dessen, Alan C., and Leslie Thomson. *A Dictionary of Stage Directions in English Drama, 1580–1642*. Cambridge: Cambridge University Press, 1999.

Dollimore, Jonathan. *Radical Tragedy: Religion, Ideology, and Power in the Drama of Shakespeare and His Contemporaries*. 2nd ed. Durham, N.C.: Duke University Press, 1993.

Donatus, Aelius. *De comoedia*. In Nugent, "Ancient Theories of Comedy," 271–75.

Draiton, Michaell. *POEMS*. London: for N. Ling, 1605.

Dutton, Richard. "*Hamlet, An Apology for Actors*, and the Sign of the Globe." *Shakespeare Survey* 41 (1988): 35–43.

Dyce, Alexander. *A FEW NOTES ON SHAKESPEARE*. London: John Russell Smith, 1853.

Eccles, Christine. *The Rose Playhouse*. London: Nick Hern, 1990.

Edmond, Mary. "The Builder of the Rose Theatre." *Theatre Notebook* 44 (1990): 50–54.

———. "Peter Street, 1553–1609: Builder of Playhouses." *Shakespeare Survey* 45 (1992): 101–14.

Egan, Gabriel. "Hearing or Seeing a Play? Evidence of Early Modern Theatrical Terminology." *Ben Jonson Journal* 8 (2001): 327–47.

———. "The Situation of the 'Lords Room': A Revaluation." *Review of English Studies* 48 (1997): 297–309.

———. *The Struggle for Shakespeare's Text: Twentieth-Century Editorial Theory and Practice*. Cambridge: Cambridge University Press, 2010.

Elam, Keir. *The Semiotics of Theatre and Drama*. 2nd ed. London: Routledge, 2001.

Else, Gerald F. *Plato and Aristotle on Poetry*. Edited by Peter Burian. Chapel Hill: University of North Carolina Press, 1986.

Enders, Jody. "Performing Miracles: The Mysterious Mimesis of Valenciennes (1547)." In *Theatricality*, edited by Tracy C. Davis and Thomas Postlewait, 40–64. Cambridge: Cambridge University Press, 2003.

Evanthius. *De fabula*. In Nugent, "Ancient Theories of Comedy," 267–71.

Fennor, William. *FENNORS Descriptions*. London: by Edvvard Griffin, for George Gibbs, 1616.

Findlay, Alison. *The Shakespeare Handbooks: Much Ado About Nothing*. Basingstoke, UK: Palgrave Macmillan, 2011.

Fitzpatrick, Tim. "From Archaeological Remains to Onion Dome: At the Upper Limits of Speculation." *Shakespeare* 7 (2011): 432–51.

———. *Playwright, Space and Place in Early Modern Performance*. Farnham, UK: Ashgate, 2011.

Fleay, Frederick Gard. *A Chronicle History of the London Stage 1559–1642*. London: Reeves and Turner, 1890.

Flecknoe, Richard. *A Short* DISCOURSE *of the English Stage*. London: by R. Wood for the Author, 1664.

Foakes, R. A. "The Discovery of the Rose Theatre: Some Implications." *Shakespeare Survey* 43 (1991): 141–48.

Foakes, R. A., and R. T. Rickert, eds. *Henslowe's Diary*. Cambridge: Cambridge University Press, 1961.

Ford, Andrew. "*Katharsis:* The Ancient Problem." In *Performativity and Performance*, edited by Andrew Parker and Eve Kosofsky Sedgwick, 109–32. New York: Routledge, 1995.

[Ford, John.] *THE CHRONICLE HISTORIE OF PERKIN VVARBECK. A Strange Truth*. London: by T.P. for Hugh Beeston, 1634.

Forty, Adrian. *Words and Buildings: A Vocabulary of Modern Architecture*. London: Thames and Hudson, 2000.

Foucault, Michel. "What Is an Author?" Translated by Josué V. Harari. In *Textual Strategies: Perspectives in Post-Structuralist Criticism*, edited by Josué V. Harari, 141–60. Ithaca, N.Y.: Cornell University Press, 1979.

Frankl, Paul. "The Secret of the Mediaeval Masons." *Art Bulletin* 27 (1945): 46–60.

Friedman, Michael D. "'Hush'd on Purpose to Grace Harmony': Wives and Silence in *Much Ado About Nothing*." *Theatre Journal* 42 (1990): 350–63.

Furness, Horace Howard, ed. *A NEW VARIORUM EDITION OF SHAKESPEARE*. Philadelphia: J. B. Lippincott Company, 1899.

Goffman, Erving. *Frame Analysis*. Harmondsworth, UK: Penguin, 1974.

Goldberg, Jonathan. *Writing Matter: From the Hands of the English Renaissance*. Stanford, Calif.: Stanford University Press, 1990.

Gordon, D. J. "Poet and Architect: The Intellectual Setting of the Quarrel between Ben Jonson and Inigo Jones." *Journal of the Warburg and Courtauld Institutes* 12 (1949): 152–78.

Greenberg, Nathan A. *The Poetic Theory of Philodemus*. New York: Garland, 1990.

Greenblatt, Stephen, Walter Cohen, Jean E. Howard, and Katharine Eisaman Maus, eds. *The Norton Shakespeare*. New York: W. W. Norton, 1997.

Greenfield, Jon. "Design as Reconstruction: Reconstruction as Design." In Mulryne and Shewring, *Shakespeare's Globe Rebuilt*, 81–96.

———. "Reconstructing the Rose: Development of the Playhouse Building between 1587 and 1592." *Shakespeare Survey* 60 (2007): 23–35.

———. "Timber Framing, the Two Bays and After." In Mulryne and Shewring, *Shakespeare's Globe Rebuilt*, 97–120.

Greenfield, Thelma N. *The Induction in Elizabethan Drama*. Eugene: University of Oregon Books, 1969.

Greer, Germaine. "The Offstage Mob: Shakespeare's Proletariat." In *Shakespeare and Cultural Traditions*, edited by Tetsuo Kishi, Roger Pringle, and Stanley W. Wells, 54–75. Newark: University of Delaware Press, 1994.

Greg, W. W. *A Bibliography of the English Printed Drama to the Restoration*. 4 vols. London: Oxford University Press, 1939–59.

———. *Dramatic Documents from the Elizabethan Playhouses: Stage Plots, Actors' Parts, Prompt Books*. 2 vols. Oxford: Clarendon, 1931.

———, ed. *Henslowe Papers: Being Documents Supplementary to Henslowe's Diary*. London: A. H. Bullen, 1907.

———. "Notes on Old Books," *The Library*, 4th ser., 2 (1922): 49–57.

Gruber, William. *Offstage Space, Narrative, and the Theatre of the Imagination*. New York: Palgrave Macmillan, 2010.

Güçbilmez, Beliz. "An Uncanny Theatricality: The Representation of the Offstage." *New Theatre Quarterly* 23 (2007): 152–60.

Gurr, Andrew. "A First Doorway into the Globe." *Shakespeare Quarterly* 41 (1990): 97–100.

———. *Playgoing in Shakespeare's London*. 3rd ed. Cambridge: Cambridge University Press, 2004.

———. "The Shakespearean Stage." In Greenblatt et al., *Norton Shakespeare*, 3281–3301.

———. *The Shakespearean Stage 1574–1642*. 4th ed. Cambridge: Cambridge University Press, 2009.

———. "The Shakespearian Stages, Forty Years On." *Shakespeare Survey* 41 (1989): 1–12.

———. "The 'State' of Shakespeare's Audiences." In *Shakespeare and the Sense of Performance: Essays in the Tradition of Performance Criticism in Honor of Bernard Beckerman*, edited by Marvin Thompson and Ruth Thompson, 162–79. Newark: University of Delaware Press, 1989.

Hammond, Antony. "Encounters of the Third Kind in Stage-Directions in Elizabethan and Jacobean Drama." *Studies in Philology* 89 (1992): 71–99.

Hardison, O. B. Jr. "A Commentary on Aristotle's *Poetics*." In Aristotle, *Aristotle's Poetics*, 53–296.

Hardy, Barbara. *Shakespeare's Storytellers: Dramatic Narration*. London: Peter Owen, 1997.

Harris, Richard. *Discovering Timber-framed Buildings*. 2nd ed. Aylesbury, UK: Shire Publications, 1979.

Herford, C. H., Percy Simpson, and Evelyn Simpson, eds. *Ben Jonson*. 11 vols. Oxford: Clarendon, 1925–52.

Herodotus. *The Persian Wars*. 4 vols. Translated by A. D. Godley. Cambridge, Mass.: Harvard University Press, 1920.

Heywood, Thomas. *AN APOLOGY For Actors*. London: by Nicholas Okes, 1612.

Hicks, Margaret R. "*Dentro:* The Imaginary World Offstage in Lope de Vega's Early Plays." In *Looking at the* Comedia *in the Year of the Quincentennial*, edited by Barbara Mujica, Sharon D. Voros, and Matthew D. Stroud, 69–74. Lanham, Md.: University Press of America, 1993.

Hilts, Carly. "Raising the Curtain: Excavating Shakespeare's Lost Playhouse." *Current Archaeology* 269 (2012): 10–13.

Hinman, Charlton, ed. *The Norton Facsimile: The First Folio of Shakespeare.* New York: W.W. Norton, 1968.

Hobson, Martha Barbour. "Action behind the Scenes in Shakespeare and in Ibsen." M.A. thesis, University of Chicago, 1918.

———. "The Development of Off-Stage Action in the English Drama." Ph.D. thesis, Northwestern University, 1932.

Holinshed, Raphael [et al.]. *THE Third volume of Chronicles*. London, 1587.

Holland, Peter, ed. *Shakespeare and Narrative*. Spec. issue of *Shakespeare Survey* 53 (2000): 1–357.

———. "'Travelling Hopefully': The Dramatic Form of Journeys in English Renaissance Drama." In *Travel and Drama in Shakespeare's Time*, edited by Jean-Pierre Maquerlot and Michèle Willems, 160–78. Cambridge: Cambridge University Press, 1996.

Holland, Peter, and Stephen Orgel, eds. *From Performance to Print in Shakespeare's England*. Basingstoke, UK: Palgrave Macmillan, 2006.

Honigmann, E. A. J. "Re-Enter the Stage Direction: Shakespeare and Some Contemporaries." *Shakespeare Survey* 29 (1976): 117–25.

Hooper, Wilfrid. "The Tudor Sumptuary Laws." *English Historical Review* 30 (1915): 433–49.

Hopkins, Lisa. *John Ford's Political Theatre*. Manchester: Manchester University Press, 1994.

Horace. *Ars Poetica*. In *Horace for Students of Literature: The* "Ars Poetica" *and Its Tradition*, translated by Leon Golden, edited by Leon Golden and O. B. Hardison Jr. Gainesville: University Press of Florida, 1995.

———. *Satires, Epistles, and Ars Poetica*. Translated by H. Rushton Fairclough. Cambridge, Mass.: Harvard University Press, 1999.

Hosley, Richard. "The Gallery over the Stage in the Public Playhouse of Shakespeare's Time." *Shakespeare Quarterly* 8 (1957): 15–31.

Howard, Jean E. *The Stage and Social Struggle in Early Modern England*. London: Routledge, 1994.

Howard-Hill, T. H. "The Evolution of the Form of Plays in English during the Renaissance." *Renaissance Quarterly* 43 (1990): 112–45.

Hunter, G. K. Introduction to *The Malcontent*, by John Marston, edited by G. K. Hunter. Manchester, UK: Manchester University Press, 1999.

Hutson, Lorna. *The Invention of Suspicion: Law and Mimesis in Shakespeare and Renaissance Drama*. Oxford: Oxford University Press, 2007.

———. "Law, Probability and Character in Shakespeare." In *Fictions of Knowledge: Fact, Evidence, Doubt*, edited by Yota Batski, Subha Mukherji, and Jan-Melissa Schramm, 61–83. New York: Palgrave Macmillan, 2012.

Ichikawa, Mariko. *Shakespearean Entrances*. Basingstoke, UK: Palgrave Macmillan, 2002.

———. *The Shakespearean Stage Space*. Cambridge: Cambridge University Press, 2013.

Ingarden, Roman. *The Literary Work of Art: An Investigation on the Borderlines of Ontology, Logic, and Theory of Literature; With an Appendix on the Functions of Language in the Theater*. Translated by George G. Grabowicz. Evanston, Ill.: Northwestern University Press, 1973.

Issacharoff, Michael. *Discourse as Performance*. Stanford, Calif.: Stanford University Press, 1989.

———. "Inscribed Performance." *Rivista di Letterature moderne e comparate* 39 (1986): 93–106.

———. "Space and Reference in Drama." *Poetics Today* 2 (1981): 211–24.

Jackson, MacD. P. "Stage Directions and Speech Headings in Act 1 of *Titus Andronicus* Q (1594): Shakespeare or Peele?" *Studies in Bibliography* 49 (1996): 134–48.

Jagger, Mick, and Keith Richards. "Wild Horses." Performed by the Rolling Stones on *Sticky Fingers*. Rolling Stones Records, COC 59100. Recorded April 23, 1971.

Janko, Richard. *Aristotle: Poetics*. Indianapolis: Hackett, 1987.

———. "Philodemus' *On Poems* and Aristotle's *On Poets*." *Cronache Ercolanesi* 21 (1991): 5–64.

Jansen, Steen. "Le Rôle de l'espace scénique dans la lecture du texte dramatique." In *Semiotics of Drama and Theatre*, edited by Herta Schmid and Aloysius van Kesteren, 254–89. Amsterdam: John Benjamins, 1984.

Johnson, Samuel. *Mr. Johnson's* PREFACE *To his* EDITION *of Shakespear's Plays*. London: for J. and R. Tonson, H. Woodfall, J. Rivington, R. Baldwin, L. Hawes, Clark and Collins, T. Longman, W. Johnston, T. Caslon, C. Corbet, T. Lownds, and the Executors of B. Dodd, 1765.

Jones, Ann Rosalind, and Peter Stallybrass. *Renaissance Clothing and the Materials of Memory*. Cambridge: Cambridge University Press, 2000.

Jones, Norman, and Paul Whitfield White. "*Gorboduc* and Royal Marriage Politics: An Elizabethan Playgoer's Report of the Premiere Performance." *English Literary Renaissance* 26 (1996): 3–17.

Jonson, Ben. *THE ALCHEMIST*. London: by Thomas Snodham, for Walter Burre, 1612.

———. *BARTHOLMEW FAYRE*. In *THE VVORKES OF BENIAMIN IONSON*. *The second Volume*. London: for Richard Meighen, 1640. A2r–M4v.

———. *CATILINE his CONSPIRACY*. London: for Walter Burre, 1611.

———. *THE DIUELL IS AN ASSE*. In *THE VVORKES OF BENIAMIN IONSON*. *The second Volume*. London: for Richard Meighen, 1640. N1r–Y4v.

———. *EVERY MAN OVT OF HIS HVMOR*. London: for Nicholas Linge, 1600.

———. *SEIANVS HIS FALL*. London: by G. Elld, for Thomas Thorpe, 1605.

———. *VOLPONE Or THE FOXE*. [London:] for Thomas Thorppe, 1607.

Jowett, John. "From Print to Performance: Looking at the Masque in *Timon of Athens*." In Holland and Orgel, *From Performance to Print*, 73–91.

Kennedy, Maev. "Did Shakespeare Write *Henry V* to Suit London Theatre's Odd Shape?" *Guardian*. November 10, 2016. Accessed November 19, 2016. https://www.theguardian.com/culture/2016/nov/10/shakespeare-write-henry-v-suit-london-theatre-the-curtain-odd-shape.

———. "Excavation Finds Early Shakespeare Theatre Was Rectangular." *Guardian*. May 17, 2016. Accessed November 19, 2016, https://www.theguardian.com/culture/2016/may/17/curtain-excavation-early-shakespeare-theatre-rectangular-shoreditch.

Kent, Joan. "Attitudes of Members of the House of Commons to the Regulation of 'Personal Conduct' in Late Elizabethan and Early Stuart England." *Bulletin of the Institute of Historical Research* 46 (1973): 41–71.

Kidnie, Margaret Jane. *Shakespeare and the Problem of Adaptation*. London: Routledge, 2009.

———. "Text, Performance, and the Editors: Staging Shakespeare's Drama." *Shakespeare Quarterly* 51 (2000): 456–73.

Kiernan, Pauline. *Staging Shakespeare at the New Globe*. Basingstoke, UK: Macmillan Press, 1999.

Kohler, Richard C. "Excavating Henslowe's Rose." *Shakespeare Quarterly* 40 (1989): 475–82.

———. "The Fortune Contract and Vitruvian Symmetry." *Shakespeare Studies* 6 (1970): 311–26.

[Kyd, Thomas.] *THE SPANISH TRAGEdie*. London: by Edward Allde, for Edward White, n.d.

Lambarde, William. *A Perambulation of Kent*. London: by Edm. Bollifant, 1596.

Le Corbusier. *Precisions on the Present State of Architecture and City Planning*. Translated by Edith Schreiber Aujame. Cambridge, Mass.: MIT Press, 1991.

Lefebvre, Henri. *The Production of Space*. Translated by Donald Nicholson-Smith. Malden, Mass.: Blackwell, 1991.

Leigh, Valentine. *THE MOST PROFITABLE AND Commendable Science of Surueying of Lands, Tenements, and Hereditaments*. London: by Robert Robinson, for Robert Dexter, 1596.

Levin, Richard. "Performance-Critics *vs* Close Readers in the Study of English Renaissance Drama." *Modern Language Review* 81 (1986): 545–59.

Loengard, Janet S. "An Elizabethan Lawsuit: John Brayne, his Carpenter, and the Building of the Red Lion Theatre." *Shakespeare Quarterly* 34 (1983): 298–310.

Long, William B. "'A bed / for woodstock': A Warning for the Unwary." *Medieval and Renaissance Drama in England* 2 (1985): 91–118.

———. "Stage-Directions: A Misinterpreted Factor in Determining Textual Provenance." *TEXT* 2 (1985): 121–37.

Loomba, Ania. *Gender, Race, Renaissance Drama*. Manchester, UK: Manchester University Press, 1989.

Love, Genevieve. "'As from the waste of Sophonisba'; or, What's Sexy about Stage Directions." *Renaissance Drama*, n.s., 32 (2003): 3–31.

Lucian. "Heracles." In *Lucian*, vol. 1, translated by A. M. Harmon, 63–71. Cambridge: Harvard University Press, 1961.

Lyons, John D. "Unseen Space and Theatrical Narrative: The 'Récit de Cinna.'" *Yale French Studies* 80 (1991): 70–89.

Mackinder, Anthony, with Lyn Blackmore, Julian Bowsher, and Christopher Phillpotts. *The Hope Playhouse, Animal Baiting and Later Industrial Activity at Bear Gardens on Bankside: Excavations at Riverside House and New Globe Walk, Southwark, 1999–2000*. London: Museum of London Archaeology, 2013.

Markiewicz, Henryk. "Ut Pictura Poesis . . . A History of the Topos and the Problem." Translated by Uliana Gabara. *New Literary History* 18 (1987): 535–58.

Marl., Ch. *THE TRAGICALL History of D. Faustus*. London: by V.S. for Thomas Bushell, 1604.

[Marlowe, Christopher.] *Tamburlaine the Great*. [London:] by Richard Iones, 1593.

Marston[, John]. *THE MALCONTENT*. London: by V.S. for William Aspley, 1604.

Masten, Jeffrey. "Toward a Queer Address: The Taste of Letters and Early Modern Male Friendship." *GLQ* 10 (2004): 367–84.

Maus, Katharine Eisaman, ed. *Four Revenge Tragedies*. Oxford: Oxford University Press, 1995.

McAuley, Gay. *Space in Performance: Making Meaning in the Theatre*. Ann Arbor: University of Michigan Press, 1999.

McDonald, Russ. *The Bedford Companion to Shakespeare: An Introduction with Documents*. Boston: Bedford Books, 1996.

McGann, Jerome J. *The Textual Condition*. Princeton, N.J.: Princeton University Press, 1991.

McJannet, Linda. "Elizabethan Speech Prefixes: Page Design, Typography, and Mimesis." In Bergeron, *Reading and Writing in Shakespeare*, 45–63.

———. *The Voice of Elizabethan Stage Directions: The Evolution of a Theatrical Code*. Newark: University of Delaware Press, 1999.

McKerrow, Ronald B. *Prolegomena for the Oxford Shakespeare: A Study in Editorial Method*. Oxford: Oxford University Press, 1939.

Meek, Richard. *Narrating the Visual in Shakespeare*. Farnham, UK: Ashgate, 2009.

Mehl, Dieter. *The Elizabethan Dumb Show: The History of a Dramatic Convention*. London: Methuen, 1965.

Middleton, T., and T. Dekkar. *The Roaring Girle*. London: for Thomas Archer, 1611.

Middleton, Tho. *NO WIT [NO] HELP LIKE A VVOMANS*. London: for Humphrey Moseley, 1657.

———. *WOMEN BEWARE WOMEN*. In *TWO NEW PLAYES*, G3r–O3r. London: for Humphrey Moseley, 1657.

[Middleton, Thomas.] *FATHER Hubbards Tales*. London: by T.C. for William Cotton, 1604.

Middleton, Thomas. *Women Beware Women*. In *Five Plays*, edited by Bryan Loughrey and Neil Taylor, 239–344. London: Penguin Books, 1988.

Monsarrat, Gilles. "John Ford's Substantive Accidentals in *Perkin Warbeck*." *The Library* 16 (2015): 446–57.

Mukherji, Subha. "Trying, Knowing and Believing: Epistemic Plots and the Poetics of Doubt." In *Fictions of Knowledge: Fact, Evidence, Doubt*, edited by Yota Batski, Subha Mukherji, and Jan-Melissa Schramm, 84–109. New York: Palgrave Macmillan, 2012.

Mullaney, Steven. *The Place of the Stage: License, Play, and Power in Renaissance England*. Chicago: University of Chicago Press, 1988.

Mulryne, J. R., and Margaret Shewring, eds. *Shakespeare's Globe Rebuilt*. Cambridge: Cambridge University Press, 1997.

Nash, Tho. *Pierce Penilesse HIS SVPPLICATION to the Diuell*. London: by Abell Ieffes, 1592.

[Norton, Thomas, and Thomas Sackville.] *The Tragidie of Ferrex and Porrex*. London: by Iohn Daye, n.d.

[———.] *THE TRAGEDIE OF GORBODVC*. London: by William Griffith, 1561.

Nugent, S. Georgia. "Ancient Theories of Comedy: The Treatises of Evanthius and Donatus." In *Shakespearean Comedy*, edited by Maurice Charney, 259–80. New York: New York Literary Forum, 1980.

Orgel, Stephen. "The Book of the Play." In Holland and Orgel, *From Performance to Print*, 13–54.

———. *The Illusion of Power: Political Theater in the English Renaissance*. Berkeley: University of California Press, 1975.

Orrell, John. "Beyond the Rose: Design Problems for the Globe Reconstruction." In *New Issues in the Reconstruction of Shakespeare's Theater: Proceedings of the Conference Held at the University of Georgia, February 16–18, 1990*, edited by Franklin J. Hildy, 95–118. New York: Peter Lang, 1990.

———. "Peter Street at the Fortune and the Globe." *Shakespeare Survey* 33 (1980): 139–51.

———. "The Private Theatre Auditorium." *Theatre Research International* 9 (1984): 79–92.

———. *The Quest for Shakespeare's Globe*. Cambridge: Cambridge University Press, 1983.

Ouerburie, Thomas. *NEW AND CHOICE CHARACTERS*. London: by Thomas Creede for Laurence Lisle, 1615.

Parker, Patricia. "Dilation and Delay: Renaissance Matrices." *Poetics Today* 5 (1984): 519–35.

Partridge, Eric. *Shakespeare's Bawdy*. London: Routledge, 1990.

Pavis, Patrice. *Dictionnaire du théâtre*. Paris: Messidor/Éditions Sociales, 1980.

———. "Remarques sur le discours théâtral." *Degrés* 6 (1978): 1–10.

Peirce, C. S. *Peirce on Signs: Writings on Semiotic by Charles Sanders Peirce*, edited by James Hoopes. Chapel Hill: University of North Carolina Press, 1991.

Peters, Julie Stone. *Theatre of the Book 1480–1880: Print, Text, and Performance in Europe*. Oxford: Oxford University Press, 2000.

Plato. *The Republic*. 2 vols. Translated by Paul Shorey. Cambridge, Mass.: Harvard University Press, 1935.

Potter, Lois. "*The Two Noble Kinsmen*: Spectacle and Narrative." In *The Show Within: Dramatic and Other Insets; English Renaissance Drama (1550–1642)*, 2 vols., edited by François Laroque, 2.235–51. Montpellier, Fr.: Publications de Université Paul-Valery, 1992.

Puttenham, George. *THE ARTE OF ENGLISH POESIE*. London: by Richard Field, 1589.

Quintilian. *The Orator's Education*. 5 vols. Edited and translated by Donald A. Russell. Cambridge, Mass.: Harvard University Press, 2001.

Rasmussen, Eric. Afterword to *Stage Directions in* Hamlet: *New Essays and New Directions*, edited by Hardin L. Aasand, 226–27. Madison, N.J.: Fairleigh Dickinson University Press, 2003.

Ratcliffe, Stephen. *Reading the Unseen: (Offstage)* Hamlet. Denver: Counterpath Press, 2010.

Rhetorica ad Herennium. Translated by Harry Caplan. Cambridge, Mass.: Harvard University Press, 1954.

Robson, Mark. "Looking with Ears, Seeing with Eyes: Shakespeare and the Ear of the Early Modern." *Early Modern Literary Studies* 7, no. 1 (2001): 10.1–23. http://extra.shu.ac.uk/emls/07-1/robsears.htm.

Rowe, N., ed. THE WORKS OF *Mr. William Shakespear*. 6 vols. London: for Jacob Tonson, 1709.

Scaliger, Julius Caesar. *Poetices libri septem*. In *Select Translations from Scaliger's* Poetics, translated by Frederick Morgan Padelford. New York: Henry Holt, 1905.

Schanzer, Ernest. "Hercules and His Load." *Review of English Studies*, n.s., 19 (1968): 51–53.

Schlueter, June, and James P. Lusardi. "Offstage Noise and Onstage Action: Entrances in the Ophelia Sequence of *Hamlet*." In *Stage Directions in Hamlet: New Essays and New Directions*, edited by Hardin L. Aasand, 33–41. Madison, N.J.: Fairleigh Dickinson University Press, 2003.

Schooler, Jonathan W., and Tonya Y. Engstler-Schooler. "Verbal Overshadowing of Visual Memories: Some Things Are Better Left Unsaid." *Cognitive Psychology* 22 (1990): 36–71.

Scolnicov, Hanna. "Theatre Space, Theatrical Space, and the Theatrical Space Without." In *The Theatrical Space*, edited by James Redmond, 11–27. Cambridge: Cambridge University Press, 1987.

A second and third blast of retrait from plaies and Theaters. London: by Henrie Denham, 1580.

[Shakespeare, William.] THE CRONICLE *History of Henry the fift*. London: by Thomas Creede, for Tho. Millington, and Iohn Busby, 1600.

Shakespeare, William. *The life and death of King Richard the Second*. In *MR. WILLIAM SHAKESPEARES COMEDIES, HISTORIES, & TRAGEDIES*. London: by Isaac Iaggard and Ed. Blount, 1623. b6r–d5r.

———. *The Life of Henry the Fift*. In *MR. WILLIAM SHAKESPEARES COMEDIES, HISTORIES, & TRAGEDIES*. London: by Isaac Iaggard and Ed. Blount, 1623. hr–k2r.

———. *A MIDSOMMER Nights Dreame*. In *MR. WILLIAM SHAKESPEARES COMEDIES, HISTORIES, & TRAGEDIES*. London: by Isaac Iaggard and Ed. Blount, 1623. Nr–O3v.

———. *Much adoe about Nothing*. In *MR. WILLIAM SHAKESPEARES COMEDIES, HISTORIES, & TRAGEDIES*. London: by Isaac Iaggard and Ed. Blount, 1623. I3r–Lr.

———. *Much adoe about Nothing*. London: by V.S. for Andrew Wise, and William Aspley, 1600.

———. *Much Ado About Nothing*. Edited by John F. Cox. Cambridge: Cambridge University Press, 1998.

———. *Much Ado About Nothing*. Edited by Barbara Mowat and Paul Werstine. New York: Washington Square Press, 2005.

———. *Pericles, Prince of Tyre*. London: for Henry Gosson, 1609.

———. *The Second Part of Henry the Fourth*. In *MR. WILLIAM SHAKESPEARES COMEDIES, HISTORIES, & TRAGEDIES*. London: by Isaac Iaggard and Ed. Blount, 1623. f6v–gg8r.

———. *THE TEMPEST*. In *MR. WILLIAM SHAKESPEARES COMEDIES, HISTORIES, & TRAGEDIES*. London: by Isaac Iaggard and Ed. Blount, 1623. A1r–B4r.

———. *THE TRAGEDIE OF HAMLET, Prince of Denmarke*. In *MR. WILLIAM SHAKESPEARES COMEDIES, HISTORIES, & TRAGEDIES*. London: by Isaac Iaggard and Ed. Blount, 1623. nn4v–qq1v.

———. THE TRAGEDIE OF KING LEAR. In MR. WILLIAM SHAKESPEARES COMEDIES, HISTORIES, & TRAGEDIES. London: by Isaac Iaggard and Ed. Blount, 1623. qq2r–ss3r.

———. THE TRAGEDIE OF MACBETH. In MR. WILLIAM SHAKESPEARES COMEDIES, HISTORIES, & TRAGEDIES. London: by Isaac Iaggard and Ed. Blount, 1623. ll6r–nn4r.

———. THE TRAGEDIE OF *Othello, the Moore of Venice*. In MR. WILLIAM SHAKESPEARES COMEDIES, HISTORIES, & TRAGEDIES. London: by Isaac Iaggard and Ed. Blount, 1623. ss3v–vv6r.

———. *The Tragedy of Richard the Third*. In MR. WILLIAM SHAKESPEARES COMEDIES, HISTORIES, & TRAGEDIES. London: by Isaac Iaggard and Ed. Blount, 1623. q5r–t2v.

[———.] THE TRAGEDY OF *King Richard the third*. London: by Valentine Sims, for Andrew Wise, 1597.

———. THE *Tragicall Historie of* HAMLET, *Prince of Denmarke*. London: by I.R. for N.L., 1604/5.

———. THE *Tragœdy of Othello, The Moore of Venice*. London: by N.O. for Thomas Walkley, 1622.

———. *The Winters Tale*. In MR. WILLIAM SHAKESPEARES COMEDIES, HISTORIES, & TRAGEDIES. London: by Isaac Iaggard and Ed. Blount, 1623. Aa1r–Cc2r.

Shapiro, I. A. "The Bankside Theatres: Early Engravings." *Shakespeare Survey* 1 (1948): 25–37.

Shirley, Frances Ann. *Shakespeare's Use of Off-Stage Sounds*. Lincoln: University of Nebraska Press, 1963.

Sidney, Philip. AN APOLOGIE *for Poetrie*. London: for Henry Olney, 1595.

———. THE DEFENCE OF *Poesie*. London: for VVilliam Ponsonby, 1595.

Simon, Scott, and Heather Knight. "Archaeologists Find Early Shakespeare Theater Was Rectangular." *Weekend Edition*. Aired May 21, 2016. Transcript accessed November 18, 2016. http://www.npr.org/2016/05/21/478962867/archaeologists-find-early-shakespeare-theater-was-rectangular.

Sinfield, Alan. *Faultlines: Cultural Materialism and the Politics of Dissident Reading*. Berkeley: University of California Press, 1992.

Smidt, Kristian. "Shakespeare's Absent Characters." *English Studies* 61 (1980): 397–407.

Smith, Bruce R. *Ancient Scripts and Modern Experience on the English Stage 1500–1700*. Princeton, N.J.: Princeton University Press, 1988.

———. *The Acoustic World of Early Modern England: Attending to the O-Factor*. Chicago: University of Chicago Press, 1999.

———. "Prickly Characters." In Bergeron, *Reading and Writing in Shakespeare*, 25–44.

Sofer, Andrew. *Dark Matter: Invisibility in Drama, Theater, and Performance*. Ann Arbor: University of Michigan Press, 2013.

———. *The Stage Life of Props*. Ann Arbor: University of Michigan Press, 2003.

Souriau, Étienne. *Les Deux cent mille situations dramatiques*. Paris: Flammarion, 1950.

Sprague, Arthur Colby. "Off-Stage Sounds," *University of Toronto Quarterly* 15 (1945): 70–75.

———. "Shakespeare's Unnecessary Characters." *Shakespeare Survey* 20 (1967): 75–82.

———. "'True, Gallant Raleigh': Some Off-Stage Conversations in Shakespeare's Plays." In *Shakespeare's Styles: Essays in Honour of Kenneth Muir*, edited by Philip Edwards, Inga-Stina Ewbank, and G. K. Hunter, 183–90. Cambridge: Cambridge University Press, 1980.

The Statutes of the Realm [1101–1713]. 12 vols. Edited by A. Luders, Sir T. Edlyn Tomlins, J. France, W. E. Taunton, and J. Raithby. London: Record Commission, 1810–1828.

Stern, Tiffany. "'The Curtain is Yours.'" In *Locating the Queen's Men, 1583–1603: Material Practices and Conditions of Playing*, edited by Helen Ostovich, Holger Schott Syme, and Andrew Griffin, 77–96. Farnham, UK: Ashgate, 2009.

———. "'You that walk i'th Galleries': Standing and Walking in the Galleries of the Globe Theatre." *Shakespeare Quarterly* 51 (2000): 211–16.

Suchy, Patricia A. "When Words Collide: The Stage Direction as Utterance." *Journal of Dramatic Theory and Criticism* 6 (1991): 69–82.

Summerson, John. *Architecture in Britain 1530 to 1830*. New Haven, Conn.: Yale University Press, 1993.

Tandon, B. G. "Off-Stage Action in *Macbeth*." In *Some Early Greek Scholars in England.*, edited by James Hogg, 62–73. Salzburg: Salzburg Studies in English Literature, Universität Salzburg, 1981.

———. "Offstage Action in the Plays of Shakespeare." In *Indian Response to Shakespeare.*, edited by Basavaraj S. Naikar, 132–38. New Delhi: Atlantic Publishers and Distributors, 2002.

———. "Why Does Ophelia Die Offstage?" *Aligarh Journal of English Studies* 15, nos. 1–2 (1993): 1–5.

Taylor, Gary. General introduction to *William Shakespeare: A Textual Companion*, by Stanley Wells and Gary Taylor, with John Jowett and William Montgomery. Oxford: Clarendon, 1987.

Taylor, Neil, and Bryan Loughrey. "Middleton's Chess Strategies in *Women Beware Women*." *Studies in English Literature* 24 (1984): 341–54.

Terence. *Guidonis Iuuenalis natione Cenomani in Terentium familiarissima interp̃tatio cũ figuris unicuiqȝ scænæ præpositis*. Lyon: Jean Trechsel, 1493.

Theobald, Lewis, ed. *THE WORKS OF SHAKESPEARE*. 7 vols. London: for A. Bettesworth and C. Hitch, J. Tonson, F. Clay, W. Feales, and R. Wellington, 1733.

Thomson, Leslie. "Playgoers on the Outdoor Stages of Early Modern London." *Theatre Notebook* 64 (2010): 3–11.

Tourneur, Cyril. *THE ATHEIST'S TRAGEDIE: OR The honest Man's Reuenge*. London: for Iohn Stepneth, and Richard Redmer, 1611.

Tribble, Evelyn B. *Margins and Marginality: The Printed Page in Early Modern England*. Charlottesville: University Press of Virginia, 1993.

Turner, Henry S. *The English Renaissance Stage: Geometry, Poetics, and the Practical Spatial Arts 1580–1630*. Oxford: Oxford University Press, 2006.

———. "*King Lear* Without: The Heath." *Renaissance Drama*, n.s., 28 (1997 [1999]): 161–93.

"The 2. Noble Ladys." British Library, M.S. Egerton 1994.

Ubersfeld, Anne. *Lire le théâtre I*. Rev. ed. Paris: Belin, 1996.

van den Berg, Kent. *Playhouse and Cosmos: Shakespearean Theater as Metaphor*. Newark: University of Delaware Press, 1985.

Varro. *On the Latin Language*. 2 vols. Translated by Roland G. Kent. Cambridge, Mass.: Harvard University Press, 1993.

von Greyerz, Georg. *The Reported Scenes in Shakespeare's Plays*. Bern: Fritz Pochon-Jent, 1965.

Walker, Jonathan. "Reading Materiality: The Literary Critical Treatment of Physical Texts." *Renaissance Drama*, n.s., 41 (2013): 199–232.

———. "Rhetorics of the Obscæne." *Theatre Survey* 48 (2007): 77–97.

Webbe, William. *A Discourse of English Poetrie*. London: by Iohn Charlewood for Robert Walley, 1586.

Webster, John. *THE TRAGEDY OF THE DVTCHESSE Of Malfy*. London: by Nicholas Okes, for Iohn Waterson, 1623.

Weimann, Robert. *Shakespeare and the Popular Tradition in the Theater: Studies in the Social Dimension of Dramatic Form and Function*. Edited by Robert Schwartz. Baltimore: Johns Hopkins University Press, 1978.

Wells, Stanley. *Re-Editing Shakespeare for the Modern Reader*. Oxford: Clarendon, 1984.

———, and Gary Taylor, with John Jowett and William Montgomery. *William Shakespeare: A Textual Companion*. Oxford: Clarendon, 1987.

West, William N. "The Idea of a Theater: Humanist Ideology and the Imaginary Stage in Early Modern Europe." *Renaissance Drama*, n.s., 28 (1997 [1999]): 245–87.

Whigham, Frank. *Ambition and Privilege: The Social Tropes of Elizabethan Courtesy Theory*. Berkeley: University of California Press, 1984.

White, Hayden. "The Value of Narrativity in the Representation of Reality." *Critical Inquiry* 7 (1980): 5–27.

Whitworth, Charles. "Reporting Offstage Events in Early Tudor Drama." In *Tudor Theatre. "Let There Be Covenants . . .": Convention et Theatre.*, edited by André Lascombes, 45–66. Bern: Peter Lang, 1998.

Wickham, Glynne. *Early English Stages 1300 to 1660*. 4 vols. in 5. London: Routledge and Kegan Paul, 1959–2001.

Wilders, John. *The Off-Stage Life of Shakespeare's Characters*. Middlebury, Vt.: Middlebury College Press, 1984.

Williams, Clare. *Thomas Platter's Travels in England, 1599*. London: J. Cape, 1937.

Williams, Gordon. *A Dictionary of Sexual Language and Imagery in Shakespearean and Stuart Literature*. London: Athlone Press, 1994.

Wilson, John Dover. "Anthony Munday, Pamphleteer and Pursuivant." *Modern Language Review* 4 (1908–1909): 484–90.

Wilson, Rawdon. *Shakespearean Narrative*. Newark: University of Delaware Press, 1995.

Womack, Peter. "Noises Off." *Textual Practice* 1 (1987): 309–28.

———. "Off-Stage." *Early Modern Theatricality*. Edited by Henry S. Turner. Oxford: Oxford University Press, 2013.

Worthen, W. B. *Shakespeare and the Authority of Performance*. Cambridge: Cambridge University Press, 1997.

Wright, Peter M. "Jonson's Revision of the Stage Directions for the 1616 Folio *Works*." *Medieval and Renaissance Drama in England* 5 (1991): 257–85.

Yates, Frances A. *Theatre of the World*. London: Routledge and Kegan Paul, 1969.

Zeitlin, Froma I. *Playing the Other: Gender and Society in Classical Greek Literature*. Chicago: University of Chicago Press, 1996.

Zhu, Bin. "Dramatic Presence and Absence: A Structural Phenomenology of Revenge Tragedy in the Tradition of Kyd." Ph.D. thesis, Boston University, 1992.

INDEX